Successful Public Speaking

A Practical Guide

William A. Haskins
McKendree College

Joseph M. Staudacher
Marquette University

Scott, Foresman and Company
Glenview, Illinois
London, England

Credits

p. 68   From "A Talk with Father Walsh, S. J." by Donald McDonald in *Marquette University Magazine,* Fall 1961. Reprinted by permission.

p. 190   From *The Milwaukee Journal,* November 25, 1978. Reprinted by permission.

p. 192   "Teen Suicide at All-Time High" by Ken Franckling as appeared in *The Milwaukee Journal,* October 30, 1984. Reprinted with permission of United Press International, Inc.

p. 193   From *Red Giants and White Dwarfs: Man's Descent from the Stars, Revised Edition.* Copyright © 1967, 1971 by Robert Jastrow. Reprinted by permission of the author.

p. 211   From *The Uses of Argument* by Stephen Edelston Toulmin. Copyright © 1958 by Cambridge University Press. Reprinted by permission.

p. 268   From the benediction given at the 1984 Democratic National Convention by Rev. Floyd A. Lotito. Reprinted by permission.

Photo credits appear on page 352, which is a legal extension of the copyright page.

An *Instructor's Manual* with test items and the DIPLOMA electronic classroom management system to accompany *Successful Public Speaking: A Practical Guide* are available through a Scott, Foresman representative or by writing to Speech Communication Editor, College Division, Scott, Foresman and Company, 1900 East Lake Avenue, Glenview, Illinois, 60025.

Library of Congress Cataloging-in-Publication Data

Haskins, William A.
  Successful public speaking.

  Includes indexes.
  1. Public speaking.   I. Staudacher, Joseph M.
II. Title.
PN4121.H266   1987   808.5'1   86-20291
ISBN 0-673-18204-5

1 2 3 4 5 6 -RRC- 91 90 89 88 87 86

Successful Public Speaking

A Practical Guide

Preface

Why another public speaking text? What can this text offer that others do not? What special features or characteristics make this text more helpful and useful than its competitors? The clue is in the title: *Successful Public Speaking: A Practical Guide*. This is not a book *about* public speaking. It is a practical handbook designed to advise and train students in the *practice* of public speaking.

This text began with an idea that a textbook should be written around the basic assignments or exercises in the public speaking course. We envisioned a text in which the student would read a chapter and then make a speech, read another chapter and make a speech, continuing in this manner throughout the text. To implement this idea, we have attempted to develop a text that correlates the basic public speaking assignments most often covered in the classroom with specific chapters in the textbook. We identify nine speech exercises as those most commonly assigned in the course:

1. a speech of self-introduction or introduction of another person
2. an "icebreaker" speech
3. a demonstration speech with emphasis on visual aids
4. a manuscript speech stressing oral style and vocal technique
5. an informative speech of reporting or complex explanation

6. a persuasive speech inducing belief through argumentation or ac-
   tivation through motivation
7. an evocative speech of inspiration or entertainment or a speech for
   a special occasion
8. impromptu speeches
9. deliberative speaking in a group or a problem-solving speech

In the list of learning objectives that precedes each chapter, you will find
one or more objectives relating to one of these assignments highlighted
with a symbol identifying them as major speaking objectives of the chapter. In the assignments at the end of the chapter, the same symbol highlights the major speaking assignment(s) of the chapter.

This introduction has told you why the text was written; the following
overview describes the contents of the book.

Overview

Chapter 1, "Introduction to Public Speaking," identifies the components
of the public speaking process and compares public speaking with other
forms of communication. Chapter 2, "The Listener in Public Speaking,"
discusses the role of the listener and suggests ways in which students
can become better listeners. Chapter 3, "Speech Preparation," lets students apply the fundamentals of speechmaking: choosing a subject; determining a purpose; organizing, developing, and rehearsing a speech;
and overcoming anxiety. A final section of the chapter deals with accepting constructive evaluation.

Chapter 4, "Conducting Interviews and Using Library Resources,"
guides the students through these two activities in the process of researching a speech. Chapter 5, "Audience Adaptation and Analysis,"
helps students learn how to adapt a speech to an audience using the
techniques of both general and specific audience analysis. Chapter 6,
"Speaker's Credibility," suggests ways in which student speakers can
develop credibility through competence, confidence, dynamism, trustworthiness, and goodwill.

Chapters 7 and 8 are both concerned with delivery. Chapter 7, "Bodily
Action and Audiovisual Aids," deals with visual technique in public
speaking. Chapter 8, "Vocal Technique in Speaking and Reading Aloud,"
discusses vocal characteristics, apparatus, and skills. Chapter 9, "Language and Meaning," describes ways in which language can be used to
foster or to impede communication.

Chapters 10 through 15 deal with the basic types of public speaking. Chapter 10, "Informative Speaking," covers both reporting and complex explanation. Persuasive speaking is examined in two chapters: Chapter 11, "Persuasion Through Argumentation," and Chapter 12, "Persuasion Through Motivation." Chapter 12 also focuses on the sales talk as a particular example of persuasion through motivation. Chapter 13, "Evocative Speaking," discusses general types of evocative speaking, speeches of inspiration and entertainment, and specific types, or speeches for special occasions. Chapter 14, "Impromptu Speaking," shows students how they can organize, develop, and present an impromptu—but not unprepared—speech. Chapter 15, "Deliberative Speaking," deals with the topic of speaking in groups and identifies the roles, duties, and responsibilities of both leaders and participants in group discussion. The chapter also discusses the problem-solving speech.

Pedagogical Aids

Numerous pedagogical aids enhance the text's usefulness for both instructors and students. Each chapter begins with an opening schematic that graphically portrays the chapter content and clearly identifies the relationships among chapter topics and subtopics. The schematic is followed by a list of chapter learning objectives, one or more of which is highlighted as a major speaking objective of the chapter. Full-length speeches and speech excerpts, some with marginal annotations, illustrate text concepts and principles. Numerous examples also apply text material to real-life situations. Each chapter ends with suggested assignments, which include both oral and written exercises, as well as group activities for the classroom.

A common complaint, frequently voiced by many beginning public speaking students, is that they cannot find a suitable topic for a speech. To help students overcome this problem, we have provided in Appendix B a list of more than one thousand suggested speech topics, grouped by type of speech for which they seem most applicable. Students may wish to choose their speech topics from the suggestions provided; they may regard the list as a beginning to which they can add their own suggestions; or they may focus on a particular aspect of one of the suggested topics. Students can use the evaluation forms and critique sheets in Appendix A to assess their classmates' and their own speaking performance.

A complete set of instructional aids is available in the *Instructor's Manual* that accompanies the text. Section 1 of the manual, an introductory section on teaching the public speaking course, includes suggestions for teaching strategies, audiovisual resources, and sample course outlines. Section 2 consists of chapter-by-chapter teaching suggestions and resources. Section 3 offers sample test questions, both objective (true-false, multiple-choice, matching, and fill-in) and essay, for each chapter. Additional evaluation forms for use by the instructor or by the students comprise Section 4 of the manual.

Acknowledgments

As with any project of this size, many people contributed to its successful completion. The publication of *Successful Public Speaking: A Practical Guide* underscores the need for and beauty of a team effort. We want to thank the members of this team for their effort and support, which have made our task so much easier. First, we thank our students. They helped create many of the ideas, examples, and stories found in our work. Their encouragement, loyalty, and good sense of humor made our task more tolerable and rewarding.

Next we thank the fine people at McKendree College and Marquette University for their encouragement, help, and support. We thank in particular Professor Alfred Sokolnicki, Dean Michael Price, Dean Ormond Smythe, and Mr. Marty Cavanaugh for their assistance and support. We also thank our colleagues in the field who gave generously of their time and knowledge to review our manuscript: Stephen D. Boyd, Northern Kentucky University; Smith V. Brand, Thornton Community College; Bruce E. Gronbeck, University of Iowa; Stanford P. Gwin, University of Southern Mississippi; Lawrence W. Hugenberg, Youngstown State University; Richard J. Jenson, University of New Mexico; Patricia P. Kluthe, Missouri Southern State College; Laura L. Nelson, University of Wisconsin at La Crosse; and Judith C. Pier, Wichita State University. Their critical insights, perceptive comments, and sound advice have contributed to the making of a better book.

We next acknowledge the effort, guidance, wisdom, and patience of the fine people at Scott, Foresman and Company. They believed in us and in our book. For that we are grateful and proud to be associated with them. We wish to thank especially Barbara Muller, Acquisitions Editor, for getting this project off the ground and Betty Slack, Developmental Editor, whose editing and leadership made a professional finished product possible. Betty Slack was one of the best teachers we ever had. We also acknowledge with gratitude the assistance of Deb DeBord, Project Editor, who copyedited the manuscript and patiently and professionally guided the text throughout all phases of its production, from manuscript to finished book.

Last, we thank our families for putting up with us during times when stress in our lives seemed to reach new highs. They encouraged us to go forward with the project. They supported our efforts and sacrificed their own time to give us time to write the book. We especially thank Rose Staudacher for her assistance and support in this project and Linda Haskins, not only for typing the manuscript, but also for her patience and wisdom, which made the impossible, possible.

William A. Haskins

Joseph M. Staudacher

Contents

15

Deliberative Speaking   **293**

Advantages of Public Speaking	Public Speaking Promotes Self-Growth	
	Public Speaking Advances Knowledge	
	Public Speaking Is Essential for Establishing a Stable Society	

Freedom and Responsibility

The Public Speaking Process	The Speaker	
	The Speech	Vocabulary Level
		Meaningful Statements
		Appropriate Material
		Organizational Pattern
	The Audience	
	Channels of Communication	
	Feedback	
	Noise	Psychological Noise
		Physiological Noise
		Semantic Noise
		Environmental Noise
	Context	Time of the Public Speech
		Location for the Public Speech
		Occasion for the Public Speech
		Format of the Speaking Event
		Importance of Speech Topic

A Public Speaking Model

Public Speaking and Other Forms of Communication	Intrapersonal Communication
	Interpersonal Communication
	Small Group Communication

1 Introduction to Public Speaking

1 Introduction to Public Speaking

As Jane walks slowly to the front of the room, she appears concerned and frightened. This is to be her first public speech. She hesitates for a few moments; she stares at the floor; then, she looks at her audience. As she speaks, Jane discovers that her classmates and teacher appear interested in her message. They listen to her and occasionally smile as she speaks. She enjoys seeing their reaction. Her confidence grows as she continues to speak. At the end of the presentation, the class enthusiastically applauds Jane. She returns to her desk, realizing that a public speaking experience can be both challenging and rewarding.

Jane's experience is not very different from other beginning public speaking students. Many students are apprehensive about giving a public speech. What topic should they select? How should they prepare their speech? How will the class respond? These are a few of the questions and concerns that most public speaking students share. But these concerns will diminish as students become more confident of their ability to deliver effective speeches.

Throughout your public speaking course you'll learn about the skills that will help you develop your communication abilities. A knowledge of public speaking and the skills involved in this art can be helpful to you both in school and in your career and activities outside the classroom. By improving your communicative abilities, you can become a more responsible and ethical speaker.

In this chapter we will explore the advantages of public speaking, examine the public speaking process, and discuss the basic differences and similarities between public speaking and other forms of communication.

ADVANTAGES OF PUBLIC SPEAKING

Public speaking has a number of advantages for those who participate in the public speaking process. In this section we will highlight these basic advantages, which include promoting self-growth, advancing knowledge, and establishing a stable society.

Public Speaking Promotes Self-Growth

As a human being you are continuously growing and developing. Public speaking can help you learn more about yourself. As a public speaker, you can discover new information through the research you conduct and the material you gather for your speeches. These discoveries help you learn more about your attitudes, beliefs, and values on various speech topics. New information can give you new reasons to view topics in ways you might not have considered before. You may find yourself growing more tolerant of views you originally thought contrary to your opinions and more sensitive to the views of others. Such changes in thinking reflect self-growth.

The reactions that you receive from your listeners influence your perceptions of yourself and your message. As your self-perception changes, you can come to realize and appreciate your self-growth.

As a public speaker, you may be criticized by your listeners. Learning to accept constructive criticism is another way in which public speaking can promote self-growth. By paying attention to your critics, you learn to improve your skills as a communicator and to develop confidence in your ability as a speaker.

Public Speaking Advances Knowledge

A second advantage of public speaking is that it helps to promote knowledge. Sometimes the truth about a particular issue is not known. Often there are a number of differing points of view on a single issue. Public speaking provides a forum in which these views are aired. As a public speaker free to express your own beliefs, you can direct your listeners' attention to important propositions, evidence, arguments, or issues.

You learn, also, as a member of an audience. A speaker who communicates effectively and ethically can provide audience members with information they need to make knowledgeable decisions.

Public Speaking Is Essential for Establishing a Stable Society

Public speaking helps maintain stability in our society. The First Amendment to the U.S. Constitution guarantees our right to freedom of speech.[1] Public speakers present a variety of views on numerous topics. Listeners often disagree with the views being presented. The public speaking process provides an avenue through which disagreement can be resolved. Public speakers air their views; listeners then decide which position to support, whose message to believe, what action to take. For example, in a presidential debate, the candidates present their views, hoping to persuade listeners to vote for them. Public speakers not only provide information for decision making, they also offer a process for peaceful resolution of societal differences.

Along with the advantages that public speaking offers come responsibilities for communicating in a free society. We will address this important point in the following section.

FREEDOM AND RESPONSIBILITY

It has been the task of every generation of Americans to *discover, define, evaluate,* and *protect* its right of free speech. Along with the right comes the responsibility of communicating intelligently and effectively. In 1972 the Speech Communication Association, the nation's largest association for people interested in the field of speech communication, endorsed the view expressed in the "Credo for Free and Responsible Communication in a Democratic Society":

> *We accept the responsibility of cultivating by precept and example, in our classrooms and in our communities, enlightened uses of communication; of developing in our students a respect for precision and accuracy in communication, and for reasoning based upon evidence and a judicious discrimination among values. We encourage our students to accept the role of well-informed and articulate citizens to defend the communication rights of those with whom they may disagree, and to expose abuses of the communication process.*[2]

These thoughts reflect the important responsibilities faced by an ethical public speaker in a free society. When you speak in public, keep in mind your right of free speech but remember also the related responsibilities that all public speakers must bear.

We have examined both the advantages and responsibilities of public speaking, but what do we mean by "public speaking"? In the following section we will explore in detail the process of public speaking.

THE PUBLIC SPEAKING PROCESS

Public speaking is *the transactional process through which a speaker delivers a speech to an audience for a specific occasion.* By *transactional* we mean that public speaking is a dynamic process in which key elements constantly interact with one another. The key elements in the public speaking process are the speaker, the speech, the audience, the channels of communication, feedback, noise, and the speaking occasion. It is the interaction of these elements that makes up the process of public speaking. As a public speaker you will learn that the public speaking process is unique. It is always different, never the same. Why? Because for each public speech the elements of the process interact in a unique fashion. In this section we will take a closer look at each of the key elements in the public speaking process. We will then examine how these elements work together in the transactional process of public speaking.

The Speaker

The public speaker is, in general, the major source or sender of information in this process. The listeners (more commonly referred to as the audience) can send information to the speaker, but generally the public speaker is expected to be the major source of information. Not only do the speaker's words communicate information, so also do the speaker's age, gender, educational background, social background, and political background. These characteristics may influence the speaker's choice of topic, language, thinking pattern, selection of evidence and sources of information, and perception of the audience.

Speakers should be aware of the image they attempt to establish in the minds of their audiences. Speakers need to be perceived as competent, honest communicators who demonstrate goodwill toward their audience. Speakers who project a negative image probably will have difficulty convincing listeners to accept their message. Wise speakers will try to avoid projecting negative images.

The Speech

The speech is a message that creates meaning in the mind of the listener. The message is both verbal and nonverbal. Some of the meaning of the message comes from the nonverbal mode (for example, body language or facial expression) surrounding the verbal mode. Listeners, however, rely heavily upon the verbal mode to grasp the speaker's meaning. In planning a speech, the speaker should be careful to consider the following areas: vocabulary level, meaningful statements, selection of material, and organizational pattern.

Vocabulary Level.
The vocabulary level of the speech must be appropriate for the audience. If the level is too high, listeners may find it difficult to understand the message.[3] If it is too low, they may be insulted, as well as bored, by the message. Audience members expect to hear a vocabulary that they understand.

Meaningful Statements.
"Ask not what your country can do for you, but what can you do for your country."—John F. Kennedy

"Give me liberty or give me death."—Patrick Henry

"You cannot depend on your eyes when your imagination is out of focus."—Mark Twain

"Nothing in life is to be feared."—Marie Curie

These are statements that have stirred the imagination of listeners. One way to generate interest in a speech is to select a statement that enhances the meaning of the message and, at the same time, sparks the excitement of the audience. Seek the phrase that adds life and vitality to your speech. Chapter 4 covers the topic of doing research in the library. The resources mentioned there should yield an abundance of meaningful statements that can enliven your speech.

Appropriate Material.   The speech should contain supporting material, arguments, or sources of information that are both interesting and believable to an audience. If, for instance, your ideas and arguments are interesting but not believable, the audience may have difficulty accepting your message. On the other hand, listeners may believe what you say but find your speech itself uninspiring. Not *all* information will appear both interesting and believable. You must work to find material that is sound and credible. It is the audience that ultimately judges the soundness and believability of your speech.

Organizational Pattern.   A logical order of the parts of a speech is essential. Listeners need to be able to follow your message. The speaker who begins with concluding remarks, then jumps to the introductory remarks, and ends with the body of the speech only confuses the audience. Listeners expect to hear introductory statements first, the body of the speech next, and final remarks last.

There are additional patterns for organizing material within each of these major parts of the speech, and we will discuss those patterns in Chapter 3. No matter which pattern is chosen, you should seek an "agreeable order" that invites communication.[4] A speech that is not clearly organized creates confusion and misunderstanding.

The Audience

If no one showed up to listen to a speech, there would be little, if any, reason to present it. The audience is obviously a vital part of the public speaking process. It would be foolish indeed to present a speech without considering the recipients of the message. Just as they did for the speaker, the characteristics of age, gender, educational background, social background, and political background affect listeners' perceptions. The listeners carry these personal characteristics with them like baggage, and these characteristics exert an influence on the speaking occasion. Sometimes the views of the audience will differ from the speaker's, thus imparting a confrontative nature to the speaking occasion. The opposite may occur. The listeners may accept the speaker's views, beliefs, and attitudes as being reasonable. If so, a more cooperative climate may emerge. Whatever the case, the personal characteristics of the listeners will influence their acceptance or rejection of the message.

As a speaker, it is your job to analyze the listeners' characteristics and then use this information to tailor your speech to them. In analyzing the audience, you should consider the characteristics of age, gender, education, economic status, political and cultural backgrounds, and psychological factors. The purpose of audience analysis is adaptation, the process by which you tailor your speech to your audience. You adjust the content, language, and structure of your speech to your audience, based on the information obtained in your audience analysis. Adaptation to the audience also affects presentation and delivery of your speech. We will discuss each of the characteristics examined in audience analysis and the process of audience adaptation in depth in Chapter 5.

Channels of Communication

A speech does not travel through a vacuum between people; it travels through a channel or several channels between speaker and listener. Generally, a message travels through the five major channels of sight, sound, smell, touch, and taste.

Studies indicate that we react differently to stimuli that affect our senses.[5] In a public speaking situation the channel or channels used are determined by the purpose of the message or the manner in which the listener chooses to receive the message. For instance, in your speech you may elect to show a visual aid, such as a graph, and then explain it. The two channels that dominate in this process are sight and sound. Speakers and listeners need to be aware that multiple channels may be in effect when a message is communicated. Sensitivity to the existence of these channels will help both speakers and listeners gain a more complete picture of the message being shared among the public speaking participants.

Feedback

Feedback is the acknowledgment that a message has been received, a response to a message is being given, or both. Feedback may be verbal, such as saying "I understand your point" or "allow me to clarify my message." It may be nonverbal—nodding the head, clapping the hands, or rolling the eyes. Feedback between speaker and audience may be given simultaneously, but it may also be delayed, as when votes are cast for a political candidate. Feedback acts as a road sign, helping participants adapt better to each other's messages. Both speakers and audience members should be sensitive to one another's feedback.

Noise

Interference in the form of noise may make it difficult, if not impossible, for listeners to hear a speech or understand its message. Noise is generally defined as anything that interferes with the reception of a message. Noise can enter any of the channels of communication; it can be located internally within the message (vague words, poor grammar, slang expressions), or it can be located in the environment (loud ticking of a clock, a door slamming, the wind howling). In this section we will discuss four common types of noise: psychological noise, physiological noise, semantic noise, and environmental noise.

Psychological Noise. This type of noise occurs when listeners are thinking about ideas or images other than the ones being communicated by the speaker. Your listener may be sitting only a few feet away from you, yet the listener's attention may not be on your message but on what happened to the listener last weekend, what the listener wants to have for lunch, or what the listener anticipates his or her exam to be next period. You can experience this same type of interference as a speaker. Psychological noise is difficult to overcome but you can attempt to counter it by keeping your speech lively and informative.

Physiological Noise. This type of noise can take the form of impaired hearing, a stomach growling for food, or the need for sleep. Listeners can attempt to reduce the effects of physiological noise by taking care of bodily needs before a speech is given, requesting the speaker to speak louder, sitting closer to the speaker, and so forth. As a speaker, you can relieve some of the physiological noise by speaking loudly enough to be heard, using visual aids that are easily seen, or getting to the point so as not to tire the listeners. Obviously, listeners and speakers are not always able to correct physiological factors that lead to noise problems, but by reducing as many potential factors as possible (such as bodily needs), they may improve the possibility for successful communication.

Semantic Noise. Semantic noise occurs when the language you use is not understandable to the audience. To say that "xenophobia leads to a prodigious gap in understanding among people" may sound impressive, but unless the audience understands that statement to mean "a fear of foreigners or strangers can cause a huge gap in understanding among people," the message will be lost. In this case, semantic noise has entered the channel of communication between speaker and listener. You can avoid semantic noise by making your message audience-centered: develop a message that the audience understands.

Environmental Noise. Poor lighting, loud air conditioners, jet planes flying overhead, and disruptive talking in the hallway fall under the category of environmental noise. At times, such noise is impossible to reduce. However, success or failure of a public speech hinges in part upon whether or not the speech is heard. Sometimes, simply opening a window or increasing the amount of lighting in the room can improve environmental conditions for both speaker and listeners. It's advantageous to both to reduce as much as possible the harmful effects of environmental noise.

Context

Every communication act, and in particular the act of public speaking, occurs within a specific context. In public speaking you need to be aware of the context in which you are speaking, especially if you want a favorable response from your audience. For example, you should be aware of the lighting, the material left on the blackboard or flip chart by the previous speaker, the seating patterns in the room, and the time of day. Lack of sensitivity to the speaking occasion invites disaster.

You need, also, to be aware of a number of factors in the speaking situation—the time, location, and occasion of the speech; the format of the speaking event; the importance of the speech topic; and the personal characteristics of the audience.

Time of the Public Speech. Some people feel they are more alert early in the day; others believe the opposite holds true for them. As a public speaker, you should be aware of the possible effects that the time of presentation will have on the speaking occasion. Depending on the time of presentation, you may need to be more dynamic, appear livelier, and present more interesting material in order to hold the audience's attention.

Location for the Public Speech. Most of you will present your public speeches in the classroom. However, some of you may have the opportunity to speak in large halls, convention centers, or houses of worship. Wherever the location, you need to be aware that it is intimately tied to the speaking occasion. Familiarize yourself with the location in which you are to speak. Know the size, acoustical quality, seating arrangement (for instance, chairs set in a linear pattern), lighting, outlet locations, and media capabilities of the speech setting. Such knowledge can help reduce your uncertainties about the location and its potential effects upon your speech.

Occasion for the Public Speech. The occasion may be a time set aside for speaking assignments, a ceremonial event, a political meeting, a debate, or some other circumstance. The occasion affects the setting and suggests to an audience that a particular kind of message will be presented.

Format of the Speaking Event.

Will the speech be delivered in a debate format, symposium format, or lecture format? (We will discuss these formats in greater detail in Chapter 15.) Each format is governed by its own rules of procedure. You should be aware of such procedures and recognize what the format is designed to accomplish within the occasion.

Importance of Speech Topic.

Most of us want to believe that the time spent listening to a speech is time well spent. We want to believe that the speeches we hear address important topics—ones that we need to be aware of. If the occasion calls for a topic of social significance (such as the topic of school segregation), then to give a speech on how to make cookies in five easy lessons fails to meet the requirements of the occasion and expectations of the audience. When you are speaking, you should provide audience members with reasons to believe that their attendance and attention are worth the effort.

As we have seen, the public speaking process involves a number of elements—the speaker, the speech, the audience, channels of communication, feedback, noise, and the speaking occasion itself. In the following section, we will discuss a public speaking model, which describes how each of these elements works together in the transactional process of public speaking.

A PUBLIC SPEAKING MODEL

Our review of public speaking as a process suggests that public speaking is transactional in nature. This transactional view of communication means that public speaking is a dynamic process in which elements constantly interact with one another. A speaker presents a speech (message) to an audience. The audience is also active in the process; the listeners communicate (verbally and nonverbally) with the speaker. Other factors, including time, occasion, location, facility, equipment, and format of the speaking event, influence the communication event. Within the public speaking process, both speaker and audience take the roles of source and receiver; both impose meaning on the message(s). And both must deal with the noise elements that can enter the process and over which they have limited, if any, control.

Figure 1.1 presents a public speaking model. Note the circularity of the model. Both speaker and audience must play active roles to avoid misunderstanding. Note also that feedback brings together the speaker and audience. As indicated in the model, noise can enter the process at any time and at any point. Both speaker and audience need to be aware of the harmful effects of noise on the transactional process of public speaking.

This public speaking model portrays important basic characteristics that exist not only in public speaking but also in other forms of communication. How is public speaking similar to and yet different from other forms of communication? We will explore this question in the following section.

PUBLIC SPEAKING AND OTHER FORMS OF COMMUNICATION

You may think you will never give another public speech after you finish this course, but the odds are that you will. As we progress through this text and see example after example of public speaking, you will discover that many times throughout your life you will be called on to speak in public, and there will be many occasions when you will *want* to speak out on a particular issue. The knowledge and skills that you gain through this course in public speaking can also be applied to other forms of communication. Clearly there are differences among the various forms of communication, but there are also many similarities. One may legitimately argue, in fact, that public speaking is often personal conversation made

FIGURE 1.1 **A Public Speaking Model**

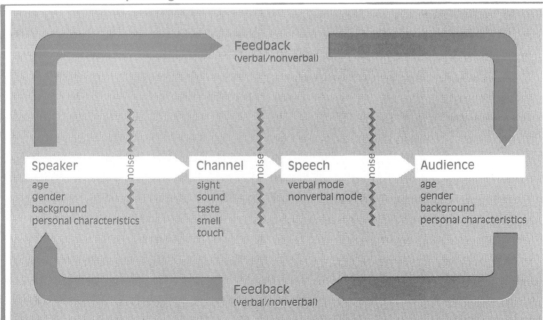

public. Knowing some of the basic similarities and differences between public speaking and other forms of communication should help you apply what you've learned in public speaking to other areas such as intrapersonal communication, interpersonal communication, and small group communication.

Intrapersonal Communication

Intrapersonal communication is that which occurs inside a person. It literally involves talking to oneself. Have you ever asked yourself, "Why did I say that?" or "Why did I put that answer on the exam?" in a moment of reflection? If so, you spoke intrapersonally.

Both intrapersonal communication and public speaking are source oriented. That is, in both forms listeners rely primarily on the source for information. Both forms are influenced by the occasion in which the message occurs. Both forms must adapt to feedback in order to make the message audience centered. Both forms need to use a language that is readily understood by speaker and listener. Both forms are dynamic, transactional processes, reflecting the interplay among components in the communication setting. Finally, both forms attempt to seek understanding and, at times, acceptance of the source's message.

Basic differences between intrapersonal communication and public speaking rest in the fact that in intrapersonal communication the speaker

Intrapersonal communication occurs within the mind of an individual. In "talking to ourselves," we send messages and react to them in ways that help us develop unique attitudes, values, and beliefs. Much of this self-communication involves the processing of a staggering amount of information that comes from daily contact with the environment.

and audience are one. The opportunity for interaction is greater in this communication setting, as is the opportunity to react immediately to a more limited amount of feedback.

In a public speaking setting, the number of listeners is greater and they vary in background. Feedback may come from multiple sources. Rarely is a speaker able to adapt to all the feedback sent by the audience.

Generally, public speaking messages are more structured in form (for example, introduction, body, and conclusion), attempt to avoid slang, follow grammatical rules, and have specific time limitations. Intrapersonal communication messages, on the other hand, are generally less formal in structure. They usually are not bound by time limitations, and they can contain any type of language or syntactical arrangement of language acceptable to the listener. Also, intrapersonal communication can occur anywhere and at anytime. This is generally not the case in public speaking.

Interpersonal Communication

Interpersonal communication occurs generally between two people who are communicating informally with each other.[6] Bill tells Linda he loves her; Ann explains to Joe the reason she wants to attend graduate school. These are just a couple of examples of interpersonal communication. Both interpersonal communication and public speaking seek understanding and, at times, acceptance of the source's message. Generally, in

Interpersonal communication usually occurs between two people in an informal situation. The effectiveness of the communication depends on the speaker's ability to send a clear, understandable message and on the listener's ability to interpret the meaning of the message as it was intended.

both forms of communication, listeners rely on the source to present reliable and pertinent information. Both forms must contain language that listeners understand. Both forms need to adjust and adapt to feedback.

The differences lie primarily in the formality of the message and occasion and in the source and audience. As with intrapersonal communication, interpersonal communication often involves the sharing of informal messages in less formal settings. This is usually not the case in public speaking. In an interpersonal setting the source of the message may shift from one person to another. This rarely occurs in public speech where the speaker is considered the principal source of information. And last, the number of audience members is less in an interpersonal communication setting than in a public speaking setting. This difference, of course, affects the amount and direction of feedback, as well as the amount of time the source and listener can interact with each other.

Small Group Communication

Most researchers agree that a small group contains a limited number of people (obviously a smaller number than usually found in a public speaking setting) who interact with each other to achieve a common goal.[7] Public speaking shares with small group communication the same simi-

In small group communication, all members interact with one another. Ideally, all communicators actively supply discussion information.

larities and differences that it does with intrapersonal and interpersonal communication. However, there is one additional difference between public speaking and small group communication—the manner in which each attempts to achieve its goal. In a small group, information for discussion can come from any or all members of the group. In a public speaking situation, speaker and audience may share the same goal, but the speaker is the principal source for supplying information needed to accomplish the goal. Thus, the speaker usually enters the event with a preconceived notion of the goal. This is not necessarily the case in small group communication.

SUMMARY

Public speaking plays an important role in the exercise of the right of free speech. Public speaking offers at least three important advantages: it is vital for self-growth, it helps to advance knowledge, and it is essential for establishing a stable society. Along with the right of free speech comes the responsibility to speak wisely and truthfully.

Public speaking is a transactional process in which speakers and listeners share formal and informal messages (verbal and nonverbal) within a specific context. The major components of the process include the speaker, the speech, the audience, the channels of communication, feedback, noise, and the speaking occasion. The components fit together in a public speaking model that emphasizes the transactional nature of the process.

There are a number of similarities and differences between public speaking and other forms of communication, including intrapersonal communication, interpersonal communication, and small group discussion. Understanding these similarities and differences should help you apply your knowledge of public speaking to other forms of communication.

ASSIGNMENTS

1. The chapter lists a number of advantages relating to the importance of public speaking in a free society.
   a. Is there one advantage that you agree with most? Why?
   b. Is there one advantage that you disagree with? Why?
   c. Would you add any other advantages to the list? What would they be?
   d. Report your views in an essay or in oral form to the class.

2. Draw a model of public speaking.
   a. How is it different or similar to the one presented in the book?
   b. Show and explain your model to the class.

3. Give a 2–3-minute speech of self-introduction.
   a. Print your name on the board.
   b. Enunciate your name clearly, particularly if it has an unusual spelling and pronunciation.
   c. Briefly describe your home town, high school, and hobbies.
   d. What is your major and what do you plan to do after graduation?
   e. What are your outside activities?

4. Give a 2–3-minute speech to introduce a classmate.
   a. Take a few minutes to interview a classmate.
   b. You may want to ask questions about his or her background, place of residence, high school or college activities, choice of major, or plans for the future.
   c. Present a brief speech that introduces your classmate. Attempt to incorporate as much relevant information about the person as possible.

NOTES

1. For an interesting review of judicial decisions on the right of free speech, see Franklin S. Haiman, *Speech and Law in a Free Society* (Chicago: University of Chicago Press, 1981).

2. "Credo for Free and Responsible Communication in a Democratic Society," *Spectra,* 9 (April 1972), p. 5.

3. Ernest C. Bormann, "Fantasy and Rhetorical Vision: The Rhetorical Criticism of Social Reality," *Quarterly Journal of Speech,* 58 (December 1972), 396–407.

4. Dominic A. LaRusso, *The Shadows of Communication* (Dubuque, IA: Kendall/Hunt Publishing Co., 1977), p. 101.

5. L. Kaufman, *Perception: The World Transformed* (New York: Oxford University Press, 1979).

6. For helpful reading on the subject of interpersonal communication see: Donald P. Cushman and Dudley D. Cahn, Jr., *Communication in Interpersonal Relations* (Albany: State University of New York Press, 1985); Dennis R. Smith and L. Keith Williamson, *Interpersonal Communication: Roles, Rules, Strategies, and Games,* 3rd ed. (Dubuque, IA: William C. Brown Co., 1985).

7. For interesting reading on the subject of small group communication see: David W. Johnson and Frank P. Johnson, *Joining Together: Group Theory and Group Skills,* 2nd ed. (Englewood Cliffs, NJ: Prentice-Hall, 1982); Donald W. Klopf, *Interacting in Groups,* 2nd ed. (Englewood, CO: Morton Publishing Co., 1985).

Definition of Listening	
Benefits of Good Listening Skills	Opportunity for Increased Knowledge and Intellectual Growth
	Opportunity to Stimulate Better Speaking
	Opportunity to Become a Better Note Taker
	Opportunity for Increased Enjoyment of Listening
Types of Listening Patterns	Appreciative Listening
	Discriminative Listening
	Evaluative Listening
	Emphathic Listening
	Dialogic Listening
Myths About Listening	Higher Intelligence Equals Better Listening Skills
	Listening Is a Natural Ability
	Hearing Is the Same as Listening
	The Speaker Is Solely Responsible for Successful Reception of a Message
	Listening Means Agreeing
	Listening Is a Passive Process
Bad Listening Habits	Pretending to Listen
	Listening Sporadically
	Dismissing the Message Because of Its Complexity
	Disliking the Speaker
	Disliking the Topic
	Listening to Argue
	Recordkeeping Listening
	Failing to Adjust to Distractions
Improving Listening Skills in a Public Speaking Setting	Skills Used Before Presentation of a Speech
	Skills Used During Presentation of a Speech
	Skills Used After Presentation of a Speech

2 The Listener in Public Speaking

OBJECTIVES

When you finish this chapter, you should be able to:

1. define listening;
2. define major myths about listening;
3. discuss bad listening habits;
4. demonstrate the steps for improving listening skills;
5. discuss the benefits of good listening skills; and
6. present an informative speech on the information gained from the listener's evaluation form located in the appendix.

2 The Listener in Public Speaking

John meets Tim in front of their dorm. Excited by the news that Pam finally agreed to go out with him, John explains in complete detail how he managed to convince Pam to date him. Tim stands quietly, occasionally nodding his head and smiling, as he hears John's story. After several minutes, John abruptly stops speaking. He looks at Tim straight in the eyes and says, "You haven't listened to a word I've said." Disgusted by Tim's alleged insincerity and rudeness, John storms away, muttering to himself how self-centered his friend Tim is.

The above example is typical for many people. Few persons listen effectively. They are easily side-tracked. Others listen to just part of the message or merely pretend to listen. Yet, a major portion of communication activities involves listening. With so much practice, everyone should be an expert listener. Unfortunately, this is not the case.

Most people would probably agree that listening plays an important role in the learning process. In the classroom, you rely heavily on the process of listening to comprehend large amounts of information communicated by professors. Robert Hirsch points out that students today must rely more on listening to process information than did their predecessors. Hirsch notes with regret that "too many teachers still downplay the importance of listening and too few people learn to listen properly or to reap its maximum benefits."[1]

Not only does listening play an important part in the classroom, it plays a major part in the working world and in everyday life as well. In the business world, for instance, listening skills are essential for effecting successful organizational communication between superiors and subordinates.[2] As much as 57.5 percent of a person's daily communication is spent in listening.[3] Still many people lack the necessary skills to be good listeners.

As with any other form of communication, public speaking is affected by the listening habits of the audience. Generally, when people listen, speakers are more apt to do a better job. When audience members don't listen, speakers may be discouraged from putting forth their best efforts. Suppose you are a speaker, presenting a message to an inattentive audience. How would you react? Would you become so outraged by their rudeness that you would somehow force them to listen to you? Would you feel so discouraged that you might stop speaking altogether? As a listener, you have a stake in the public speaking process. Your activities as a listener can help or hinder this process. Remember, when you speak, you'll want people to listen to you; as a listener, you should show speakers the same courtesy. Good speaking and good listening go hand in hand.

In this chapter we will explore several aspects of listening. We will examine the benefits of good listening and talk about several types of listening patterns. We will discuss obstacles that prevent effective listening: myths about listening and poor listening habits. We will also suggest some ways in which you can improve your listening skills. Before we turn to these topics, however, we will begin with a definition of listening.

DEFINITION OF LISTENING

Have you ever been accused of not listening? You may have responded, "But I heard what was said." But were you listening? What is the difference between hearing and listening? Generally, hearing implies the receiving of sounds through the aural channel (ears) but not necessarily the understanding and remembering of those sounds.[4]

A universally agreed-upon definition of listening does not yet exist. As researchers A. D. Wolvin and C. G. Coakley explain, "The definition of listening is still in the process of being developed."[5] But many definitions of listening include the elements of hearing, aural stimuli, discrimination among aural input, remembering, and understanding.

We define listening as *an activity that involves both hearing and the transactional process of attempting to understand and remember particular symbols within a specific context.* Particularly in the public speaking context, listening is a transactional process: a dynamic interplay among the components within a specific context. Figure 2.1, a model of listen-

FIGURE 2.1   **A Model of Listening**

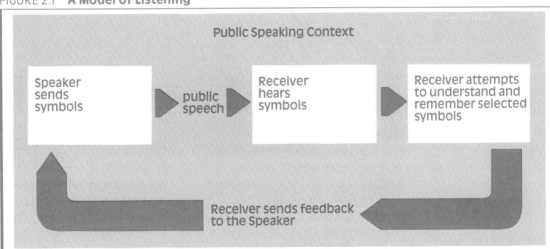

ing, illustrates stages involved in the process of listening. Notice that the model designates the speaker as the sender of the symbols. Remember, however, that at any time the speaker and the receiver may reverse their roles in this transactional speaking process.

Although it is basic, the model contains most of the major components in listening. Within the public speaking context, there is generally an aural symbol in the public speech that triggers the listening process. The listener selectively hears the symbol in the speech. The symbol is then processed for purposes of understanding (meaning is assigned to the symbol) and remembering. The listener responds to the message, source of the message, or both.

The interactive listening process promotes the sharing of meaning between speaker and listener. As both attempt to adapt the message to each other, they may alter the meaning of the message for clarity and understanding. As we can see, then, listening is an interactive, transactional process between speaker and listener. It will be to your advantage as a speaker to understand the benefits of listening and to become a good listener.

BENEFITS OF GOOD LISTENING SKILLS

Listening is an essential part of the communication process in general and public speaking in particular. As such, good listening skills may lead to advantages that you may not yet be aware of in public speaking. Such advantages include the opportunity for increased knowledge and intellectual growth, the opportunity to stimulate better speaking, the opportunity to learn how to become a better note taker, and the opportunity to derive increased enjoyment from the activity of listening.

Opportunity for Increased Knowledge and Intellectual Growth

During your lifetime, you will listen to many public speeches. These speeches may ask you to support a candidate, to support a bond issue, to join a branch of the service, to buy a particular product, to consider specific information, or to praise an individual. Moreover, you'll have to evaluate a large quantity of information, attitudes, beliefs, and values. How will you learn how to manage all these messages?

One important way to manage such messages is to master the process of listening. Good listening skills can help you organize and retain more information in a message. Your ability to grow intellectually is as important as your ability to retain information. With a wider base of information from which to operate, you'll be more likely to expand your knowledge. There is, of course, no guarantee that increased knowledge creates a more responsible citizen, but your chances of making informed decisions are improved when you can base your decisions on a wide base of knowledge.

Opportunity to Stimulate Better Speaking

As both a speaker and a listener in public speaking, you can appreciate the time, effort, and energy it takes to perform both these roles successfully, and you probably appreciate the effort put forth by others who perform these roles. Have you given much thought to the possible interplay between these roles? Do they affect each other? Research does suggest that effective speakers tend to score higher on standardized listening tests.[6]

As a speaker, how do you feel when you present a speech to an audience? Are you encouraged to do a better job if your audience is listening? Are you discouraged if they appear inattentive? As a listener you can help create a positive climate—one that encourages a speaker to put forth his or her best effort. In such a situation, all participants gain from the public speaking experience.

Good listening skills can stimulate you to become a better speaker. When, through attentive listening, you encourage others to speak well, you may learn from them (as models) the skills and abilities that help you be a better speaker. Obviously, much can be gained in an environment that encourages effective public speaking.

Opportunity to Become a Better Note Taker

Sometimes a listener taking notes at a speech or lecture will try to record *every* word he or she hears. The listener may not be listening carefully and may miss much of the nonverbal communication surrounding the speaker's message. How often have you gone back to your notes and then asked yourself, "What did the speaker mean?" Probably, this happens more than we wish to admit.

It is not advisable to stop taking notes altogether. Rather, you should concentrate on the *quality* rather than the *quantity* of note taking. Effective listening can help. We will present some suggestions for effective note taking later in this chapter.

Opportunity for Increased Enjoyment of Listening

Do you find yourself enjoying activities that challenge you? As you improve your skills to meet these challenges, do you appear to enjoy the activity even more? If so, you'll probably find this true with the art of listening. (Hopefully, a similar feeling will occur with the art of public speaking.)

As you practice to improve your listening ability, you'll want to test it. Seek challenges. Try to listen effectively in your private conversations, in small group meetings, or at public speaking events. With your increased confidence, you'll learn to trust more in your listening ability. A sense of active, responsible participation in the communication process will help you enjoy even more the acts of listening and communicating. There are several ways in which you can listen effectively. In the next section we will explore the types of listening patterns.

TYPES OF LISTENING PATTERNS

A variety of listening patterns exists within the communication process. People generally have multiple goals and reasons for listening. For example, when you listen to a public speech, you may want to asses the strength and weaknesses of the message, as well as appreciate the content of the speech and the manner in which it was delivered. Or you may want to listen openly, to accept the speaker as a fellow human being, and to offer genuine feedback. Rarely is only one type of listening pattern present when a person listens actively; most often a combination of patterns is in use. It may help you listen more effectively and enjoyably if you know how and why you are listening. In this section we will discuss several common types of listening patterns.

Appreciative Listening

People who listen appreciatively attempt to satisfy their sensory appetite. They want to appreciate the style of language used, the forcefulness of ideas presented, the environmental sounds that surround the message, or the clash of ideas on a particular issue. Appreciative listening yields several benefits:

1. A greater awareness of rhythm and rate of time in a message.
2. A greater awareness of the different types of delivery patterns.
3. A greater awareness of the different types of organizational patterns of messages.
4. A greater awareness of the different types of nonverbal modes of communication.

Discriminative Listening

People who listen discriminatively attempt to distinguish between ideas in order to find those that are of value to them. Discriminative listeners focus their attention on the speaker's main ideas, weigh the evidence presented, listen attentively to other listeners' questions and the speaker's responses, and ask their own questions to clarify the message.

Evaluative Listening

Evaluative listening is a process that attempts to assess the value of a persuasive message. After evaluating the message, listeners ask themselves if they are willing to change their attitudes, beliefs, or values in a direction advocated by the speaker.

Empathic Listening

To listen empathically is to attempt to understand the speaker's attitudes, beliefs, and values, while suspending judgment about the speaker. The focus is not on how the listener feels about the speaker but on how the listener *believes* the speaker feels about the message. Empathic listening is frequently used in counseling situations: the counselor tries to understand better the feelings of the client.

Dialogic Listening

Dialogic listening, like empathic listening, builds on a sense of genuine communication. The dialogic listener tries to understand the speaker's feelings and to provide honest feedback that allows the speaker "to agree to or correct [the listener's] interpretation of the message."[7] The dialogic listener respects the speaker's right to freely voice his or her opinion. The listener attempts to "stick with" the speaker's thoughts. Active dialogic listening invites and promotes communication between speaker and listener.

No one pattern or combination of patterns can guarantee effective listening. Several obstacles can still stand in the way. Among these obstacles are myths about listening, which we will discuss in the next section of this chapter.

MYTHS ABOUT LISTENING

Myths about listening foster a general belief that effective listening is a natural ability that entails minimum effort, which is usually not the case. (Such a view is sometimes also heard regarding the act of public speaking.) In the following section we will discuss some of the myths associated with effective listening.[8]

Higher Intelligence Equals Better Listening Skills

Some people are gifted with high intelligence. Standard levels of academic work are less challenging for them than for other people. Often those capable of comprehending and assimilating information quickly believe that this natural skill automatically makes them good listeners. It seems logical to conclude that higher intelligence equals better listening skills. This is not necessarily the case, say researchers Wolff, Marsnik, Taey, and Nichols in their work, *Perceptive Listening*.[9] They suggest that no clear correlation exists between a person's intelligence and listening ability. No matter what your intelligence level is, you must *work* at improving your listening skills. As with public speaking, you must practice good listening skills if you are to improve as a communicator.

Listening Is a Natural Ability

Very little formal training is available on how to listen. Although the topic of listening is slowly gaining respect as a subject for academic study, far too few schools offer any serious study of this subject. Part of the reason for this rests in the mistaken belief that listening is a natural ability that can be acquired easily. The commonly heard statement "Pay attention!" assumes that people automatically possess the natural ability to listen. Perhaps some people do. But most people must work hard to improve their listening skills. You must learn and practice the theories and skills of listening, just as you must learn the theories and practice the skills of public speaking if you hope to improve your communicative ability.

Hearing Is the Same as Listening

As we said earlier, hearing and listening are not the same. Hearing involves receiving aural symbols but not necessarily understanding and remembering them. Listening encompasses hearing but also includes the stages of understanding and remembering aural symbols. The danger of equating hearing and listening rests in the belief that when an aural symbol is heard, the receiver is also *listening* to it. Such a belief makes the receiver a passive participant in the communication process. Forcing yourself to be a good listener helps you understand and remember the message.

The Speaker Is Solely Responsible for Successful Reception of a Message

According to this myth, whoever presents the speech is responsible for successful reception of its message. If it's a good message, the members of the audience will listen to it; if not, they'll ignore it. Do the listeners carry no responsibility? Of course they do. Good, attentive listeners not only gain more from the message; as we have discussed, they can also stimulate better speaking. A speaker may be more inclined to communicate more clearly if he or she feels the audience is truly listening. Both speaker and listener contribute to the successful reception of a message.

Listening Means Agreeing

This myth says that if you're listening, you must be agreeing with the speaker. Is this always the case? Certainly there are times when you both listen to and agree with the speaker, but listening does not automatically translate into agreement. The act of listening involves understanding and remembering particular aural symbols—not necessarily agreeing with them. If you agree with the speaker, you do so not because you listen but because you understand the speaker's message and find it acceptable.

Listening Is a Passive Process

A person who listens plays an active part in the communication process. An active listener uses most, if not all, of his or her senses when receiving messages. An active listener does not just hear a speaker describe the shape and fragrance of a rose; an active listener imagines smelling it and seeing it as well. On the other hand, the receiver who simply hears the aural symbol without attempting to use the other senses is acting passively and gains only a minimal amount of content from a limited number of senses.

As you can see, a number of myths about listening exist, but there are also other obstacles to developing good listening skills. Sometimes it is not a myth about listening that stands in the way of good listening; it may be a bad listening habit. In the next section, we will discuss some bad listening habits and examine how they prevent people from becoming good listeners.

BAD LISTENING HABITS

Have you ever tried to learn a new sport without being properly instructed? If you used the process of "trial and error" to learn the sport, you probably developed a number of bad habits. Similarly, many persons have developed bad listening habits. The first step in correcting bad habits is identifying them. You may find it easier and less threatening, at first, to recognize the bad listening habits of other people, then compare and contrast their listening habits with your own. In this section we will discuss some of the most common bad listening habits—habits that may prevent you from becoming a good listener and an effective communicator.

Pretending to Listen

Some people are quite adept at pretending to listen. They don't want to offend the speaker so they politely pretend to listen. They look at the speaker, their facial expressions suggesting interest. They may even nod occasionally or otherwise acknowledge the message. Still, they are not listening. By merely pretending to listen, they defeat the very purposes of listening—to understand and remember. Continually pretending to listen forms a habitual response. Insincere listeners condition themselves to act politely while tuning out the speaker and the message.

Listening Sporadically

Unlike the person who pretends to listen, a person who listens sporadically actually listens, but only for short periods of time. At first the listener focuses on the message but then shifts his or her attention to another idea external to the speaker's message. Later the listener shifts back again to the original message. For example, a speaker may be talking about the problems related to declining enrollments in college. At first, the listener hears the speaker's message. The listener, however, then shifts his or her attention to the topic of his or her plans for the weekend. After a few moments, the listener's attention shifts back to the speaker's message. This pattern of listening may continue many times through the remainder of the speech. When the listener's focus shifts frequently, he or she has difficulty remembering and understanding the speaker's message.

Do you find yourself listening sporadically? Do you tend to shift your focus from one message to another? If so, you accumulate only fragmentary parts of the original message. Any decisions you can make or meaningful responses that you may provide are limited by the fragmentary information you have gained.

Dismissing the Message Because of Its Complexity

Sometimes you give up too quickly when listening to a complex message. If it contains complex sentences, vocabulary, pieces of evidence, or thoughts, you excuse yourself from listening to the message. You may prematurely believe that nothing can be learned from so complicated a message. This may be true, but unless you seriously try to listen, to challenge yourself, you'll never know. Worse yet, you may deny yourself the possibility of learning new information that may help broaden your base of knowledge and develop your potential.

Disliking the Speaker

You may not like the speaker's clothing, accent, or attitudes. For whatever reasons, if you dislike the speaker, you may not listen attentively to the message. Does this mean that to listen well you must like the speaker? No, but you do need to take stock of your beliefs, values, or attitudes toward the speaker. If you have strong negative feelings, you'll want to recognize and control them as much as possible. If you fail to do so, you may "tune out" the speaker. The speaker may have something worthwhile to say, but you'll never know that if you don't overcome the obstacle of dislike.

Disliking the Topic

You may dismiss the speaker's topic as uninteresting, simplistic, offensive, complex, or vague. For example, a speaker may be discussing the national debt. Most of the listeners in the audience, however, may not be interested in topics related to economics. They may dismiss the speaker's message as being too dull for them. As noted in Chapter 1, public speaking is a vital vehicle for self-growth. When you prematurely dismiss a topic because you don't like it, you severely limit your development as a thinking, caring individual.

Listening to Argue

Sometimes referred to as defensive listening, argumentative listening suggests that you listen not to understand but to refute. You "know" that you're right and the speaker is wrong. You generally react immediately to views with which you disagree either by verbally stating your objections or by thinking of points to counter. Perhaps you are highly involved with the subject chosen by the speaker. As a result, you may feel threatened by the message and compelled to defend yourself. Perhaps you simply enjoy arguing. You don't care about what the subject is or the reasons given on its behalf. When you listen argumentatively, you listen only to the part of the message with which you disagree. Any serious understanding of the speaker's entire message evaporates when you listen simply to argue and refute.

Recordkeeping Listening

Do you find yourself taking detailed notes during a speech or lecture? If so, you may have developed the bad habit of recordkeeping listening. This means that you rely on note taking for your listening. Your attention focuses more on recording all or most of the speaker's words for later reference than on actively listening to the message as it is being presented. The solution to this problem is to attempt to observe and listen to the speaker while selectively and *periodically* taking notes. By freeing yourself from excessive note taking, you can, even if momentarily, observe the speaker's nonverbal messages as you listen to the verbal ones. Taken together, these messages may provide you with greater insight and understanding of the speech. Effective listening can help you become a better note taker, just as learning how to take selective notes can help you listen more effectively. Later in this chapter we will discuss some methods of effective note taking.

Failing to Adjust to Distractions

Do you find that you are easily distracted when listening to people? Do you focus on irrelevant material written on a blackboard or tacked on a wall? Many people are easily distracted when listening to a speaker, especially if they aren't interested in the message. You may be tempted to excuse this common listening habit as a natural human shortcoming. However, consider how deeply rooted this habit is. Do you attempt to minimize the internal and external distractions that may affect the listening process (recall the discussion of noise elements in Chapter 1)? If not, you may find yourself focusing more on distractions and less on the speaker's message.

Perhaps you have recognized some of your own bad listening habits among those discussed in this section. Now that we have identified some habits of poor listening, we turn to the topic of correcting these faults. How can you improve your listening habits and maximize the advantages that can accrue from good listening skills? In the next section we will explore several ways to improve listening skills.

IMPROVING LISTENING SKILLS IN A PUBLIC SPEAKING SETTING

Most people speak within a range of speed of 125 words to 180 words per minute. People are able to listen to 450 to 800 words or more per minute.[10] Effective listening occurs at a speed somewhere between these two ranges; at a speed slow enough for a speaker to effectively use the language but fast enough to keep the listener's attention. Furthermore, as John Stewart observes, the listener must be "open to the meanings that are being developed 'between' one's self and one's partner."[11] Thus, the exchange of meaning between listener and speaker promotes shared understanding.

You can develop the skills needed to improve your listening habits. These skills fall into three broad categories: skills used before the message, skills used during the message, and skills used after the message.

Skills Used Before Presentation of a Speech

When time permits, as a listener you'll want to assess the public speaking situation, topic, speaker, and any of your attitudes toward these elements *before* the speaking event occurs. By doing this, you'll identify any of your attitudes, beliefs, or values that may interfere with the reception of the message. Obviously, you cannot completely suspend all of your feelings. You should use them to help you understand the emerging meanings in the speech. The danger comes when your attitudes, beliefs, or values prevent you from listening to the speech. Recognize this danger. Let yourself listen as completely as possible to the *entire* speech. As a result, you should be able to listen more objectively when the message is presented.

There are some measures you can take before presentation of the message that will help you listen completely and objectively. For example, try to eliminate as many of the external distractions as possible. You may be able to do this simply by turning on some lights, closing windows to cut down on outside noise, or opening windows to improve ventilation. Anticipate your own internal needs so as to minimize their potential disruptive force on your reception of the message. When possible, satisfy such needs as hunger or thirst before the speech occurs. Doing a pre-analysis of potential distractions may make you more aware of problems that can affect your ability to listen effectively.

Skills Used During Presentation of a Speech

During this stage the interval between speaking and listening exerts a crucial impact on listening habits and abilities. Remember that you are able to listen much faster than a speaker can speak. During the presentation of a speech many distractions can direct your attention away from the message. Distractions can include uncomfortable chairs, poor acoustics, outside interruptions, or a poorly constructed speech. Exercising good listening skills during the presentation of a speech can help you make better use of the "gap of time" between speaking and listening.

While listening to the speech, construct a brief mental outline of the speaker's message. Let the outline focus mainly on the major purpose and ideas of the message. Transfer this outline to paper. Seek out the important words that identify major topic areas, subpoints, and evidence. Capture as briefly but as accurately as possible the central parts of the speech. As you become a more skillful listener, you will be able to take more detailed and accurate notes. Likewise as you develop your note-taking skills, you'll sharpen your listening ability. Keep your notes simple, referring to major ideas, evidence, and sources. As you complete your outline, attempt to recycle it several times. Good times to recycle are during periods when the speaker is using several examples to illustrate a point, when the speaker seems to be wandering from the topic, or when you need to listen more actively and thus reconstruct as much of the message as possible.

Suppose you were listening to a speech on experimentation using prison inmates. Your notes on the speech might look something like this:

Major purpose: To persuade audience that experiments using prison inmates can be dangerous.

   I. Experiments on humans can be dangerous
      A. Effects of drugs and procedures are unknown (*Society*, 1974)
      B. Experiment may require contracting disease
         1. Malaria project exhibited problems at Statesville prison in
            Illinois
         2. Experiments conducted in Ohio prisons (*Atlantic Monthly*,
            1973)
      C. Some experiments in prisons are not done carefully
         1. Experimenter, Dr. Hodges, reported problems concerning
            scurvy experiment (*Atlantic Monthly*, 1973)
         2. Dr. Austin Stough responsible for causing a hepatitis out-
            break in experiments with Alabama prisoners
  II. Inmates are particularly useful in experiments
      A. Prisoners make convenient, stable population
      B. Prisoners generally healthy and mentally competent

At first, your notes may not be as complete as those in the example, but
as you improve your listening skills, your note-taking ability will improve.

There are other listening skills that you can use during the presentation of a speech. Try to anticipate some of the points that the speaker may
make. By anticipating the line of development, you keep your mind on the
topic and maintain your interest in the message. Just don't get too far
ahead of the speaker. Assess briefly the strengths and weaknesses of the
speaker's arguments, evidence, and sources. For example, is the evidence
current, from reliable sources, and consistent with other evidence on the
same or similar topics? Are the arguments valid? Are the conclusions
supported by sound evidence?

Be aware of the noise elements that can interfere with the reception of
a message and try to minimize their effects. For example, if you have
difficulty hearing the speaker, ask the speaker to talk louder or move
closer to the speaker. You may do a perception check by asking such
questions as "Do you mean this?" or "Am I to understand that you feel
this way toward the subject?" Such questions allow you, as a listener, to
check the accuracy of your perception of the message.

During the presentation of a speech, be in command of your role as
listener. Recognize your feelings toward the speaker and the message.
Try to listen as actively as possible. Tolerate as few distractions as possible
that interfere with your goals of listening to understand and remember
the message. While you are listening to the speech, keep in mind that the
speaking event may provide you with the opportunity to learn new, useful,
information.

Skills Used After Presentation of a Speech

Listeners seldom develop one of the most important phases in listening. This phase occurs *after* the speech has been delivered. You use listening skills after the presentation of the speech to recycle and reinforce the message. You are, in a sense, doing an instant replay of the speech. You probably will not remember the entire speech, but you attempt to "listen" once again to the message. After the speech has been presented, use your listening skills to recycle the outline, focusing on the speaker's purpose, main points, supporting points, and source material. Try to recall the main elements that gave rise to the purpose and meaning of the message. If possible, you should recycle the outline in a quiet area where there are as few distractions as possible. You may not have this opportunity in a public speaking class. However, if you can, retreat to a quiet part of the room to evaluate the speech.

In your evaluation, ask how the message relates to you. Ask why it is important that you remember and understand it. You are likely to feel closer to the speaker's message if you can understand its relationship and importance to you.

By using these listening skills before, during, and after the presentation of a speech, you should be able to increase your effectiveness as a listener—which is, after all, the task you hope to accomplish as an active listener. You may discover, too, that not only will your effectiveness as a listener increase, but so also will your enjoyment of listening to speeches.

SUMMARY

The art of listening involves the flexible application of principles. Listening is defined as the active, transactional process of hearing and attempting to understand and remember particular symbols within a specific context.

Good listening skills yield benefits for both the listener and the public speaker. Among these are the opportunity for increased knowledge, the opportunity to stimulate better speaking, the opportunity to become a better note taker, and the opportunity for increased listening enjoyment.

Types of listening patterns include appreciative listening, discriminative listening, evaluative listening, empathic listening, and dialogic listening. Knowing these patterns can help one listen more effectively and enjoyably.

Several common myths associated with the listening process can interfere with effective listening. Common listening myths include the beliefs that higher intelligence equals better listening skills, that listening is a natural ability, that hearing is the same as listening, and that the speaker is solely responsible for the successful reception of a message. Other widely held myths include the views that listening means agreeing and that listening is a passive process.

Some of the major bad habits commonly associated with listening involve pretending to listen, listening sporadically, dismissing the message because of its complexity, disliking the speaker, disliking the topic, listening to argue, record-keeping listening, and failing to adjust to distractions.

There are several ways in which you can improve your listening skills in a public speaking situation. The skills fall into three broad areas: skills used before the presentation of a speech, skills used during the presentation of a speech, and skills used after the presentation of a speech.

By recognizing the myths and bad habits often associated with listening and by practicing the skills for improving listening, receivers of speeches can increase their listening effectiveness and come to a greater enjoyment of the public speaking process.

ASSIGNMENTS

1. Draw your own model of listening. Display and explain its components and functions to the class.

2. Practice note taking as described in this chapter. As you listen to a speaker, make a brief outline of the speaker's
   a. major purpose
   b. major points
   c. subpoints
   d. important supporting material
   Briefly explain your outline to the class.

3. In a group of three people, assign one person to be the speaker, one to be the listener, and the third to be the judge. Perform the following activities:
   a. Have the speaker give a one-minute speech on a topic of interest.
   b. Have the listener attempt to remember what the speaker says without taking notes.
   c. Have the judge take notes of the speaker's message.
   d. After the speech, have the listener paraphrase what he or she heard.
   e. Have the judge evaluate the accuracy of the paraphrase.
   f. Perform these activities two more times, with members of the group exchanging roles.

4. Attempt to take control of the listening situation. During the next speaking assignment, make an effort to minimize physical and psy-

chological distractions. Make a list of items (such as sitting closer to the speaker, asking the speaker to talk louder, getting a drink of water before class) that you attempted to control. Share your list.

5. Use the listener's evaluation form in the appendix to critique a speaker and yourself as a listener. In a two-minute speech present your findings to the class.

NOTES

1. Robert O. Hirsch, *Listening Processing Information Annually* (Dubuque, IA: Gorsuch Scarisbrick, 1983), p. 4.

2. Cal W. Downs and Charles C. Conrad, "Effective Subordinacy," *The Journal of Business Communication,* 19 (1982), 27–38.

3. Andrew D. Wolvin and Carolyn Gwynn Coakley, *Listening* (Dubuque, IA: Wm. C. Brown Co., 1982), p. 4.

4. John Stewart, "Interpretive Listening: An Alternative to Empathy," *Communication Education,* 32 (1983), 379.

5. Wolvin and Coakley, p. 31.

6. Larry L. Barker, Kitte W. Watson, and Robert J. Kibler, "An Investigation of the Effect of Presentations by Effective and Ineffective Speakers on Listening Test Scores," *Southern Speech Communication Journal,* 49 (1984), 317.

7. James J. Floyd, *Listening: A Practical Approach* (Glenview, IL: Scott, Foresman, 1985), pp. 122–23.

8. For a more complete listing of myths, see Florence I. Wolff et al., *Perceptive Listening* (NY: Holt, Rinehart and Winston, 1983), pp. 24–44.

9. Wolff et al., pp. 25–26.

10. Wolff et al., p. 159.

11. Stewart, p. 384.

Developing the Speech	Analyzing the Audience	
	Analyzing the Occasion	
	Choosing the Right Subject	A Subject in Which You Are Already Interested
		A Subject About Which You Already Know Something
		A Subject on Which You Can Do Extra Research
		A Subject Worth Your Listeners' Time
	Determining the General Purpose	
	Determining the Specific Purpose	
	Researching the Material	Researching Yourself
		Researching Others
	Organizing Ideas	Patterns of Organization
		Principles of Outlining
	Developing Ideas	The Body of the Speech
		The Introduction of the Speech
		The Conclusion of the Speech
Rehearsing the Speech	Methods of Presentation	Written Out and Memorized
		Written Out and Read
		Spoken Impromptu
		Outlined and Extemporized
	Visual and Vocal Techniques	
Building Confidence in Public Speaking	Experiencing Anxiety	
	Analyzing the Situation	
	Converting Fear into Action	
	Getting and Holding Listeners' Attention	External Competition
		Internal Competition
Accepting Constructive Evaluation		

3

Speech Preparation

When you finish this chapter, you should be able to:

1. analyze an audience in a specific occasion;
2. describe the criteria for choosing a speech topic and choose a subject to speak on that you can handle successfully;
3. determine a general and a specific purpose for your speech;
4. research yourself and others for your speech material;
5. identify the patterns of organization and organize your speech according to one of the patterns;
6. explain the principles of outlining and use them to develop an outline for your speech;
7. rehearse your speech from an outline;
8. incorporate visual and vocal techniques in your speech;
9. recognize the symptoms of anxiety and know how to cope with them; and
10. give a short extemporaneous speech of 3–5 minutes from an outline on a subject of your choice.

3 Speech Preparation

Richard Spaulding dreaded his first prepared speech. He dreaded it mainly because he didn't know how to go about it—what steps to take and how to put it all together. He solved his problem, he thought, by choosing the Star Wars defense system as a subject and lifting large chunks of information from articles in the library. Richard realized the speech was heavy in content, but, he rationalized, the audience wouldn't listen too carefully, and, after all, he was just trying to give the listeners an overview of the topic. When he finished, no one, not even the instructor, knew exactly what his point was or how he wanted the audience to react to it. What, Richard wondered, had gone wrong?

In this chapter we will discuss the fundamental procedures of speech preparation. By the time you finish this chapter, you should be able to prepare an effective presentation, one that has a good chance of achieving the purpose you determine from the start.

As we discussed in Chapter 2, listening to many other public speakers can help you become an effective speaker. You will notice many personalities and styles at work. It won't be long before you will conclude that there are many acceptable ways to give a speech in public, and yet there are certain techniques that are fundamental to all successful speakers.

There are four basic procedures to follow to be an effective public speaker: develop your speech, rehearse your presentation, build your self-confidence, and accept constructive evaluation. In this chapter we will examine each of these techniques.

DEVELOPING THE SPEECH

To build a speech you need to analyze your audience and the occasion, choose the right subject, determine your purpose, do research, and organize and develop your material. If you follow these steps one at a time, you will simplify what seems at the start to be a complicated process.

Analyzing the Audience

Students in a public speaking class sometimes think that a speech is mostly standing up, performing, and getting it over with. Yet a speech is much more than that. An effective speech is tailored to a particular audience with the hope of getting a specific response. Almost all beginning teachers have had the confusing experience of teaching the same subject to two classes in a row. The teacher begins the first class in a certain way, and the class responds favorably, even to the point of enjoyable laughter. Feeling successful, the teacher starts the second class in the same way and gets little response. Then, if never before, the teacher learns that all audiences are different, even seemingly homogeneous classes in the same school.

In the same way, the wise public speaker recognizes that all audiences are different and learns to tailor the speech to the particular audience being addressed. Tailoring the speech to the audience begins with audience analysis. There are a number of ways to analyze an audience. For example, you can determine whether the audience is friendly, hostile, or indifferent. Specifically, you should consider age, economic level, education, knowledge of the subject, national origin, race, occupation, politics, religion, gender, and social status. You may also consider beliefs, attitudes, and values.

Speakers who address older people might talk about security, stability, and contentment, whereas those who speak to college students might introduce ideas related to jobs, adventure, and romance. We will examine audience analysis in detail in Chapter 5. What you need to consider right now is adapting your subject matter to your classmates as you present your first prepared speech. For example, if you plan to persuade your listeners to join the Young Democrats, you might ask yourself how you can adjust your material to those who come from Republican family backgrounds.

Analyzing the Occasion

The public speaking occasion deals with the setting, conditions, and circumstances. The possibilities are limitless. To analyze the occasion, the public speaker might consider the following questions:

1. What is the function of the gathering: A business luncheon? A graduation? An honors banquet? A religious ceremony? A classroom lecture? A sales meeting? A political rally? A prison setting? A wake? A patriotic event? An ethnic celebration?
2. What is the nature of the gathering: An orderly audience? An unruly crowd with hecklers? A dangerous mob?
3. What has preceded the speaking event: A cocktail party and dinner?
4. What kind of mood are the listeners in: Happy? Silly? Bold? Rude?
5. What will follow the speech: Other scheduled speakers at a certain time? A dance? Getting back to work after a luncheon?
6. What is the physical makeup of the room: What is the seating arrangement—regular, in arcs, or listeners surrounding the speaker? Can visual or auditory aids be used? What about light, heat, ventilation, noise, and acoustics?

Perhaps not many of these questions will pertain to your first prepared speech for the classroom, but some of them will. You should be aware, for example, of how the time of day will affect your presentation. A hungry 11:00 A.M. audience will react much differently than an after-lunch, sleepy one.

The important consideration is to look ahead and try to anticipate any occasional problems that may get in the way of your presentation. Then you can make adjustments.

Choosing the Right Subject

No one can speak well on every subject, but everyone can speak well on some. In the conquest of fear and development of self-confidence, your choice of the right subject is more than half the battle. The following checklist will help you select the right subject. If you can answer "yes" to the following four questions, your speech subject is likely to be right for you and your listeners:

1. Is the subject one in which you are already interested?
2. Is it a subject about which you already know something?
3. Is it a subject on which you can do some extra research?
4. Is it a subject worth your listeners' time?

A Subject in Which You Are Already Interested.

What are your special interests? Are you interested in popular music, symphony, astronomy, poetry, politics, religious writings, the economy, architecture, international relations? Few individuals are completely knowledgeable on all of these subjects, but perhaps you are conversant with some phases of one or another. You will find it easier to generate excitement among your listeners if you choose to speak on a subject in which you're already interested.

A Subject About Which You Already Know Something.

You have only a limited number of prepared speeches to make in your public speaking class. Why not start with those subjects about which you've earned the right to talk, at least to some degree? Does it make sense for you, in your beginning speech class, to choose a subject about which you know very little, research for hours in the library, and then with little ease or fluency try to communicate to your listeners?

One young man stumbled through a highly researched speech on the deficit of the United States Treasury. He was not fluent; he was glued to his notes and showed minimal visual variety. His voice was monotonous, and he presented so much compressed economic material that the audience lost interest. The instructor asked him if he was an economics major or had been following the problem for a long time. The answer was no. The speaker just didn't have enough background to tackle a subject so complicated in so short a time. If you speak on a topic you know, you won't have to pump up your speech from a dry well.

A Subject on Which You Can Do Extra Research.   Once you have found a subject in which you're already interested and know something about, the research step is exciting. You supplement and enrich your knowledge with the information that others can supply. You fill gaps in your own background and come out of the experience well rounded and fulfilled.

A Subject Worth Your Listeners' Time.   While it is true that there are no uninteresting subjects, only uninteresting speakers, some care should be taken to meet the needs, wants, and values of the audience.

Determining the General Purpose

Once you have analyzed your audience and chosen your subject, you need to determine your purpose. The universal purpose of all kinds of speaking is to gain a response from the listener. Within this universal purpose are several general purposes of public speaking:

1. To inform
2. To persuade
3. To evoke
4. To deliberate and problem solve

Each general purpose, in turn, can be further subdivided:

1. To inform
   a. To report objectively
   b. To explain thoroughly
2. To persuade
   a. To convince through argumentation
   b. To actuate through motivation
3. To evoke
   a. To inspire
   b. To entertain
4. To deliberate and problem solve
   a. In a group
   b. As an individual speaker

A public speaker might use any of these general purposes in the speech, no matter what the topic. For example, suppose the speaker chooses to speak on the topic of inequities in education. The informative speaker who chooses to report objectively might focus on the lack of good educational facilities in a slum area, while the speaker who wants to explain the problem thoroughly might talk about the political technicalities of revenue sharing between the federal and local governments. A speaker who wants to persuade listeners through argumentation might present statistical evidence, whereas a speaker who wants to persuade through motivation might describe the experiences of the downtrodden. The speaker who wants to evoke a response from listeners might choose to describe inspirational examples of those who have risen above their environments or entertaining examples of humorous incidents in the classroom. You can see, therefore, how helpful it is to determine one main general purpose even though you may use other general purposes. After you have determined your general purpose, you are ready to determine the specific purpose of your speech.

Determining the Specific Purpose

What is the relationship between the general and the specific purpose? General is to specific what vegetables are to carrots or meat is to steak. The specific purpose, therefore, is a species of a general purpose. It is like an arrow taken from a quiver to be directed toward a specific audience. The specific purpose determines exactly what you as a speaker intend to do. Suppose for example, your topic is the curve ball in baseball. Note the difference between the following two specific purposes.

1. I want to explain to you *how* a baseball pitcher throws a curve ball. Information on this subject can be obtained from the Physical Education Department.
2. I want to explain to you *why* a baseball curves. Information on this subject can be obtained from the Physics Department.

Consider these examples of specific purposes as they relate to the general purposes already listed. Notice how they use short, simple, direct phrases.

1. *Reporting.* To give a report on the courses necessary for teacher accreditation in the state of Wisconsin.
2. *Explanation.* To explain how to grade tests on the bell-shaped curve.
3. *Conviction.* To convince the audience that the cultural aspects of education are as important as the vocational aspects.

4. *Actuation.* To motivate the listeners to take as many cultural courses as they can while in college.
5. *Inspiration.* To inspire the listeners with examples of how students overcame fear and discovered their potential in a public speaking class.
6. *Entertainment.* To entertain the listeners with examples of amusing happenings in a public speaking class.
7. *Deliberation.* To help the listeners solve the problem of fear in speaking before a group.

Researching the Material

Once you have determined your specific purpose, you are ready to research your material. Determining your specific purpose will help you identify exactly what sources to research.

Research is the process of finding and recording information in an orderly, systematic manner. Material can be found mainly by researching yourself and others.

Researching Yourself.
Have you ever thought of yourself as a library, a center of resources? You are filled with a world of experience and knowledge. You've been exposed to more information than Aristotle, Plato, or Socrates. You may not be smarter than these individuals were, but you probably have been more generously informed.

What about the trip you may have taken to another part of the United States? Did you experience different attitudes, expressions of language, environmental concerns, values, and customs? Any of these areas can lead to a fruitful discovery of information for speech topics. Your own background can serve as a resource center for information.

In addition to your personal experience, you have your personal resources of textbooks, magazines, scrapbooks, and other volumes in your personal library. Don't overlook these rich resources so close to you and so easily available.

Researching Others.
As excellent as your personal background and experiences may be, they are usually limited in range and scope. To supplement your incomplete knowledge, turn to experts for help. Who is an expert? One who has adequate training, sufficient experience, emotional maturity, and good judgment is the kind of person you can consult for intensive investigation on more difficult subjects.

In Chapter 4 we will discuss researching others through interviewing and using the library. For your present speech, your instructor may accept research of your own background and personal resources.

Organizing Ideas

After you have chosen your subject, determined your purposes (both general and specific), and researched your subject matter, you are ready for the next step in building your speech: organizing your ideas. How do you go about accomplishing this task?

The basis of learning how to organize your ideas is to understand the various patterns of organization and the principles of outlining. The patterns of organization will give you general hints or clues for ordering your material, and the principles of outlining will help you identify the specific divisions and subdivisions within your ideas.

Patterns of Organization.

A pattern of organization is a diagram of parts as they fit together into a unified whole. In public speaking, a pattern of organization is simply a general method of ordering your material to get a preliminary overall view. We will consider several patterns of organization: chronological, spatial, topical, pro and con, logical, psychological, and deliberative or problem-solution.

1. *Chronological pattern.* The chronological pattern refers to the happenings of an event in the order of time. The time order in a chronological pattern moves consistently forward or backward in time and does not jump around. For example, suppose the topic of a speech is "making pancakes." Using a chronological pattern, a speaker might arrange the ideas in the following sequence:

a. preparing the ingredients;
b. mixing the ingredients;
c. preparing the griddle;
d. frying the batter.

The chronological pattern could involve the narrative steps in a story, personal experience, anecdote, or joke. Chronological order simply means the time sequence in which something happens.

2. *Spatial pattern.* The spatial pattern is concerned with the physical extension of matter in all directions: how wide, how long, how high, how deep, and so on. A spatial pattern moves in a consistent direction—top to bottom, right to left—and does not jump around. In public speaking the spatial pattern might be used to explain the offense and the defense in football or basketball, how the campus is laid out, or the floor plan of your home.

3. *Topical pattern.* The topical pattern is a list of informational points subordinate to the main topic. The points may be ordered in various ways: from least to most important, from general to specific, or from simple to

complex. For example, in a speech describing a baseball player, you might talk about the subtopics of hitting, fielding, running, and throwing abilities.

4. *Pro and con pattern.* Pro and con refers to arguments for and against a proposal. The word "pro" comes from the Latin *pro* meaning "for," and "con" is from the Latin *contra* meaning "against." The pro and con pattern is used when the speaker wishes to point out the advantages and disadvantages of two points of view. This pattern might be used, for example, with such topics as the physical punishment of children, capitalism versus socialism, or a cultural versus a vocational education.

5. *Logical pattern.* The logical pattern is a defense of one side of one view; it takes a pro *or* con stand. This pattern is frequently used with controversial topics such as abortion, capital punishment, or nuclear weaponry. Taking a logical stand, the public speaker might address any of the following questions:

   a. Is the proposition right or wrong in principle?
   b. Is there a real need for a change from present policy?
   c. Is there a plan to meet the need for a change?
   d. Do the advantages of the plan outweigh the disadvantages?

6. *Psychological pattern.* The psychological pattern is based on choosing evidence that appeals to the needs, wants, and values of the listeners. The speaker organizes the speech around evidence that relates to the listeners' interests. For example, a speaker who appeals to the listeners to avoid drugs, to join a certain organization, or to donate money to a worthy cause might use a psychological pattern of organization.

7. *Deliberative or problem-solution pattern.* The deliberative or problem-solution pattern is based on the exploratory sequence of determining a problem, ascertaining its causes, proposing possible solutions, choosing the best solution, and suggesting a plan of action.

Each of these patterns of organization can help give you a general idea of the plan to use in your speech. The general pattern of organization will help you determine how to arrange the major points of your topic. After you have selected the major ideas, you are ready to identify and organize the specific subpoints and subdivisions of your speech. You are ready to prepare the specific outline.

Principles of Outlining. An outline is a summary of a subject in phrase or sentence form with major points governing minor points. An outline is to a speech what floor plans are to a builder or an itinerary to a traveler. The outline serves as a functional cue card for the speaker's extemporaneous delivery, the method of presentation most commonly used. There are several guidelines to follow in preparing an outline. As you develop the outline for your speech, keep the following rules in mind.

1. *Use a consistent set of symbols throughout the outline.* No absolute agreement exists on what symbols are to be used. Generally, however, Roman numerals are used to indicate main points, capital letters indicate major subdivisions, Arabic numbers indicate minor subdivisions, and lowercase letters indicate further subdivisions. Thus, the symbols in an outline might be:

I.
   A.
   B.
      1.
      2.
II.
   A.
      1.
         a.
         b.
      2.
      3.
   B.
   C.

No matter what symbols you choose to use, the important point is that you be consistent.

2. *Less important points should be subordinated to main points.* Main points are coordinate to each other; that is, they hold the same degree of importance. The minor points are subordinated to the main points. Subordination is indicated by indentation and by the symbols used in the outline. The ability to arrange your outline with the proper coordination and subordination is important to prevent confusion as you speak. The following outline violates the rule of proper subordination. Can you identify the word that is misplaced?

   I. Foods Recommended for a Healthful Diet
      A. Fruits
      B. Oranges
      C. Vegetables
      D. Lean Meats

The answer, of course, is "oranges" because oranges are not coordinate with fruits, vegetables, and lean meats. Oranges are subordinate to fruits.

3. *Use only one idea per main point.* Suppose that the topic of your speech is the programming of a radio station. Can you identify the error in the following outline?

I. Programming
   A. Hit tunes and news
   B. Other kinds of music

As you can see, point A covers two ideas. A better outline would be:

I. Programming
   A. Music
     1. Hit tunes
     2. Other kinds of music
   B. News

4. *Avoid overlapping in categorization and classification.* Although it may be difficult to determine perfect, exclusive categories and classifications, strive for as little overlap as possible. Notice the error in overlapping in the following example of classification.

I. People Attending the Conference
   A. Democrats
   B. Doctors
   C. Men

The overlap is clear. Democrats could be doctors; doctors could be men or women; men could be Democrats or Republicans. In fact, one individual might belong to all three categories.

Two kinds of outlines are available to the speaker: the key phrase and the complete sentence. The key phrase outline is used for simple communication, whereas the complete sentence outline is used for complex explanation or speech material heavily supported with evidence: studies, statistics, and quotations. After you have made your outline, put it away for a day and let your subconscious go to work. Then, make another outline. Repeat this process several times until a balanced outline starts to jell. Your material should fall into the general divisions of introduction, body, and conclusion.

This sample shows what the speaker wants to accomplish in each division of the speech.

Introduction of the speech

    I. Get attention with something amusing.
   II. Establish goodwill by saying something nice.
 III. Break down prejudice by some explanation.

IV. Orient the audience.
   A. Give the title of the speech unless someone is introducing you.
   B. State your specific purpose,
   C. Enumerate the subpoints, arguments, motives, or other modes of procedure such as the stories or problem-solving steps that will be covered in the body of the speech.

Body of the speech

   I. State the first subtopic, argument, or benefit: let listeners know you are taking up subtopics A and B.
      A. Give an example.
      B. Use an analogy.
   II. State the second subtopic, argument, or benefit: let listener know you are taking up subtopics A and B.
      A. Cite expert opinion.
      B. Dramatize statistics.
   III. State the third subtopic, argument, or benefit: let listener know you are taking up subtopics A and B.
      A. Recall personal experience.
      B. Give a demonstration.

Conclusion of the speech

   I. Restate specific purpose.
   II. Summarize subtopics, arguments or benefits.
   III. Conclude with something inspirational or entertaining.

The following example demonstrates how a speech on "How to Have a Successful Garden" might be outlined.

Introduction of the Speech

I. Get attention:	If you were home all alone, would you like to go out to your garden and cut some fresh lettuce and pick a ripe tomato for a salad?
II. Establish goodwill:	You look healthy enough to be a gardener. Maybe you're at it already.
III. Break down prejudice:	Please don't misunderstand me. I don't think you're ready for retirement, but gardening can be fun and profitable.
IV. Orient audience:	
A. Title of speech/general purpose:	My general subject is gardening.

B. Specific purpose: Specifically I'd like to explain how you could have a successful garden.

C. Enumerate subpoints: The steps I'd like to cover are the conditioning of the soil, seeding, controlling the gardening, and harvesting.

Body of the Speech

I. First subtopic   I. Conditioning the soil
                                   A. Clay as a basic problem
                                      1. Organic materials
                                         a. Peat moss
                                         b. Residue from mulch box
                                      2. Top soil
                                      3. Sand
                                   B. Good fertilizer

II. Second subtopic   II. Seeding
                                   A. Getting disease resistant seed
                                   B. Starting seedlings in flats
                                   C. Carefully organizing planting

III. Third subtopic   III. Controlling the garden
                                   A. Watering
                                   B. Weeding

IV. Fourth subtopic   IV. Harvesting
                                   A. Early growing season
                                   B. Later growing season

Conclusion of the Speech

I. Restate specific purpose: I hope I've shown you how to have a successful garden.

II. Summarize subtopics: I. Conditioning the soil
                                   II. Seeding
                                   III. Garden control
                                   IV. Harvesting

III. Inspirational/entertaining close: Happy gardening and good health to all!

Developing Ideas

After researching and organizing your material, you are ready to develop your ideas. Recall your general and specific purposes. Are you reporting, explaining, convincing, actuating, inspiring, entertaining, or helping the audience solve a problem? In this section we will first discuss the development of the body of the speech and then the development of the introduction and conclusion.

The Body of the Speech.

Although all kinds of speeches can use just about any of the forms of development, informative speeches generally use definitions, examples, and analogies (comparisons). Teachers, for example, use many definitions, examples, and analogies. Persuasive speeches use facts, statistics, and expert opinion directed toward the listeners' needs, wants, and values. For example, an attorney uses facts and expert opinion, while a salesperson is concerned with directing information to the listeners' needs, wants, and values. Evocative speeches of inspiration and entertainment use stories, anecdotes, and literary quotations. For example, the after-dinner speaker tells stories and fits quotations into the presentation.

We will discuss these various types of speech development in the chapters on informative, persuasive, evocative, and deliberative speaking. In these chapters we will investigate the various ways to develop a speech according to its particular purpose.

The Introduction of the Speech.

The introduction is a very important part of the speech because it is here that you the speaker determines who will listen to your speech. If you can't get attention and arouse interest in the introduction, your listeners may not listen to you at all. The functions of the introduction are to get attention, establish goodwill, break down prejudice, and orient the audience as to the specific purpose of the speech and its organization.

1. *Get Attention.* There are several methods you can use to get your listeners' attention. You can ask for a show of hands, arouse suspense, say something amusing, use a visual aid, talk in terms of the listeners' interests, reveal conflict between two forces, start with an anecdote, arouse curiosity, or tell a story. These methods create interest and help you bridge the gap between your listeners and your subject matter.

2. *Establish Goodwill.* You can establish goodwill by being in a good emotional state, by having a good attitude toward yourself and your listeners, by playing yourself down a little, by being objective and fair, and by showing no prejudice. Listeners tend to like and give a fair hearing to that kind of speaker.

3. *Break Down Prejudice.* By establishing goodwill, you will already have broken down much prejudice, but you can do more. Sometimes some factual information may help give a balanced picture of a person or situation. Suppose you're talking about a person with some obvious faults. Suppose you mention that this individual does many benefit performances for charity. You have helped break down prejudice.

4. *Orient the Audience.* To orient the audience to the topic of your speech, state your specific purpose and the steps, arguments, or values you intend to develop. In this way you make it easy for the audience to follow what you will develop in the body of the speech.

It isn't necessary to follow all of these introductory steps every time, but follow those that seem most helpful. In general, the most important step is to make the introduction audience centered rather than speaker centered. See how the following examples illustrate the values of audience-centered introduction.

Poor: Self- centered	Today I'm going to discuss with you the topic of facial care and explain how you can have a beautiful complexion just like mine. I didn't always have this radiant glow. At one time, I had zits like some of you.
Better: Audience- centered	You're getting ready to go on that special date, that party of the semester, or to have your senior picture taken. You look at your face and don't like the condition of your skin. What can you do? Cosmetics will help, of course, but the best time to start is now, long in advance of the big moment. And so, today I'd like to analyze with you the basic causes of a bad complexion and therapies for a good one.
Poor: Self- centered	Today I'm going to tell you about blues music and its influence on popular music. I've researched this topic extensively and I probably know more about it than anyone in this class.
Better: Audience- centered	Popular music plays a big part in the lives of most of us. We may be awakened by it on our clock radio. We dance to it at parties or bars. Maybe we listen to it for enjoyment or relaxation. Did you ever consider what influences there are behind popular music? Today I'd like to explain to you how popular music has been influenced by the blues.

The Conclusion of the Speech.   In general, the conclusion should restate the specific purpose, summarize the subtopics, arguments, or values, and end with something inspirational or entertaining. Specifically, a conclusion should have more than just those general mechanics. The speaker should examine what kind of speech is being made—reporting, explanation, conviction, actuation, inspiration, entertainment, or deliberation—and then compose the conclusion according to the original purpose of the speech.

Often, the general purpose of the speech will determine the type of conclusion used. A speech of reporting and explanation, for example, needs a restatement of the specific purpose and a summary of the subtopics. To conclude a speech of conviction, restate the proposition or proposal and summarize the arguments. The speech of actuation needs a summary of the benefits and a request for action. Speeches of inspiration or entertainment can end in many creative ways—with a big lift, a high moment usually achieved through emotional appeal, an amusing personal experience, or a quotation from literature. To conclude the speech of deliberation the speaker can summarize the possible solutions or, if the speech is developed up to and including the action step, summarize the entire process of reflective thinking explained in Chapter 15.

Once you have researched, organized, and developed your ideas, you have satisfied the compositional requirements of speech preparation. Now you are ready for rehearsal.

REHEARSING THE SPEECH

The value of rehearsing your speech is twofold: it builds confidence in you and credibility in the listener. With rehearsal behind you, the speech will become part of you, and your listeners will perceive easily that you are in control of the situation.

In rehearsing your speech, decide on your method of presentation and how you will capitalize on visual and vocal technique.

Methods of Presentation

There are four generally recognized methods of presentation. Each has distinct advantages and disadvantages; no one method is best for all occasions. In this section we will examine the four methods of delivery: written out and memorized, written out and read, outlined and extemporized, and spoken impromptu.

Written Out and Memorized.
With this method the entire speech is written out and memorized word for word. If you have the trained memory of an experienced actor and the talent to go with it, the memorized method has advantages. You are not bound by notes and your body is free for dramatization and showmanship. In fact, you look the part of the finished, polished speaker. Unfortunately, few of us are talented enough to use this method and create the illusion of reality and the ring of honesty.

When reciting from memory, you tend to have a faraway look in your eyes and a distant ring to your voice. Most importantly, you are in danger of forgetting parts of your message and spoiling whatever contact you may have established with the audience. In addition, it takes too much time to memorize a speech. Memorization as a speech method, therefore, is not recommended except for brief passages, such as quotations. Even here, however, it's wise to have the quotations written out in the outline, just in case you should forget.

Written Out and Read. On very important occasions when accuracy, time limits, and precise language are desirable, a manuscript speech written in an oral style is recommended. An oral style is simply the way we talk well, not too flippantly and not too formally. It's advisable to write out the speech and then speak it aloud, asking yourself if it sounds like one person conversing with another. Once the speech is written, it should be rehearsed aloud until your ear tells you that your written and oral style sound believable. Don't assume, however, that you have found the perfect method of speechmaking and that from now on all you need to do is write out your speeches, get up, and read them.

Almost always, speeches read from a manuscript suffer the same weaknesses as memorized speeches. The visual and vocal deliveries suffer, and immediate, on-the-spot creativity is hampered.

Spoken Impromptu. Speaking off the cuff, without preparation, should be used only when necessary. It can produce a disorganized, non-fluent delivery. There are times when a speech must be delivered impromptu. Sometimes when we are called on at a meeting there is no other choice. The best training for effective impromptu public speaking is sound training in extemporaneous public speaking—and much practice. We will discuss impromptu speaking in greater detail in Chapter 14.

Outlined and Extemporized. Extemporaneous speaking is delivered from a written or memorized outline, although a written outline is most generally used. Its biggest advantage is adaptability. If something unforeseen happens, additions or deletions are easily made. The written outline poses no serious memory problems and promotes effective visual and vocal presentation. Although the speech is prepared in advance, most of the actual words are selected at the moment of presentation. Even an extemporaneous speech, however, requires rehearsal. After you have practiced your speech several times, you will notice that your flow of words will develop easily and efficiently. Don't expect to use exactly the same words each time. Express yourself as the spirit moves you at the particular moment of utterance. Your research, organization, and developed outline will give you the background you need to have confidence.

Remember that the points in your outline are to serve as prompters for ideas, not rigid guides of exact wording. If your outline is too long and you are too dependent on it, you begin to lose contact with your audience. A concise, easily read outline allows you to express yourself more freely and to use your body and voice to communicate more effectively.

The preparatory outline from which you construct your speech should be analytic and well developed with complete sentences for the main subpoints, arguments, or benefits. The performance outline that you take to the speaker's stand is generally shorter and written or printed in large letters so that you can see your next point at a glance. For a 5–7-minute speech, a performance outline of one to two pages, with introduction and conclusion, should suffice.

Visual and Vocal Techniques

We communicate with more than words. A strong handshake, the fragrance of sophisticated perfume, and the taste of warmed-over green beans, all play a part in communication. In public speaking, however, the two most common sensory stimuli are the visual and the vocal. The visual refers to anything we see, and the vocal, anything we hear.

The speaker's visual communication is significant because listeners instinctively believe first what they see, that is, the speaker's general bodily posture, gesture, facial expression, and eye contact. Visual communication should be an outer expression of inner ideas and feelings, and should spring from the speaker like branches growing from a tree trunk. Speakers will be more effective if they let themselves be guided by inner enthusiasm, vivid dramatization, and modified showmanship. Effective use of visual aids will also promote good visual communication. We will explore the topic of visual communication more thoroughly in Chapter 7, "Delivery: Bodily Action and Audiovisual Aids."

In addition to using visual communication, the speaker expresses a message through vocal communication. Voice quality reflects personality and vice versa. They go hand in hand. Vocalization of words can communicate more than do the words themselves.

The basic techniques of effective vocalization are adequate volume and projection, conversational directness, meaningful emphasis, logical or dramatic phrasing, emotional tone-coloring, change of pace, and the use of pause. The finished product is expressed in acceptable pronunciation and distinct enunciation. We will discuss the method of vocal communication in Chapter 8, "Delivery: Vocal Technique in Speaking and Reading Aloud."

Don't try too hard with your visual and vocal techniques. Make your art an easy one. However, it takes time. You may find yourself struggling at first, but in time you can develop an easy, fluid delivery. How much time? That depends on your desire, native talent, and practice.

Quintillian, the ancient Roman speech teacher, believed that the greatest art conceals art. In other words, we can say that effective speech is disarming in its apparent spontaneity and effortlessness, ease, and simplicity.

Have you ever sat next to someone at a dinner or banquet whose table manners were so perfect they made you feel uncomfortable? Have you ever ridden with someone who has just learned to drive an automobile and was so precise that you wanted to get out and walk? If so, then you have a basic understanding of this principle of easy art. Precise understanding is one thing, but smooth application is another. Rehearsing your speeches as much as possible will help you learn how to deliver your speech in a spontaneous, sincere, disarming manner.

BUILDING CONFIDENCE IN PUBLIC SPEAKING

You have built your speech and rehearsed its delivery. Now is the time to think about the conquest of anxiety, how you will overcome apprehension and acquire self-confidence. In fact, when students in a beginning public speaking course are asked what they would like most to derive from the course, many respond, "Self-confidence." They would like to be able to stand before an audience with self-assurance and a solid faith in their ability to think and create on their feet. They would like to be able to express their ideas and feelings clearly, persuasively, and enjoyably.

Building self-confidence is not an easy task, but neither is it insurmountable. In this section we will examine some guidelines for developing self-confidence—or more of it.

Experiencing Anxiety

Almost everyone experiences some anxiety before and during a public performance, especially in the first few minutes. This anxiety is revealed in various ways: a feverish feeling, rapid heart beat, dizziness, difficulty in breathing, dry mouth, sweaty palms and forehead, nausea, vomiting, diarrhea, knocking knees, general bodily tremors, and many related phenomena. As a result of these subtle, subjective reactions to anxiety, frequently more noticeable to the speaker than to the audience, the speaker may display the more obvious signs of fear: staring, wandering eyes, weak and trembling voice, vocalized pauses, tense or slovenly posture, leaning, swaying, rocking, and sometimes even laughing or crying. These disturbances are not limited to amateurs. Even the professionals confess similar reactions. The celebrated Metropolitan Opera star Lily Pons once confessed she was sick to her stomach for several hours before every concert performance. Broadway stars have reported the feeling of being a caged wild animal and have sought release in heightened conversation, physical exercise, and even prayer. The important thing to remember is that many people have experienced these same feelings; you're not alone. Furthermore, there are some things that you can do to lessen or overcome your anxiety.

Analyzing the Situation

Analyze why you are afraid. An emotion tends to fade away and lose much of its impact when it is taken apart and analyzed. For example, are you uneasy because the situation is strange? Then get up and make the mystery disappear. Follow Emerson's sage advice concerning self-conquest: "Do the thing you fear to do, and the death of fear is certain." Do the think you fear to do. Get up and speak. Follow the method of George Bernard Shaw who, when asked how he became an effective speaker, said, "I did it the same way I learned to skate—by making a fool of myself until I got used to it." Somewhat differently, Shakespeare expressed the same thought: "Our doubts are traitors and make us lose the good we oft might win by fearing to attempt." If the situation seems strange, therefore, take every opportunity you can to gain experience. Get up and speak.

Converting Fear Into Action

Recognize the fact that some fear, anxiety, and tension are good. They motivate you to prepare well and help you speak with sincerity. Whenever actor John Barrymore had to face an opening night audience, his hands would begin to tremble and the butterflies in his stomach would flutter furiously. It was a nerve-shattering ordeal but one he understood and respected. It kept his performance at a high pitch. One opening night, shortly before the curtain was to go up, the customary feelings of fear were missing. His hands were steady, the butterflies were in repose, and he was calm and confident. He was so calm and confident that it scared him. His hands began to shake, the butterflies took flight, and suddenly everything was back to normal again, and he was able to give a performance worthy of his talent.

Apply John Barrymore's experience to your own situation. Realize that some anxiety is normal and that the adrenalin rushing through your system can be used to your own advantage by motivating you to be well prepared and by energizing your presentation.

Getting and Holding Listeners' Attention

Despite the fact that you may think the biggest problem in speaking is self-confidence, there is another equally serious problem: listener apathy. Often, listeners are neither critical nor friendly. They may be passive, indifferent, or preoccupied with their own problems. Members of an audience may look at a speaker and appear to be listening, but their thoughts may be miles away. What appears to be listening may be merely pretending to listen. As a speaker, you may be misled by this make-believe attention. When members of your audience pretend to listen, they pretend to give you their full and undivided attention. They may be hearing the sounds you are making, but they are not necessarily listening to your message.

Since listeners may be apathetic, you as the speaker must realize that the primary responsibility is yours. It is your job to be well informed and organized and to say something worth your listeners' time. It is your job to be animated and enthusiastic, to use the artistry of public speaking. If you take the attitude that your content is good in itself and that you need not exert yourself in presenting it, then you are not facing the reality of audiences as they are. Through your delivery, you can motivate your listeners to be attentive, thoughtful participants in the transactional process of public speaking.

The problem of getting and holding attention is just that—getting and holding. It is relatively easy to *get* attention. Talking in terms of the listeners' interests, building a bridge from their backgrounds to your message, motivating them to see vital relationships between their lives and your message—these are obvious approaches. The really difficult problem is *maintaining* the listeners' attention. Audiences tend to listen in spurts that are often interrupted by internal and external competition.

External Competition. A wise old teacher once said, "I need three conditions in my classroom before I can even consider teaching anything at all—lots of fresh air, plenty of light, and quiet." Maintaining attention in a poorly ventilated, inadequately lit room with competition from building construction noises next door is a challenge to anyone. While this may be an exceptional case, the fact remains that many physical stimuli compete with speakers as they attempt to maintain listeners' attention. Be aware of such stimuli and their potential impact on your listeners.

Internal Competition. Stronger than the external stimuli that compete with getting and holding attention are the internal stimuli inside the head and heart of the listener. Personal problems compete in a thousand ways. Think of the thoughts and emotions that were running through your mind the last time you listened to a speaker attempting to reach you. Recall the stimuli within you that presented competition to the speaker. Multiply these stimuli by the number of persons in the audience. Now you have some idea of what every speaker has to compete with.

Getting and holding listeners' attention, therefore, is a major problem, more serious and difficult than the problem of the speaker's feelings of anxiety. The listeners are so preoccupied with their own thoughts that in many cases they aren't even aware of the speaker's apprehension.

Your final big step in speech preparation is evaluation. Perhaps, in your rehearsal step, a friend consented to listen to you and offer a few suggestions. Certainly your instructor will offer a written or oral critique, and you can use those comments as you prepare your next speech. Therefore, you must be prepared to accept constructive evaluation.

ACCEPTING CONSTRUCTIVE EVALUATION

Much of life is trial and error. We try and fail. We try again and succeed to some extent. Sometimes we try again and go backward. Generally, however, we improve.

You can do much to improve your speaking ability. You can speak on topics with which you are familiar, you can research and rehearse more, and you can apply constructive evaluation from others. Evaluation need not be all negative. Much can be constructive, pointing out what you did well, at least to some degree. Pay close attention to an evaluation of your good points—it will help you build confidence. But in addition, consider those points that indicate a need for improvement. It's not always easy to accept these evaluations, but if you apply the suggestions, you can improve. Trial and error become trial and improvement.

You may become defensive when evaluation is offered. Your ego may be bruised; you may feel threatened or humiliated; you may try to defend your performance by offering excuses. After a while, the critic may stop providing suggestions, and then you will be the loser. Invite constructive criticism. Allow yourself to grow as a thoughtful, intelligent speaker. Listening to constructive criticism is worth the risk.

Look at the Speech Critique Sheet in the appendix. On it you will find various points a listener might use to evaluate you. Be aware of your strong points and sharpen those that may be weak. Remember Lincoln's observation, "I believe that I shall never be old enough to speak without embarrassment when I have nothing to say or when I failed to take the time to prepare." In other words, the better you are prepared, the greater are your chances for decreasing anxiety and for increasing self-confidence.

If you follow these basic suggestions, you can develop into an effective public speaker. Once you have experienced success, you will make the same discovery as every swimmer who accepts the challenge of the cool pool: "C'mon in! The water's fine!"

SUMMARY

Speech preparation involves four major steps: developing the speech, rehearsing it, building confidence, and accepting constructive evaluation.

You develop the speech by analyzing your audience and the occasion and then choosing a subject that you can adapt to their interests. You determine a general and then a specific purpose, which will direct your research, organization, and development of ideas into a unified, coherent, and proportioned presentation.

Rehearsing the speech entails choosing a method of presentation and the use of visual and vocal techniques. The method of presentation most frequently used is extemporizing from an outline. Effective use of visual and vocal techniques raises audience attention to a higher level, thus strengthening communication.

Building confidence in speaking is accomplished by realizing that anxiety is a common problem. Analyzing the situation helps objectify the problem. Converting fear into action puts nervous energy to use in a positive way. Realizing that the big problem in building self-confidence is not so much the anxiety of the speaker as it is the indifference of the audience can help put the situation in perspective. Finally, the best therapy of all is thorough preparation and much practice.

The speaker who wishes to improve and have a series of successful experiences should accept constructive criticism graciously and use the comments offered to improve with each opportunity to speak.

ASSIGNMENTS

1. Listen to a public speaker in person or on television, radio, or film. The speaker may be in church (sermon), the classroom (lecture), or any other situation in which an oral address is presented.
   a. Make a critical evaluation of what you listen to, based on the suggestions in this chapter and the critique sheet in the appendix. You aren't expected to cover all of the suggestions. Use three or four of the ones most applicable.
   b. Present your report in class within 3–5 minutes. Be sure to have specific examples, dramatizations, and even impersonations to illustrate your observations.

2. Compose your own ten commandments of public speaking for your own needs. Explain your selections. Hand them in to your instructor for evaluation.

3. Make a list of ten subjects on which you have "earned the right to speak." Explain your reasons in essay form.

4. With a group of four or five other students make a list of ten subjects the average college student should be able to use as speech material.

5. Listen to a presentation on TV. Take notes. Make an outline that you could use to make a report on the content of the presentation.

6. Who do you think is a good speaker? Explain the reasons for your choice in a written report of less than 300 words.

7. Prepare a 3–5-minute speech for class presentation on any subject you choose, one in which you're interested and know something about. You might choose to talk about a personal experience, such as a vacation or an embarrassing moment. Perhaps you would like to describe or explain something, such as a summer job or a hobby. Remember to choose the right subject for you. See the list of topics in the appendix for suggestions.

8. By prearrangement with your instructor, give class members a short objective quiz after your speech. Investigate how many listeners remember your specific purpose, the divisions of your speech, and any particular information you may have given. Analyze this data in a short written report to your instructor. How could you, as the speaker, develop your next speech to help your listeners improve their understanding and remembering of the information you present?

Conducting an Interview	Defining an Interview	Conversation
		Planning
		Specific Purpose
		Questions
	Preparing the Interview	Selecting an Interviewee
		Structuring the Interview
Researching Library Resources	Recording Information	
	Dialogue with Librarians	
	Major Informational Guides and Indexes	
	Other Library Guides to Reference Sources	Guides to Reference Books
		Indexes to Books
		Indexes to Periodicals
		Newspaper Indexes
		Indexes of Government Publications
		Government Publications
		Guides to Essays
		Guides to Legal Documents
		Almanacs and Fact Books
		Dictionaries
		Encyclopedias
	Recording Research Material	

4 Conducting Interviews and Using Library Resources

OBJECTIVES

When you finish reading this chapter, you should be able to:

1. identify the fundamental components of an interview;
2. discuss the steps to follow in preparing an interview;
3. conduct an interview;
4. identify important reference sources in the library for locating appropriate material;
5. record research information efficiently and effectively; and
6. give an informational speech on how to conduct an interview or how to do research in the library.

4 Conducting Interviews and Using Library Resources

Jim left his public speaking class angry and frustrated. His instructor had just assigned a speech to be prepared from researched material. The assignment suggested interviewing knowledgeable persons, researching the library, or both. "Why should I have to go through all that effort when I can get up and make a good talk out of my own experience? I did that in my first few speeches and got B's," said Jim. Although he complained about the assignment, Jim followed the instructor's directions and found there was much more information on his speech topic, teenage crime, than he had anticipated. As a result, when the time came to speak, he stood up in front of his classmates with more confidence than he ever had before. He knew the information inside-out, and he felt better informed on the topic than anyone in the room because of the research he had done.

Up to this point your investigation for speech-making, like Jim's, most likely has been limited to your own background and experience. In this chapter we shall discover the value to be found in seeking help from others, thereby enriching and broadening our own limited knowledge and experience. Two important ways to explore others' ideas are to conduct interviews and to use library resources to do research. We will discuss both topics, beginning with an examination of the interview process.

CONDUCTING AN INTERVIEW

In order to conduct a successful research interview, you must first know what an interview is, how to prepare for it, and how to record the material you gain from the interview.

Defining an Interview

An interview is a prepared conversation usually between two persons and planned for a specific purpose by means of predetermined and follow-up questions.

The purpose of a research interview is to gather information and opinion from a reliable source, someone with training, experience, and good judgment.

Let us explain some of the more important terms in these definitions: conversation, planning, specific purpose, and kinds of questions.

Conversation.   Conversation is *interaction* between at least two individuals. Conversation is not two persons playing golf side by side. It is more like two baseball players playing catch. In interviewing, the focus is on the interviewee, but occasionally he or she may reverse the process and become an interviewer when greater clarity is desired. For example, the interviewee may respond to an interviewer's question, "What kinds of crimes are you referring to?"

Planning.   Normally, we do not use prepared questions when talking to others. In interviewing, however, questions prepared and written out are acceptable. The journalist's notebook with spaced questions is the classic example.

Specific Purpose.   Like a speech, an interview should have a specific purpose, for example, "The specific purpose of my interview is to determine what can be done to lessen juvenile crime." A specific purpose unifies your procedure and saves time for you and the interviewee.

Questions.   To be able to ask good questions in an interview, you should know the difference between open and closed questions, primary and secondary questions, and neutral and leading questions.

1. *Open and Closed Questions.* An open question is one that invites all possible responses. A closed question restricts the answer to one possibility. An open question to the women's intramural basketball coach could be, "How do you think women's intramural basketball will develop here at the college?" A closed question would be, "How many teams will there be in the league?" Closed questions are used in the survey interview, which seeks facts or opinion. The survey interview shown in Figure 4.1 provides examples of closed questions.

2. *Primary and Follow-up Questions.* A primary question is usually a prepared question, whereas a follow-up question takes its cue from the interviewee's answers to the primary question. Here is a crucial point for beginning interviewers. Frequently, in their haste and inexperience, they fail to listen carefully to the answer to the primary question and do not probe the interviewee with a follow-up question or two. If you've ever watched Barbara Walters conduct an interview on television, you may have noticed her skill in asking follow-up questions. Her famous, "Why not, Dr. Kissinger?" is a classical example.

3. *Neutral and Leading Questions.* A neutral question is objective, fair, and unbiased; a leading question steers the interviewee in the direction in which the interviewer wants to go. For example, a neutral question would ask, "How is the pizza at Angelo's?" A leading question would be, "The pizza at Angelo's is pretty good, isn't it?"

Any or all of these kinds of questions can be used in an interview. The kind of question you ask depends on the circumstances. Usually you would start with an open question and proceed with follow-up questions. Sometimes you want a specific answer, so you ask a closed question. Normally you would not ask leading questions, but you could, for example, to clear up what the interviewee is saying, such as, "You mean you are opposed to that plan?" Understanding the fundamental components of an interview and recognizing the differences between types of questions are first steps in learning how to conduct a thorough interview. Conducting a worthwhile and useful interview demands careful and specific preparation.

FIGURE 4.1   **A Survey Interview**

Hello.
I'm (name), and I'm conducting a survey of grocery shopping habits, particularly about shoppers' use of coupons clipped from newspapers. May I have a few minutes of your time to answer five brief questions?

1. Are you the person who usually does the grocery shopping for your household?
   The choices are:

                              Yes   No

2. Which one of these statements best describes your use of newspaper coupons?
   The choices are:

   I redeem at least one newspaper coupon per week when grocery shopping.
   I rarely use newspaper coupons when grocery shopping.

3. How many newspaper coupons do you usually redeem during a week's time?
   The choices are:

                    1 to 5   6 to 10   11 or more

4. About how much money do you usually save in a week's time by using newspaper coupons?
   The choices are:

                    $1 to $3 $4 to $10 $11 or more

5. If a company were to produce a new beverage that will be sold for $1 each, how high a value must the newspaper coupon have before you would be willing to buy the beverage for the first time?
   The choices are:

   I would purchase it with a coupon for at least 10¢ off.
   I would purchase it with a coupon for at least 35¢ off.
   I would purchase it with a coupon for at least 50¢ off.
   I would only purchase it with a coupon for a free beverage.

Preparing the Interview

To have a successful interview you need to follow some basic preparatory procedures. These procedures, if followed carefully, will simplify your task and make your experience rewarding. Two basic steps to follow are first selecting an interviewee and then structuring the interview.

Selecting an Interviewee.
The first step in selecting an interviewee is to choose someone who is knowledgeable in the subject area you are investigating. To find a knowledgeable interviewee, you should ask yourself some questions about the person's credentials. Is the person educated in the subject area? Does the person have years of practical experience in the subject area? Has the person published articles or books about the subject? Is the person recognized as an expert or authority in the area by other people? Sometimes you may find it helpful to know something about your potential interviewee's religious, political, economic, or social beliefs and attitudes. You can obtain information about your interviewee by consulting material that has been written about the person (books or newspaper or magazine articles) or by talking to others who know the individual.

When you are looking for an interviewee, remember that you might not be able to interview every person you choose. Very important persons do not grant interviews except for serious purposes. You may have to make a number of telephone calls to find someone who is both available and willing to be interviewed. You may need to write a follow-up letter to the proposed interviewee suggesting various dates and times convenient to both your schedules. If you are using this research interview to prepare for a speech, remember to allow enough time in advance and not wait until the last minute to select the interviewee and schedule the interview.

Structuring the Interview.
Like a speech, an interview has an introduction, body, and conclusion. This structure is helpful for getting started, proceeding with the questions in a patterned sequence, and finally selecting the important kernels from the harvest of ideas.

1. *Introduction.* The opening moments of the interview are very important because they set the tone. A nice appearance, good manners, and a professional approach are basic. In establishing rapport and orienting the interviewee to the purpose of the interview, your integrity, goodwill, and competence should be evident early in the interview and persist until the end. To achieve this good impression, begin with a pleasant self-introduction and clearly explain the purpose of the interview. A sample introductory statement might be: "Coach Brown, I'm planning to give a talk in my

speech class on women's intramural basketball, and I'd be grateful for any information you can give me."

2. *Body*. Your questions should be arranged according to a specific pattern or sequence:

   a. A topical sequence, which follows a series of natural or logical steps, parts, ways, or divisions: three ways to develop a successful women's basketball program.

   b. A time sequence, which follows events in their chronological or narrative order: the important events that took place in the development of women's basketball from its beginning to the present.

   c. A cause and effect sequence: the main causes that still stand in the way of a perfect women's basketball program.

   d. A problem-solving sequence: the problems, causes, possible solutions, and best solution to today's low attendance at women's basketball games.

You might choose any combination of these sequences as dictated by the circumstances and your own good judgment. No matter what pattern is chosen, the important consideration is organization.

3. *Conclusion*. The conclusion is usually brief. Do not start the interview over, but take advantage of the opportunity to summarize the main points for accuracy and verification. Express your thanks to the interviewee for his or her time and cooperation.

Once the interview is under way, keep it moving in an orderly manner. Keep your purpose in mind: to secure information. Be mindful, too, of the amount of time you have, and do not spend too much time on any one question. On the other hand, do not rush your interviewee, who may need time to consider what the best answer might be.

As you listen, evaluate what you hear. Some of the answers may be more helpful than others. Try to be flexible. If the interviewee brings up an important point that you hadn't thought of, be prepared to consider it, asking the necessary questions even if they aren't on your list.

Critical listening will help make your note taking easier, too. It isn't necessary to know shorthand or to write down every spoken word. You can take down key words or phrases provided that you understand later what they mean. If you plan to quote, however, you must get the words exactly. Do not hesitate to read back your quote to the interviewee for accuracy.

And don't forget that the interviewee should do most of the talking. You ask the questions, follow up the points, and tactfully steer the interviewee back if he or she gets off the subject. Do not use valuable time to express your own opinions or show off your knowledge. You are there to listen and to gather information.

Recording Information

The most frequently used method of recording the information in an interview is taking written notes. Another commonly used method is recording the interview with a tape recorder. If you plan to use a tape recorder, ask the interviewee's permission, and be sure you have pre-tested the recorder to be sure it works properly.

Should you take written notes or tape record the interview? It depends on many circumstances. How much tape do you have time to listen to? If you don't record, will you be able to take down all the information you want? The safest method may be to record the entire interview and take notes on the important ideas. As soon after the interview as possible, listen to the taped interview and take notes. Your memory will be fresh, and insights may elude you later.

You can take written notes during an interview or tape record it for playback later. Be sure to review the tape while the interview is still fresh in your mind so that the recording will clarify and enhance the information in your written notes.

The interview in Figure 4.2 illustrates several of the points covered in this discussion. The figure is a portion of an interview with Father John J. Walsh, S.J., former director of drama at Marquette University, Milwaukee, Wisconsin.

Notice in the interview that the reporter does not show off or try to be the "star." In fact, Father Walsh does a majority of the talking. Notice that the reporter uses a variety of approaches, a technique that helps sustain interest for both parties and elicits the kind of information the interviewer is seeking.

As we mentioned at the beginning of this chapter, conducting an interview is one way to explore others' ideas to find supporting material for

FIGURE 4.2   An Interview with Father John J. Walsh

Primary Question	REPORTER: Father, of the fifty plays you have put on here, which did you most enjoy directing?
	WALSH: That's hard to answer, because I enjoyed some plays from one respect and others from another respect. But I think the one that I enjoyed most of all was *The Carnival of Thieves.*
Follow-up Question	REPORTER: Why do you say this, Father?
	WALSH: In the performance of a play you depend upon so many different elements in being perfect—talented, trained people; a good play that appeals to you personally; someone very good on lights and very good on sets. I think we had all the elements at this particular time.
Probing	REPORTER: What determined your selection of plays for the summer session?
	WALSH: I wanted a play that had some literary stature, because I wanted the fiftieth play to be something a little on the special side.
Letting Walsh Talk	REPORTER: And then you have *The Lesson* scheduled to be performed.
	WALSH: Yes, and the reason is that the most important part of our job here in the University is to train not just the drama students who are specializing in acting or directing, but the playwrights; you can't have anybody developing into much of a playwright if he's unaware of the current trends in drama.
Word "presume" Is a Modest Approach	REPORTER: I presume that you not only aim at developing artists but also at the audience, the student body.
	WALSH: Definitely, definitely, because dramatic appreciation, of course, is essential. If you don't have an audience, you don't have theater.
Nicely Challenging	REPORTER: On the other hand, is it not true that the majority of your audience does not consist of university students?
	WALSH: That's true, regrettably.
Follow-up question	REPORTER: Why is this?
	WALSH: Because it takes a while to develop a taste for the theater. This is something that has to be acquired; it's not simply immediate. You'd rather stick

your speeches. The library is another storehouse of others' ideas. In the next section, we will investigate the various guides to resources found in the library and examine how to use these guides to uncover supporting material for speeches.

RESEARCHING LIBRARY RESOURCES

At first glance, the library can be an intimidating sight. High walls, stacks of books, serious facial expressions, subdued sounds, and rows of card catalogs present a challenging environment. However, if used prop-

with what you've known all your life. So these people who have been brought up on movies and television don't immediately see the value of the theater. It's an entirely different kind of experience.

REPORTER: This is a higher level of artistic endeavor, drama as compared to TV and the movies?

Probing

WALSH: Of its nature, it's a different kind of experience. The movies can be a great art form. They're developing into that; they're reaching maturity. I think television has a long way to go, but, it has moments when it promises a great future, too. The thing about the theater is that it's essentially different. At its greatest, it deals with universals—man's universal relationships. Whereas both television and the movies are essentially attuned to dealing with realistic problems which deal with particular phases of man's existence, not the universal aspects.

REPORTER: There is more lasting value in this?

Follow-Up question

WALSH: Well, yes, because the theater at its greatest is supposed to be an experience in which we extend our knowledge of life. We come away with a deeper appreciation of what man can become, his possibilities for greatness, his possibilities for failure.

REPORTER: Would you enumerate the basic differences between the stage and the screen?

Direct Question

WALSH: Theatricality and no theatricality. The theater can't exist without theatricality. We shouldn't try to emulate the realism of the movies by having a stove that cooks real eggs and steam that comes out of the shower room door when you open it. The theater was never adept at naturalism and realism because of the limitations of the stage.

With a movie camera you can go all over the world. You can cover as much time and as much space as you want, just the way you can in a novel. That's why the novel and the movies work so well together, but not the stage. The stage is like a poem. Life has to be distilled. Have I made my point about the difference in form?

REPORTER: Yes, very clearly. Thank you very much, Father.

Mannerly

WALSH: Thank you.

erly, the library can become a cornerstone in your educational experience. Certainly, in preparing your speech, you'll find the library an invaluable resource. So, don't be afraid to use it. As one of the authors of this text was once advised, envision your research in the library as a dialogue. You ask questions; the librarians and related sources help provide answers. Good research dialogues can lead to exciting discoveries of information.

Dialogue with Librarians

Librarians are highly educated, competent, individuals who genuinely want to help. Their knowledge of relevant reference sources, location of material, interlibrary loan procedures, computer searches, or microfilm usage can prove invaluable in your research. They can teach you the "hows" and "whys" of library research. Don't hesitate to learn from them. Seek their assistance. You'll find the effort and dialogue worthwhile when researching your speech topic or, for that matter, any topic during the balance of your academic or professional career.

Major Informational Guides and Indexes

Three major sources of material in the library are the card catalog, the *Readers' Guide to Periodical Literature*, and the library's listing of periodical holdings. The card catalog will help you locate books on your sub-

The card catalog classifies books by call numbers, a system that indicates their location in the library. If you are unfamiliar with a particular library's physical layout, ask a librarian to help you locate the books you need.

ject of interest. Books provide detailed, in-depth information, although this material is likely to be more dated than that found in periodical literature.

Generally, the card catalog is divided alphabetically into three sections: a) title section, b) author section, and c) subject section. Suppose you are investigating the subject of communication. You go first to the subject section of the card catalog where you'll find cards listing the names of authors and books on the subject. If you already know a specific title or author, then you can consult the title or author section of the card catalog. Once you have located a particular card, copy down the call number of the book. Most libraries have a system that divides the library into sections based on the call number classification system used for the books. The book's call number tells you the book's location in the library.

When you have located a book, you can quickly assess its content by checking its table of contents and index. In this way you can tell at a glance whether the book contains the type of material you are looking for. Figure 4.3 shows typical title, author, and subject cards you might find in a card catalog.

The major guide for locating general-interest periodical articles on a wide variety of subjects is the *Readers' Guide to Periodical Literature.* This reference source lists articles found in many of today's mass market periodical publications, such as *Time, Newsweek, Fortune, Business Week, Sports Illustrated,* and *Vital Speeches of the Day.* The *Readers'*

FIGURE 4.3 **Sample Card Catalog Listing for a Book**

```
                              a. Title Card

Title ──────────────────────Communication:  methods for all media
Author ─────────────────
Call Number ────────┌─301.16    Read, Hadley,
                    └─ R22      Communication:  methods for
Place of Publication ─────     all media.  Urbana,
Publisher ──────────────────University of Illinois Press
Date ───────────────────────[1972] xii, 307 p. 24 cm.

                            1.  Communication
                            2.  Mass media

                            I. Title
                            P90.R35          CUMA          301.16
                                                           75-18 2196
                            ISBN 0-252-00209-1 A7-852981 A MARC
```

Guide indexes articles alphabetically by subject and author. You use the *Readers' Guide* to find periodical articles on particular subjects. Suppose your topic is nuclear reactors. Figure 4.4 on page 74 shows a typical *Readers' Guide* listing on this topic.

After you have found a relevant article in the *Readers' Guide*, your next task is to locate the specific issue of that periodical in the library. To do this, consult the library's listing of periodical holdings. This listing will tell you if the library receives the periodical you are looking for, which issues of the periodical the library holds, and where in the library the specific issue you are looking for is located. Often the periodicals are on microfilm or are bound and stored on shelves in a separate section, arranged alphabetically by title rather than by call number.

The library's listing of periodical holdings may take any one of a variety of forms—in a bound volume or on microfilm. One form of microfilm reader of periodical listings is the serials record reader. This catalog, which lists periodicals, newspapers, and other serials, provides a quick way to locate the call number of a particular source. You simply scan through the reader to locate the periodical, newspaper, or other serial you are looking for. Once you have identified the call number and title of the source, you go to the section of the library where the source is located. A typical serials record reader is shown in Figure 4.5 on page 75.

Figure 4.5 shows the serials record reader's on/off switch, fast scanner button, pointer, index listing, manual selector, and focus button. The first

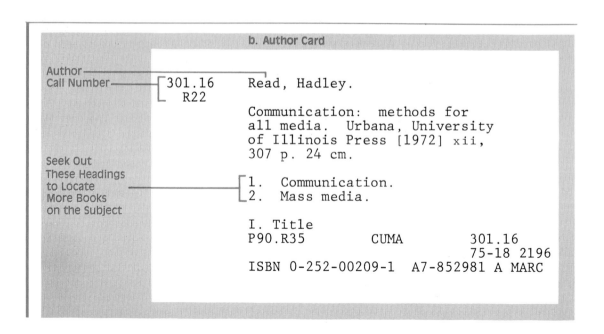

step in using the serials record reader is to turn on the switch. The fast scanner buttons move both the index of publications and the pointer (arrow) up or down. The top button moves the pointer upward; the bottom button moves it downward. By fast scanning you can position the pointer as close as possible to the title of the publication you are seeking. Turn the manual selector to slowly move both the pointer and the index. The manually controlled focus button adjusts the visual clarity of the index listing.

Figure 4.6 on page 76 is an example of a typical listing from the serials record reader. The entry number indicates the numerical position of the title in the serials record reader. The title is the name of the publication. "Library" indicates in which library the periodical is located (there may be more than one library at some institutions). "Holdings" tells you what volumes and issues of the periodical the library has. Microfilm indicates from what year, if any, microfilm copies of the periodical are contained in the library.

The card catalog, the *Readers' Guide*, and the listing of periodical holdings are major sources for locating important library material, but the library also contains other sources that provide useful information for locating additional material. These sources include guides and indexes to reference books, books, periodicals, newspapers, government publications, essays, and legal sources. Almanacs and fact books, encyclopedias, and dictionaries are additional reference guides.

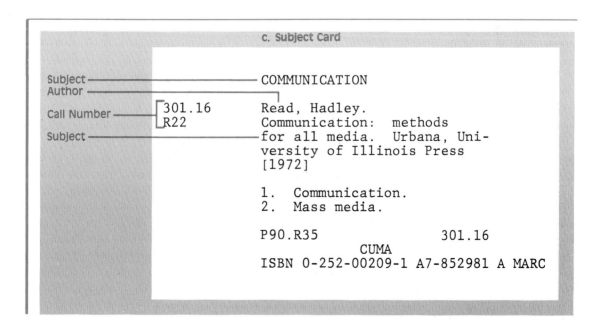

c. Subject Card

Subject —————————————— COMMUNICATION
Author ——————————
Call Number ——— ⌈301.16　　Read, Hadley.
　　　　　　　　⌊R22　　　　Communication:　methods
Subject ——————————————for all media.　Urbana, Uni-
　　　　　　　　　　　　　versity of Illinois Press
　　　　　　　　　　　　　[1972]

　　　　　　　　　　　　　1.　Communication.
　　　　　　　　　　　　　2.　Mass media.

　　　　　　　　　　　　　P90.R35　　　　　　　301.16
　　　　　　　　　　　　　　　　　CUMA
　　　　　　　　　　　　　ISBN 0-252-00209-1 A7-852981 A MARC

Other Library Guides to Reference Sources

There are a number of reference guides to library holdings. Usually these guides are located in a designated reference section of the library. By learning to identify the appropriate guides and familiarizing yourself with how to use them, you'll find doing research a more pleasant and rewarding experience.

Guides to Reference Books.   Reference books are important keys for unlocking important sources of information. Such works are invaluable for locating sources of information or for gathering material useful in speech preparation. If you are uncertain about what reference books to use, ask the librarian or consult some of the basic guides to reference books. Some useful guides are *A Guide to Reference Books*, *Reference Books: A Brief Guide for Students and Other Users*, and *Reference Books in the Social Sciences and Humanities*.

Indexes to Books.   As we have already mentioned, the card catalog tells you what books are contained in the library. But suppose you need to find a book that is not located in the library. Where can you go to locate

FIGURE 4.4   **Sample Listing in *Readers' Guide to Periodical Literature***

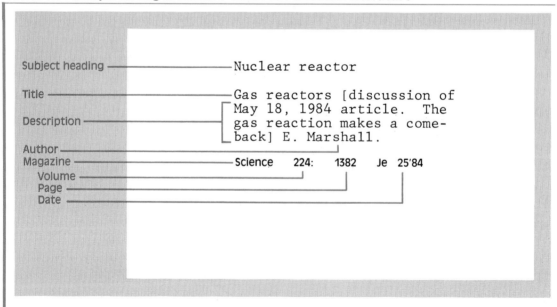

it? A good place to start is the *Cumulative Book Index*. This guide lists by year all the books published in the United States. The books are indexed alphabetically by author, title, and subject. The author section is more detailed than are the other two sections.

Indexes to Periodical Material.   The most common guide to articles in periodicals is the *Readers' Guide to Periodical Literature*, which indexes articles in many of the most popular magazines in the United States. It does not, however, list articles in some of the more specialized professional journals. Instead, there are specialized indexes for current research material published in professional journals. Students are often encouraged to consult articles in these journals when preparing speeches or papers. Some of the more commonly used specialized guides to articles in professional journals are the *Humanities Index*, the *Social Sciences Index*, and the *Public Affairs Information Service Bulletin*. Both the *Humanities Index* and the *Social Sciences Index* list articles alphabetically by author and subject. The *Public Affairs Information Service Bulletin* lists articles in political science, government, economics, and sociology. The guide is organized alphabetically by subject. Once you have located the particular article you want, you can again consult the library's listing of periodical holdings to see if the library has the particular issue that you need.

Indexes to Newspapers.   Generally, the most complete index of an American newspaper is the *New York Times Index*. There may also be indexes for such newspapers as the *Chicago Tribune, Chicago Sun-Times,*

FIGURE 4.5   **A Serials Record Reader**

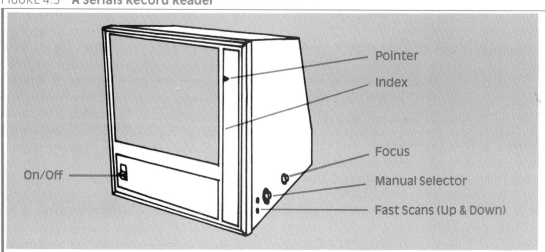

Christian Science Monitor, Detroit News, Washington Post, and *Wall Street Journal.*

The newspaper indexes list articles alphabetically according to subject. If your library contains only the *New York Times Index* but also holds some other newspapers, you can cross-reference your search by checking the *Times Index* for the date on which an article appeared in the *New York Times.* Odds are, if the topic is a newsworthy one, of national or international importance, it will be reported by other newspapers on approximately the same date.

Indexes of Government Publications.   The U.S. government is a major publisher of information on a wide range of topics. Reports on congressional meetings, agricultural production in the United States, environmental impact studies, and national and international economic conditions are but a few of the topics on which the government publishes reports. An important source for locating relevant federal government publications is the *Monthly Catalog of United States Government Publications.*

Government Publications.   This guide provides a comprehensive listing of publications from federal agencies and departments in the United States. The listings in the *Monthly Catalog* are arranged alphabetically by federal department and agency. The catalog also contains in-

FIGURE 4.6   **Typical Listing from a Serials Record Reader**

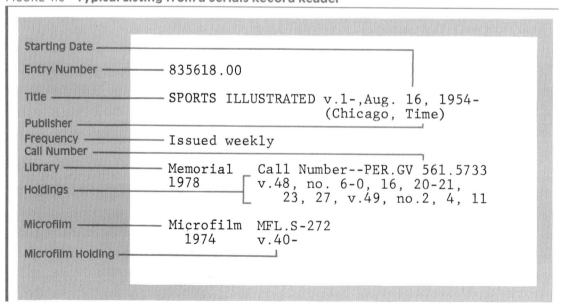

Starting Date

Entry Number ———— 835618.00

Title ———— SPORTS ILLUSTRATED v.1-,Aug. 16, 1954-
                                         (Chicago, Time)

Publisher

Frequency ———— Issued weekly

Call Number

Library ———— Memorial   Call Number--PER.GV 561.5733

Holdings   1978   v.48, no. 6-0, 16, 20-21,
                                   23, 27, v.49, no.2, 4, 11

Microfilm ———— Microfilm MFL.S-272
                    1974   v.40-

Microfilm Holding

dexes, such as a title index, author index, and subject index, which are helpful for locating appropriate material.[1]

Guides to Essays.   Sometimes the material you need may not be found in books or periodicals, but it may exist in other sources, such as essays in edited collections. An excellent guide for locating such material is the *Essay and General Literature Index*. This source lists essays alphabetically, primarily by author and subject.

Guides to Legal Documents.   Legal research can be a fruitful source of valuable information when you are preparing a speech. Material regarding legal information on a variety of topics (e.g., divorce, censorship, employment, zoning) exists in legal documents. An excellent source of relevant material is the *Index to Legal Periodicals*. It catalogs articles in many of the legal publications according to subject headings. This source is indispensable for anyone who is serious about doing legal research. Other valuable legal sources are *American Law Reports, American Jurisprudence, Federal Regulation of Employment Service,* and *Federal Procedure, Lawyers Edition*.

Almanacs and Fact Books.   Of the almanacs and fact books, probably the best known is the *World Almanac*. It contains a variety of historical and contemporary information on such topics as countries, people, resources, and sports. It is organized alphabetically by subject, profession, and occupation. Some other widely used resources of this type include the following:

1. *Statistical Abstract of the United States*. Probably one of the best sources for finding information (e.g., population, death rates, income levels) about the United States, this work covers a wide range of political, social, and economic topics.

2. *Facts on File*. This resource is a weekly (made cumulative monthly, quarterly, and yearly) encyclopedic summary of important facts from events recorded in major metropolitan newspapers. One important drawback with this work, however, is that it does not identify sources that provide the information.

3. *Dissertation Abstracts*. This is a monthly compilation of abstracts of doctoral dissertations submitted to University Microfilms by institutions of higher learning. Each dissertation is listed under one or more subject headings as assigned by the Library of Congress. Microfilm copies of dissertations can be purchased on request.

Encyclopedias.   These reference guides are useful for finding historical or background information for speeches. Information is usually arranged alphabetically according to subject. Often encyclopedias include a short bibliography at the end of an article. This bibliography is a good place to look for additional sources. The encyclopedia is a good place to begin, but in your college research you should move on from the encyclopedia to other, more specialized sources to find material for your speeches.

Some of the most commonly known and widely used general information encyclopedias are *Collier's Encyclopedia, Academic American Encyclopedia, Encyclopaedia Britannica, Encyclopedia Americana,* and *World Book Encyclopedia.* There are also specialized encyclopedias that contain articles in a particular field. Some well-known specialized encyclopedias are the *Encyclopedia of Education, Encyclopedia of Philosophy, McGraw-Hill Encyclopedia of Science and Technology, International Encyclopedia of Social Science, Encyclopedia of World Art,* and *Encyclopedia of Religion.*

Dictionaries. When doing research, you may come across a word that is unfamiliar to you. The dictionary can be a vital research tool. Most major dictionaries indicate the proper pronunciation of the word and its derivation. Some of the most popular dictionaries are *Webster's Ninth New Collegiate Dictionary, Webster's New World Dictionary, Dictionary of Word and Phrase Origins,* and *Webster's New Dictionary of Synonyms.*

Recording Research Material

As you compile your research material, you'll need to record sources and information pertinent to your speech. Obviously, with the scope of material available, you cannot record all the information you uncover. The following procedure is one way in which you can record and organize your research material. The procedure calls for the use of two sets of file cards: one for bibliographic facts and the other for informational notes and quotes.

1. On each bibliography file card, record the call number and, if given, the author, title, place of publication, publisher, date, and page number(s). Add a brief description of the material to remind you of the material in the stated source. Keep this card filed in alphabetical order with the other bibliographic file cards. Figure 4.7 is a sample bibliography card.

2. On each information card, cite the topic heading in the upper right-hand corner. This will make it easier to file and identify the card.

3. Record only a single idea on each card and use only one side of the card. If the card contains more than one idea, it may be impossible to file, especially if the ideas are on different topics. Keeping the information on one side of the card restricts the amount of information recorded for a

single idea and helps prevent you from omitting material because you failed to turn over the note card.

4. Record information exactly the way it appears in the source. If you must paraphrase or edit, be careful to keep it within the context in which it appears. That is, do not have your evidence suggest a different idea from the original.

5. The length of the recorded material should be restricted according to its anticipated use in the speech. For example, if you are to present a five-minute speech you won't be able to cite lengthy quotes.

6. Record abbreviated bibliographic material at the end of each note card. This will help you identify quickly the source of the material. You'll find this especially useful when you have to identify the source of your material in your speech. Figure 4.8 on page 80 is an example of an informational note card.

7. File your informational note cards under appropriate headings. The headings may not correspond exactly to those in your speech, but, as you prepare and develop your speech you'll find it easier to retrieve relevant note cards under some system of logically arranged headings (for example, chronological, spatial, topical).

Library research is indispensable in finding useful and interesting material for public speeches. Dialogues with librarians can help you find material that perhaps you would otherwise not locate. Informational

FIGURE 4.7 **Sample Bibliography Card**

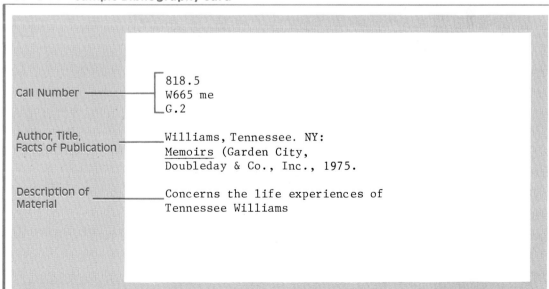

guides, indexes, and references are valuable tools for locating material that adds intellectual rigor and interest to messages. After finding appropriate information, you, as a public speaker, need to record it in a manner that helps you quickly locate the sources of information as well as the information itself. An efficient, effective filing system allows you to feel confident that your material stands ready for use when needed.

SUMMARY

Gathering material for your speech can be a rewarding exercise. You need not approach the prospect of research as a dull, laborious task. Instead, consider it an opportunity to further your knowledge in an interesting and stimulating manner.

Two major methods for gaining information are the interview and library research. An interview is defined as a prepared conversation, usually between two persons and planned for a specific purpose by means of predetermined and follow-up questions. The fundamental components of an interview include conversation, planning, specific purpose, and prepared questions, which may be either open or closed, primary or follow-up, and neutral or leading. In preparing an interview, you should select an interviewee who is knowledgeable on the subject under investigation. You should structure your interview into an introduction, body, and conclusion. Information from an interview can be recorded by taking

FIGURE 4.8   **Sample Informational Note Card**

Topic Heading ———————— High school years of Tennessee Williams

Direct Quote ———————— It was still almost entirely impossible
for me to speak aloud in the classroom.
And, teachers stopped asking me questions,
because when they did, I would produce a
voice that was hardly intelligible, my
throat would be so tight with panic.

Abbreviated Citation
(Full citation on ———————— Tennessee Williams, Memoirs, p. 23.
bibliography card)

written notes, by taping the interview, or both. Interviews can prove valuable for gaining information sometimes not contained in other sources of information.

The library contains numerous resources for locating material. Some of the more traditional listings are the card catalog, *Readers' Guide*, and the library's listing of periodical holdings. Most libraries also contain guides and indexes to reference books, general works, professional and specialized periodicals, essays, government publications, and legal references. Almanacs, fact books, encyclopedias, and dictionaries are other types of reference guides. Information from your library research should be recorded and filed on two types of cards. One card file is for bibliographic information; the other is for information on your subject. On the informational note cards, cite the topic, record only a single idea per card on one side only, record material exactly, monitor the length of the information you record, and note bibliographic information.

Information obtained through interviews of other people and from research in the library supply important, useful, and interesting material for public speeches.

ASSIGNMENTS

1. Interview one of your classmates on his or her hobby, major, plans for the future, or other subject you choose. Prepare some questions in advance and make adaptations as you go along. What did you learn about interviewing from this experience? Explain your conclusions in a written report to your instructor.

2. Make arrangements to interview one of your instructors on one aspect of the person's expertise. Give a two-minute oral report of what you learned from conducting the interview: the things that went well, what mistakes if any, and how you might improve the interview if you could do it over.

3. Interview a newspaper reporter and a broadcast newsperson on how they interview to get a story. What do they have in common? Any differences? Write a one-page report of your findings.

4. Give a five-minute speech on a topic in which you are interested, know something about, is worth your listeners' attention, and which lends itself to interviewing an expert. For example, for a speech on cars, interview a garage mechanic. For a report on supermarket shopping, interview a supermarket manager. For a speech on a particular type of crime, arrange an interview with an assistant district attorney.
Incorporate the information from the interview into your five-minute speech.

5. Locate six library reference sources not mentioned in this chapter. Identify the purposes of these sources. Compare your findings with those of other class members and compile and distribute a complete list of these new sources to your class.

6. Start a file box of information on a speech topic that you will be presenting in class. Using the ideas suggested in this chapter, record and file your information for possible future use. Report to the class how your file system is arranged. Suggest advantages and disadvantages for having such a system.

7. Give a five-minute informative speech on how to conduct an interview or how to do research in the library. In your speech discuss methods of gathering information, either through the interview process or by library research for a particular topic. Consult the appendix for suggested topics.

NOTES

1. We want to thank Mr. Marty Cavanaugh, librarian at McKendree College, for his assistance in this section.

Audience Adaptation

General Audience Analysis

Demographic Analysis

- Age
- Gender
- Educational Background
- Economic Status
- Political Orientation
- Cultural Background

Psychological Analysis

Analysis of Specific Audience

- Audience Size
- Interest in the Speaker
- Interest in the Subject
- Interest in the Speaking Occasion

Methods for Analyzing Audiences

- Focus Group Analysis
- Dry-run Analysis
- Questionnaire Analysis

5 Audience Adaptation and Analysis

OBJECTIVES

When you finish this chapter, you should be able to:

1. explain the general characteristics of audiences;
2. identify specific characteristics of your immediate audience;
3. apply methods for audience analysis; and
4. use the techniques of audience analysis and adaptation to present a five-minute speech to a specific audience.

5 Audience Adaptation and Analysis

Two speakers were to address the local PTA group on the issue of gun control. The first speaker, Marion, began:

> *I'm happy to see such a fine turn out tonight. By your presence here, you must consider the occasion and topic important enough to warrant your attendance. Tonight, I want to discuss a topic that affects men and women alike. The topic is guns. Many of you are farmers, who, as I understand from informal conversations with some of you, enjoy hunting. So do I! I enjoy most outdoor activities when done in a climate of safety and common sense. I think that most of you would agree with the view that gun safety is important in the handling and use of guns. But, when this right is abused, we need to protect ourselves. More specifically, we need to protect ourselves from the abuse of specific guns in our society. You may not agree with this point, but I sincerely hope that you will at least consider it in tonight's discussion.*

The second speaker was Tom. In part, he said:

> *Let me start with my conclusion. We have a problem in our society. Too many people are dying because of our misuse of guns. Too many handguns are being carried by too many men. Each year thousands of men and boys die because they were shot by people who did not know how to use firearms. The NRA would have us believe that it's our constitutional right to bear arms. I say "bull" to that view. We don't have a constitutional right to kill each other. What we need to do is to ban the use of handguns. Don't let anyone carry a gun. If men want to hunt, they can use rifles, bows and arrows, or knives. They don't need to carry guns.*

As Tom proceeded with his speech, his listeners grew increasingly hostile. Finally, one woman stood up and said to Tom, "Look, sir, you may not realize it, but most of the people in this audience are farmers and members of the NRA. We also like to hunt. We believe in the intelligent use of firearms, not in the banning of them."

Why did Tom have such a problem with his audience? In his preparation and presentation he made several mistakes that affected the effectiveness of his speech. His listeners seemed confused about why he started with the conclusion of his speech. Tom failed to understand the make-up of his audience. He addressed only the male members. He overlooked his listeners' economic, social, and educational backgrounds. He failed to consider their attitudes, beliefs, or values on his subject. Tom should have considered how interested the audience members would be in his subject, in the occasion, and in himself as a speaker. He failed to adjust his message to them. He should have used language that recognized the gender differences within his audience. His style of delivery appeared abrasive. If Tom had analyzed his audience carefully, he could have learned that many of the members belonged to the National Rifle Association. He then could have avoided attacking the organization and instead focused on some common goals that he shared with the audience.

If he had been working within a framework of common goals, Tom would have been in a better position to present the specific purpose of his address. His listeners might not have agreed with him, but they might have been more inclined to listen to his message.

In contrast, Marion was much more successful. Her message was organized. She recognized the characteristics of her audience and used this information to shape her message. Through her speech, Marion attempted to "build a bridge" between herself and her listeners. Unlike Tom, Marion adapted her message to her specific audience.

AUDIENCE ADAPTATION

A speech needs to be "tailor made" for an audience. Speakers who present speeches for their own benefit and not for that of their audiences risk alienating their listeners. Mistrust, lack of confidence, and boredom are some of the reactions of audience members toward speakers who don't adapt their speeches to the audience.

Audience adaptation is the process by which a speaker adjusts a message to an audience. This process occurs in two fundamental stages. The first step is audience analysis, in which the speaker attempts to discover information about the audience. In the second stage, the speaker uses this information to adjust the language, content, structure, and presentation of the message.

Public speakers need to adapt to a wide variety of audience characteristics through the entire speech. As speakers receive feedback, they should adjust their message to their listeners' reactions. For example, if some listeners seem confused, speakers need to introduce new material or redefine points that appear confusing.

As a speaker, you need to understand the characteristics of your listeners in order to adapt your message to them and to the occasion. This process is similar to that of a basketball coach, for example, who prepares his or her team by analyzing the opposition and adapting the game plan to the characteristics of the opposing team. To discover information about your listeners, focus on both general audience characteristics and characteristics of the specific audience you are addressing. We will examine first the factors investigated in general audience analysis.

GENERAL AUDIENCE ANALYSIS

Have you ever listened to a speaker who presented a message that most audience members failed to understand? What about a lecture you once heard that offended you because of the cultural or sexual stereotypes it contained? If you answer "yes" to either of these questions, then you listened to a message in which the speaker possibly misunderstood the general characteristics of the audience. Sensitivity to audience characteristics is an essential component of speech adaptation. Ancient scholars to present-day communication scholars share in this fundamental belief.[1]

When you, as a speaker, analyze the characteristics of your listeners, you are attempting to discover how homogeneous (similar) or heterogeneous (dissimilar) they are. Homogeneity suggests similarity of attributes between or among interacting individuals. Heterogeneity suggests differences.

Demographic Analysis

"Hey," said Crista, "I can speak to anybody. I treat everyone the same. So, when I give a speech I don't worry about who's in my audience. They're all the same people to me." Are people all the same? Should speakers address their audiences as if no differences existed among them?

You are a unique person, as is every person in your audience. While similarities may exist, each person has specific characteristics, backgrounds, and interests that make him or her a unique individual. Crista neglected this important point. Her failure to adjust her message to her listeners limited the effectiveness of her speech.

One way in which you can discover information about the general characteristics of your audience is to undertake a demographic analysis in which you investigate the age, gender, educational level, economic status, political orientation, and cultural background of the audience members. You look for similarities and differences among audience members in each of these areas. You can gain some knowledge of an audience's general demographic characteristics by speaking informally with the people who will make up your audience as you begin to prepare your speech.

Age.   One author once addressed his audience with stories about national politicians prominent in the 1950s and 1960s. Unfortunately, although the author was familiar with the political figures and their backgrounds, most of the members of his audience were not. As a result, blank stares greeted his message. The author failed to realize that most of the people in his audience had been born in the late 1960s. They were simply too young to remember the political figures of the 1950s and early 1960s. They recognized the politicians' names but knew little else about them.

Age is a factor that needs to be considered in audience analysis. Language, perceptions, style of dress, and political views are, in part, influenced by a person's age. As a speaker, you'll need to estimate the age range of your audience members. By having some idea of the range in ages, you are in a better position to select a style of language, examples, stories, testimony, and sources that are more understandable and relevant to your listeners.

If, for instance, your audience consists primarily of teenagers, they may not be interested in listening to a speech on social security, which may be more appealing to an audience of older persons. The younger listeners may not yet have realized the importance of the topic. You may need to present to these listeners reasons why they need to be concerned about social security. For example, you may want to hit them in the pocketbook. That is, show them that their taxes may continue to rise as the need for higher social security payments increases. As a result, they may have less spendable income for dating, paying off college loans, and so forth. Obviously, not all members (even those of the same ages) will interpret the message identically. Yet, you still need to recognize the factor of age in analyzing the audience.

Do not automatically assume, however, that people's ages necessarily exclude them from being able to understand or appreciate messages designed for a different age group. As a speaker, you face a real challenge in adapting your message to an audience.

Gender. Bill approached his public speaking class with a firm determination to make a strong initial impression. Looking the class members straight in the eye, he began: "Guys, I want you to be aware that car accidents are one of the leading causes of death in our country." Confident that he had accomplished his initial objective, Bill continued to address his listeners as "guys." Self-assured, feeling that he understood his listeners and that he had adapted his message to them, Bill concluded his speech, "Guys, I hope today that you follow my advice of being men, not boys, when it comes to smart driving."

Only scattered applause followed Bill's speech. He seemed puzzled and somewhat stunned by the audience's reaction. What, he wondered, had gone wrong? Bill failed to realize that most of the audience members were women. Many of them objected to his sexist language. They felt excluded from a message that was directed only to "guys" and "men." Bill should have considered the demographic factor of gender of the audience members when preparing his speech.

Your general public speaking audience will probably contain members of both sexes. You may be tempted to see your audience members not as they are but as they appear in your stereotypical perceptions of them. If so, you may inadvertently make statements that insult or offend them. Let your language reflect the gender differences in your audience. Avoid using only masculine pronouns—*he, him, his*. Instead of saying "for the preservation of mankind," you can say "for the preservation of the human race." The latter expression recognizes that more than one gender exists.

Educational Background.

Another factor to consider in your demographic analysis is the educational background of the audience members. You may assume, for example, that all the members of your class are high-school graduates, but within the audience there may be those who major in such different fields as engineering, chemistry, nursing, business, or liberal arts. It's rare when all members in your public speaking class share the same educational background.

You need to be sensitive to the differences in educational level among your audience members. To present a highly technical speech to an audience not familiar with the subject matter beckons disaster. On the other hand, take care not to insult your listeners with too simple a message. Part of the excitement in doing an effective speech lies in tailoring a message to fit the listeners' general educational backgrounds. The more widely varied their educational backgrounds, the more challenging will be your task.

Economic Status.

Rosali attempted to persuade her class that tuition at the university should be raised by 20 percent. She thought that her speech contained just the right amount of persuasive arguments. When

A general audience is usually made up of men and women who differ widely in age, educational background, economic status, political orientation, and culture. Analyze your audience in terms of these factors and adapt your message accordingly in order to communicate as effectively as possible.

her speech ended, she received no applause, only a chorus of complaints. What was her mistake?

She misjudged one important demographic factor of her listeners: their economic status. Most students in her class were not well-off financially; many had taken loans and were working part-time to pay for their college education. Asking them to support a 20 percent increase in tuition obviously clashed with their economic background.

Economic status is usually an important factor in our lives. As a speaker, you'll need to be sensitive to the economic status of your listeners. You'll want to seek a common ground on economic matters: one that listeners perceive does not threaten their economic condition but may perhaps improve it.

Political Orientation.   In his speech, Matt asked his listeners to support a particular candidate for a local political office. Defending his view, Matt stated that the opposing candidate represented a political view "alien to most red-blooded Americans." In Matt's audience, however, were persons who shared or respected the political views of the candidate whom Matt attacked. As a result, many in Matt's audience rejected his speech.

Unlike Matt, you'll want to be more sensitive to the political beliefs of the members of your audience. While you need not share these views, it is wise to recognize the differences that exist. Attempt to focus your speech on the important issues. Avoid using personal attacks against those who do not agree with your political beliefs. Such attacks tend to divide people.

Cultural Background.   Religious, ethnic, racial, age, gender, social, economic, educational, and political backgrounds influence and are, in turn, influenced by culture. For many of us, cultural upbringing has a strong influence on the way we view the world. Sometimes, we compare our culture to others. This type of comparison is not in and of itself bad. When we take an ethnocentric view—a view that suggests our culture is superior to others—we may quickly find ourselves in trouble.

As you do with any of the other demographic factors, you'll want to be sensitive to the different cultural backgrounds that exist among your listeners. Seek a common ground of understanding that reflects your sensitivity to and respect for cultural differences. This is not always easy to do, as sometimes demonstrated in addresses given in the United Nations. Yet, as the world grows smaller and international trade and exchange increase, we must learn to expand our awareness of cultures different from our own. This increased awareness will help us be more effective speakers when addressing audiences of mixed cultures.

Psychological Analysis

Much of what we have discussed so far about the demographic characteristics of audience members touches on their psychological characteristics as well. Their attitudes of liking or disliking someone or something, their beliefs of what is true or false, and their values of what is or is not important or worthy are all intimately tied to their demographic characteristics. To simply consider, for instance, the gender of your listeners without considering their beliefs, values, and attitudes toward your speech subject limits your ability to adapt your message. There are several ways to obtain information about the psychological characteristics of your listeners. You can conduct formal or informal interviews, circulate questionnaires, or do a focus-group analysis. We will discuss these methods of audience analysis later in this chapter.

Other ways in which you can obtain information about the psychological characteristics of your listeners are to analyze the listeners' responses to other speeches or to ask questions of the persons who will make up your audience before you begin your speech. For example, you may ask, "How many of you strongly favor the idea that students should be allowed to select their own college advisors?" Responses to this question will give you some indication of the listeners' attitude toward this position. Such psychological information can be incorporated into your speech in several ways:

1. by using startling statistics;
2. by developing examples that may be familiar to your listeners;
3. by introducing interesting visual aids; and
4. by asking rhetorical questions, telling humorous stories, or building your message to a climactic point.

ANALYSIS OF SPECIFIC AUDIENCE

To do adequate audience analysis, you must do more than focus on the general demographic and psychological characteristics that apply to audiences. You must also investigate the characteristics that apply to an immediate audience. These immediate audience characteristics include audience size, interest in the speaker, interest in the topic, and interest in the speaking occasion. These factors, too, have an impact on the differences or similarities among audience members.

Audience Size

Your audience will probably consist of more than one person. This probably is not startling news to you. What you may not know is that group size can affect audience members' feelings toward each other, interaction with each other, and manner of response to the speaker.[2] Smaller audiences may feel more compelled to provide feedback, interact more frequently with each other, or feel closer bonds of friendship with each other. Larger audiences may exhibit a wider range of interaction patterns, listening patterns, and seating patterns.

Obviously, you want to be sensitive to the size of your immediate audience. Note the seating arrangements of your listeners. Do the same people seem to sit in the same general area? If so, they may tend to interact more frequently with those nearest them. This can be important, especially if some of them tend to be influential, opinionated, or disruptive. You may need to devote more attention to these people. If the audience is small, you may discover that the listeners are more willing to provide you with feedback than if they were members of a larger audience.

With a larger audience, you may find it more difficult to discover common characteristics of the listeners. You may have to speak louder or use an audio aid (a topic we will discuss in Chapter 7). Your visual aids must be large enough to be seen by all the listeners. Other factors to consider may include facial expressions (they may need to be exaggerated in order to be seen), restricted bodily movement if the speech is presented from a platform, or limited opportunity to hand out material to a large audience. Consider further your ability to maintain eye contact with your listeners, the speaking level you select, and the manner in which you present visual aids. Clearly, the size of the audience affects the way in which you will speak.

Interest in the Speaker

How interested will your audience be in you as a speaker? You may assume that your classmates will automatically be interested in you simply because you are a classmate. This may be true initially, but don't assume that you can maintain their interest without continually working for it. What if you are the fourth speaker to address them that day? You may assume, probably correctly, that they're tired, restless, and perhaps not as interested in you as they might have been had you spoken first. You'll have to work harder to get and maintain their interest.

As they listen to you, members of your audience will probably assess your credibility as a speaker. They may want to know if you are a competent speaker, if you can be trusted, and if you demonstrate goodwill toward them.

Henry assumed that his listeners liked him because he was, after all, a likable person, but he insulted his audience by being ill-prepared, by mispronouncing words, and by appearing self-centered in his presentation. He did little to generate interest in his message. Henry misjudged his audience's level of interest and respect in him as a speaker. Unlike

Henry, you'll want to nourish and amplify whatever level of interest your listeners have in you. Show them that their trust in you is not misguided.

Interest in the Subject

Kedron assumed that her subject alone would generate and maintain audience interest. Everyone, she thought, would like the subject of earthquakes. To her dismay, however, as she spoke, her listeners soon grew tired and appeared bored with her subject. "Weren't they interested in earthquakes?" she thought to herself. "What did I do wrong?" Kedron muttered as she sat down.

Kedron made a mistake common to many beginning public speaking students. She assumed more audience interest in her subject than was the case. It is wise to assume that your audience possesses a limited degree of interest in your subject. You will need to generate more interest in your speech topic. Work at increasing interest in your speech topic throughout your entire presentation.

Interest in the Speaking Occasion

Naturally, you as the speaker will regard the speaking occasion as a special one. Ideally, the audience members should view it in a similar manner. At times they do, but too often the opposite is true. In class, they often view the situation as an artificial one, where they are a captive audience who must listen to a number of speeches.

Your presentation can create a special climate that encourages your listeners to view the occasion as interesting and special. If you doubt this, ask yourself why you look forward to hearing messages from particular people, such as clergy, teachers, politicians, friends, or classmates, who present effective public speeches. Don't they, through their speeches, help generate interest in the occasion? You, too, can work at developing similar interest among your listeners.

To generate your listeners' interest in the occasion, consider the following points:

1. The manner in which you approach your topic sends your listeners a message about the importance of the occasion. If you give the impression that the occasion is unimportant, don't expect your listeners to think otherwise.

2. Let your introduction help create a climate of importance that surrounds the occasion. For instance, you may suggest, "Today I hope to challenge your beliefs on a topic important to us all."

3. Use examples, quotes, stories, and facts throughout your speech to demonstrate why the occasion is important.

4. In your conclusion remind your listeners that this occasion was an important one for them.

As we've seen, there are a number of factors to consider both in general audience analysis as well as in analysis of your immediate audience. In the next section we will discuss some specific methods that you can use to gather information for audience analysis.

METHODS FOR ANALYZING AUDIENCES

No one method of audience analysis is superior to the others, but each may be useful in one or another situation. Three useful methods for audience analysis are focus group analysis, dry-run analysis, and questionnaire analysis.

Focus Group Analysis

Focus group analysis is a helpful exploratory tool used in marketing research.[3] Essentially a loosely structured group interview, focus group analysis is used to discover beliefs, values, or attitudes toward a particular product or service. The size of the group usually runs between five to seven people, and sessions usually last from one hour to one hour and a half. It is generally recommended that the session be repeated with a similar group. A modified focus group analysis can be adapted to your public speaking class to help you identify your classmates' values, beliefs, or attitudes toward your subject.

In class, your focus group session can contain fewer people and run for a shorter period of time. For example, two or three days before your presentation you may select a random sample of classmates to meet in a focus group setting. By selecting a random sample, you guarantee that every member of your class has an equal chance to be included in the group.[4] One way in which you can select a random sample is to select every eighth name (or fifth name, etc.) from your instructor's class list and invite those persons to be members of your focus group. You may have greater success in selecting a focus group if your instructor encourages participation in such groups.

In the focus group, interview the members on your topic (recall the skills for interviewing discussed in Chapter 4). You may ask them questions orally, have them complete questionnaires, or both. You can then evaluate this information and use it to adapt your speech to the whole audience.

Dry-run Analysis

One of the most common types of audience analysis used in public speaking is a dry-run analysis. This simply means that you deliver a practice speech to a number of friends. This procedure can be particularly helpful, especially if the friends are similar to the people who will constitute the audience. At the end of the practice speech, you the speaker can ask for a critique of the message.

Valuable insight can be gained from this type of analysis. Did the listeners find the message interesting? Was the speech organized? Did they feel the message related to them? These are just some of the types of questions that can be raised in the critique session. The information you obtain from the critique can be used to help you polish and adapt your speech for the actual presentation. Doing two or three dry runs will give you needed help and practice, but beware: too many dry runs may make your speech sound less spontaneous and more memorized.

Dry runs can also help you build confidence in your speaking. As you gain experience by speaking to different audiences, you can develop more confidence in your public speaking ability. As this confidence grows, you may find the challenging art of public speaking becoming more enjoyable.

Questionnaire Analysis

Questionnaires may be dichotomous (stating two answers to choose from), multiple-choice (stating more than two answers to choose from), or open-ended, using questions such as "Why do you like this class?" An audience analysis questionnaire is best kept brief and simple. Use these general steps as a guide for developing a questionnaire:

1. Specify the information that will be sought. Are you seeking specific attitudes toward your subject? Are you interested in discovering the audience's level of knowledge about your subject? Are you seeking a list of subjects that interest your listeners?

2. Determine the type of questionnaire and method of administration. Will your questionnaire contain structured, predetermined questions that seek fixed responses? Will your questionnaire contain open-ended questions that allow for a wider range of responses? Will it contain both types of questions? How will you administer your questionnaire? Will it be a telephone questionnaire, mail-order questionnaire, or survey questionnaire that you administer in a face-to-face manner?

3. Determine the content of your individual questions. What do you want your questions to ask? Will their content focus on demographic information (for example, gender, age, college major)? Will their content seek information about psychological characteristics (for example, attitudes, beliefs, or values)? Is it going to produce the type of data you need?

4. Determine the form of response to each question. Will it be a fixed response (for instance, yes or no) or will it be open-ended? Sample questions in fixed and open forms may look something like the following:

(Fixed-response)	Do you agree with the university's plan for a 5 percent tuition increase?
	_____ Yes _____ No
(Scale-fixed response)	What is your attitude toward a 5 percent tuition increase to pay for increased faculty salaries?
	_____ Strongly agree
	_____ Mildly agree
	_____ Neutral
	_____ Mildly disagree
	_____ Strongly disagree
(Open-ended response)	What can a university do to raise money other than increase tuition?
	Your response: _____
	_____
	_____

The form of the response is particularly important to the type of data you wish to collect and to the manner of data evaluation. Fixed-response or scale-fixed-response questions may be more useful if you are interested in tabulating a statistical analysis of the responses. If you want to do a content analysis, then the open-ended responses may be more beneficial.

5. Determine the number of questions and their sequence. If you want to find out only a limited amount of information, then your questionnaire should be relatively brief. Seeking more detailed information will require a more elaborate questionnaire. Generally, it is better to ask critical questions early in case people fail to complete the questionnaire.

6. Pretest the questionnaire. See how long it takes your friends to fill it out. If you estimate that it will take fifteen minutes but your friends need half an hour, then you need to reexamine your questionnaire. Through pretesting you may discover that certain questions are vague or confusing and need to be reworded or discarded.

SUMMARY

Audience analysis and adaptation are essential in public speaking. Audience adaptation is the process by which a speaker adjusts a message to the audience. The first step in this two-stage process is audience analysis, in which the speaker attempts to obtain information about the audience members. In analyzing an audience, the speaker needs to consider both general audience factors and characteristics of the specific audience being addressed. In general audience analysis, the speaker seeks information about the audience's demographic characteristics, such as age, gender, educational level, economic status, political orientation, and cultural background. The speaker also investigates the listeners' psychological attributes, such as their attitudes, beliefs, and values. Analysis of the specific audience focuses on consideration of its size, interest in the speaker, interest in the subject, and interest in the speaking occasion.

Several methods can be used to gather information for purposes of audience analysis. Three commonly used methods are focus group analysis, dry-run analysis, and questionnaire analysis. In questionnaire analysis, the questions used may ask for fixed responses, scale fixed responses, or open-ended responses. The type of data sought and the manner in which it will be evaluated affect the type of questions used on the questionnaire. The three methods of gathering information can be used individually or in combination with one another to help the speaker discover information about audience members.

Analyzing the audience, however, is only a means to an end. The goal is audience adaptation. A speaker must be able to use the information gained to adapt his or her message to the listeners. Through selection of language, style of delivery, content, and organizational pattern a speaker attempts to tailor a message to the immediate audience being addressed. Through audience analysis and adaptation, a speaker builds bridges, not walls, between the speaker and the listeners.

ASSIGNMENTS

1. Choose a speech topic. Construct an audience questionnaire with which you can gather information on the audience's perceptions of that topic. Include questions that ask for both fixed and open-ended responses. Have your classmates complete the questionnaire and report on the results at the next class meeting.

2. Ask three to five classmates to participate in a focus group analysis. Plan a series of questions that relate to their attitudes, beliefs, and values on a speech topic you select. Give a report in class on how you can use the information gained from the focus group analysis to prepare your speech.

3. Obtain a copy of a survey poll such as a Gallup or Harris poll. Analyze its findings. What does it reveal about the audience's demographic characteristics? What does it reveal about the audience's psychological attributes? Report your findings to the class.

4. Do a dry run of a speech before friends who are not members of your public speaking class. At the end of your presentation, ask them what they liked or disliked about your speech and why. Write down their specific comments and use their criticisms to adapt your speech before delivering it to your public speaking classmates. Following your speech, give a short oral report on your friends' criticisms and explain how you adapted your speech in light of their comments.

5. Give a five-minute speech on a topic of your choice. Use information gained from your audience analysis to adjust your message to the audience. Select language, content, organizational pattern, and delivery style that you believe appropriate for your audience.

NOTES

1. Theodore Clevenger, Jr., *Audience Analysis* (New York: Bobbs-Merrill Co., 1966).

2. John E. Baird, Jr., and Sanford B. Weinberg, *Group Communication: The Essence of Synergy*, 2nd ed. (Dubuque, IA: William C. Brown, 1981), pp. 167–69.

3. Gilbert A. Churchill, Jr., *Marketing Research: Methodological Foundation*, 3rd ed. (Chicago: Dryden Press, 1983), pp. 178–84.

4. Charles T. Clark and Lawrence L. Schkade, *Statistical Analysis for Administrative Decisions*, 4th ed. (Cincinnati: South-Western Publishing Co., 1983), p. 153.

Speaker's Credibility Defined

Advantages of Having Credibility

- Listeners' Perception of Competence
- Listeners' Perception of Confidence
- Listeners' Perception of Trustworthiness
- Listeners' Perception of Goodwill

Developing Speaker's Credibility

- Developing Competence
- Developing Trustworthiness
- Developing Goodwill Toward the Audience
- Developing Dynamism
- Developing Identification
- Introduction of a Speaker

6

Speaker's Credibility

OBJECTIVES

When you finish this chapter, you should be able to:

1. define the term *credibility;*
2. list several advantages of having credibility;
3. explain the factors believed to influence credibility;
4. evaluate a speaker's credibility; and
5. present an informative speech in which you demonstrate the qualities of speaker's credibility.

6 Speaker's Credibility

In her speeches, Rose always seemed to be effective in persuading her listeners to believe her. She was always in command of the subject; she always seemed to know what she was talking about. Her speeches were not any more complex than most of the other speeches presented in class, but the listeners always seemed to believe Rose more than they did the other speakers. One day Rose's friend Kristen asked Rose why people believed her so much. "I'm not sure," replied Rose. "I don't think I do anything special. I try to make sure that I understand my material and be prepared, and I make an effort to be interesting and talk about something that I think will be helpful to most people. Maybe they just appreciate the effort I make."

SPEAKER'S CREDIBILITY DEFINED

What quality did Rose have that made her audience believe her and respond favorably to what she had to say? Rose had *credibility*. Her listeners believed her to be a competent, confident, trustworthy speaker who displayed goodwill toward them. Rose seemed to understand her audi-

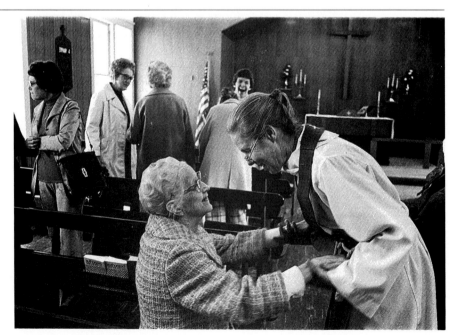

Audience members form perceptions of a speaker's personality and speaking skills. These perceptions help the audience assign a level of credibility to the speaker. Highly credible speakers are perceived to be competent, confident, trustworthy, and full of goodwill.

ence's trust in her. She respected this honor and did not try to take advantage of it.

Does every speaker have credibility? No, not all speakers do, and others may possess it in varying amounts. Speakers must work to develop credibility so that their audiences will believe them and what they say. Speakers can't simply assume that good looks or a charming personality will automatically create and maintain a high level of credibility. Credibility, like fame or success, can be fleeting. A speaker perceived to have credibility at one time may not be deemed credible at another time if he or she does not work to maintain that credibility.

Credibility can be defined as *the amount of belief a person has in some person or some thing, such as an institution.* At the core of credibility rests the concept of belief, which suggests trust or confidence in someone or something. Thus, when we speak of credibility in public speaking, we mean that listeners trust and have confidence in the speaker and the message. Speakers must take care not to abuse that trust. Listeners' belief in the speaker is an important factor, especially if the speaker hopes to inform, entertain, or persuade them.

ADVANTAGES OF HAVING CREDIBILITY

Doctors, lawyers, salespeople, teachers, engineers—for that matter, almost everyone—can benefit from having a high level of credibility. Jamie and Laurie discovered this when they applied for teaching positions at a local college. Their credentials, strong letters of recommendation from colleagues, and previous teaching experience gave them a high level of credibility. They were both hired at higher ranks and at higher salaries than some of their peers. In addition to the advantages of greater monetary reward and advancement, other advantages exist for an individual who is considered to be a highly credible person. In this section we will explore the favorable components of credibility, which include being perceived as competent, confident, trustworthy, and as having goodwill.

Listeners' Perception of Competence

"Ron really knows what he's talking about," said Barbara. "He has great command of the subject matter. I certainly believe what he says." Barbara's belief in Ron's mastery of the subject is an advantage for him. As long as Barbara perceives him to be competent on the subject, she is likely to continue to believe and be influenced by him. She may not automatically agree with him or blindly follow everything he says, but she is in a state of mind that predisposes her to perceive Ron as a competent individual.

Being perceived as competent by others is an advantage for you as a speaker. If they see you as competent, people trust what you say. They believe you to be well versed on your subject, and they may support your positions on issues. They accept your decisions more readily if they believe them to be wise ones. Competence is not easily earned but, if achieved, will enhance your credibility.

Listeners' Perception of Confidence

Lisa knew her subject inside and out. She believed that her audience trusted her views on the critical issues. She honestly felt that she spoke with her listeners' best interests in mind. As she approached the podium, her confidence grew in her ability to present an honest and persuasive message.

A person who is perceived as credible has earned the right to speak or perform a certain task. Earning this right presupposes a degree of confidence in one's own ability to master or be in command of a particular task. The confident person is self-assured and is perceived as being competent in what he or she says or does. Confidence in yourself can help increase the amount of trust and belief others have in you. If you believe what you say, others are more likely to trust you.

Of course, there is the danger of appearing too confident. This can quickly undermine your credibility. They may view you as a know-it-all who cares more about what you think than what others think. Confidence with a touch of humility go a long way in helping your listeners perceive you as a confident, caring individual.

Listeners' Perception of Trustworthiness

Everyone enjoys working with Stan. He always keeps his word. He never undermines his workers. He supports their decisions and evaluates their work fairly and honestly. Stan is indeed an exceptional supervisor—his workers trust and support him.

Trust exists in many relationships—between husband and wife, parent and child, doctor and patient, lawyer and client, teacher and student, clergy and laypeople, and politician and constituent. Trust can be defined as *a reliance or dependence on the honesty or truthfulness of someone or something.* We are likely to trust people we believe to be honest, sincere, and truthful. We are also likely to respect, support, and have confidence in those we trust.

Listeners' Perception of Goodwill

Kathy was always willing to help and seemed to simply enjoy doing good for other people. As a result, she was welcomed wherever she went. Kathy never felt lonely; she felt needed and loved by her friends.

When you are perceived as being willing to help other people, you may find that they in turn may be willing to help or support you. Goodwill involves your ethical choices between right and wrong. When people believe that you are saying or doing something that helps them, they believe that you are displaying goodwill. By combining sound, ethical decisions with goodwill, you can help people see you as an actively concerned and caring person. They then may be willing to return the favor by helping and supporting you.

As we have seen, there are many advantages associated with having credibility. As a public speaker, however, you must do more than recognize these advantages. You must learn how to develop a high level of credibility in order to increase your effectiveness as a speaker.

DEVELOPING SPEAKER'S CREDIBILITY

Attempting to establish your credibility is not an easy task. Gaining credibility involves developing competence, confidence, trustworthiness, and goodwill. Two other factors, dynamism and identification, also contribute to credibility. In this section we will examine each of these qualities and explore some specific ways to develop credibility in each area.

Developing Competence

Chad greeted his audience with a smile. After a brief introduction, he began to stumble over his words. He mispronounced important terms and forgot essential facts. He cited material that most listeners either could not understand or did not believe. In his arguments Chad often advanced sweeping generalizations instead of specific points. His content was vague and incomplete. At the end of his speech, he asked for a show of hands from those who supported his position. To Chad's dismay, no one responded.

Chad's listeners responded unfavorably to his presentation because, in their view, Chad acted incompetently. His failure to pronounce words correctly, offer specific arguments or analyses, and present credible material chipped away at his credibility as a speaker. What should Chad—or any speaker—consider when attempting to convey an impression of competence? The following list provides some suggestions.

1. Have a narrow, well-defined purpose that allows you to make your content concrete and specific. Avoid sweeping generalizations and vague abstractions.

2. Present current material from credible sources. Cite the sources that you use.

3. Be organized and clear in your presentation.

4. Be knowledgeable on your topic and appear in control of the subject matter.

5. Rehearse your presentation. Have command of the correct pronunciation of words in your speech. If uncertain about pronunciation, consult a dictionary. Practice the correct pronunciation until it is automatic so that you will not stumble in the delivery of your speech.

6. If unusually qualified to address your subject, inform the listeners of your qualifications.[1]

Developing Trustworthiness

Trustworthiness is closely connected to the factor of competence. It is difficult to establish trust between a speaker and members of an audience if they perceive the speaker as incompetent. But an image of a competent speaker does not always elicit trust. Note what black activist Malcolm X did when addressing an audience. Speaking in 1964 in New York City to an audience composed primarily of white persons, he said in part:

> Friends and enemies: Tonight I hope that we can have a little fireside chat with as few sparks as possible being tossed around, [e]specially because of the very explosive condition that the world is in today. Sometimes, when a person's house is on fire and someone comes in yelling fire, instead of the person who is awakened by the yell being thankful, he makes the mistake of charging the one who awakened him with having set the fire. I hope that this little conversation tonight about the black revolution won't cause many of you to accuse us of igniting it when you find it at your doorstep . . . .[2]

In attempting to build trust, Malcolm X encouraged his audience not to jump to a hasty conclusion. Rather, he hoped that the audience members would first listen to his message before making a judgment. He acknowledged all those in his audience, even his enemies. By doing this, he showed that he was not speaking to any one person but all. And, by speaking to all the members, he hoped that they would listen to his frank message without accusing him of causing the black revolution. In short, he attempted to use their perception of his frankness, honesty, sincerity, and competence to build trust.

There are a number of specific techniques that you can use to present an image of trustworthiness:

1. Adapt your message to your audience by appearing sincere and honest in the presentation of your message and by showing your listeners that you have their best interests in mind. (Recall the procedures for audience analysis and adaptation discussed in Chapter 5.)

2. Show that other people have trusted your views on the subject. Cite specific examples.

3. Be in control of your subject matter.

4. Present sound reasons and analyses in support of issues.

5. Use trusted sources to support your material and cite the sources that you use.

Developing Goodwill Toward the Audience

As a public speaker, you need to be, in a sense, a "goodwill ambassador." Both ancient and contemporary communication scholars have recognized the importance of goodwill in influencing an audience's perception of a speaker.[3]

Consider this student's attempt to display goodwill toward her audience.

> Today I want to present a message that I believe is beneficial to each person here. I encourage you to donate blood to the local blood center in our city. Your contribution may help save the life of a friend, relative, or classmate or even your own life. On occasion I have donated blood. I believe that my time and effort are well spent, especially if my small contribution helps a fellow human being.

Clearly, the speaker has the audience's interest in mind. She attempts to be honest about her feelings and the need for donating blood. She accentuates her feeling of goodwill by demonstrating her personal commitment to the cause.

The following suggestions list some ways in which you can help establish goodwill toward your listeners.

1. Through audience analysis, attempt to discover what qualities your listeners admire and respect as well as those qualities they dislike. Then, in your speech, develop those qualities that they admire and respect.

2. Demonstrate that you have your listeners' best interests in mind. One way to do this is to point to yourself as a person who actively pursues your own suggestions (as did the speaker in the example above). Another way is to suggest that the listeners may reap particular benefits if they follow your recommendations.

3. Use a clear and orderly pattern of organization that your listeners can easily follow.

4. Use personal pronouns—*we, our, us*—to personalize your message.

5. Make your message honest and your arguments reasonable.

6. Be warm, friendly, pleasant, and sincere.

Developing Dynamism

Pat approached her audience sheepishly. She stood in a semi-erect posture with her head tucked close to her chest. She spoke in a mono-tone with little, if any, variation in rate or pitch. Numerous "ahs" and "ums" punctuated her speech. She kept her arms and hands glued to the podium and used no gestures to accentuate the important points in her speech. She did not lift her eyes from her notes. Pat ended her speech, then walked quickly back to her seat, without once looking at her audience.

As a speaker, Pat personified a lack of confidence. Her presentation lacked dynamism, which can be defined as *a sense of confidence conveyed through a lively and energetic delivery.* Pat appeared neither dynamic nor confident and interested in her subject. Her audience probably found it difficult to listen to her speech or to be interested in it. Too often public speaking students exhibit the same delivery characteristics that Pat displayed, characteristics that can undercut the dynamism and effectiveness of their delivery.

Consider the following suggestions for ways to increase your dynamism and add variety and interest to your presentation.

1. Try to limit the nonfluencies ("ahs," "ums") in your delivery. These can hurt your credibility.[4] Being adequately rehearsed and in control of your subject matter will help you avoid using nonfluencies in your speech.

2. Avoid repeating words and phrases ("you know," "like," "okay"), which draw attention to themselves and weaken the life of your presentation. Make yourself aware of when you use these expressions and try to break the habit. Start and end sentences without using these expressions.

3. Vary your physical movements (gestures, posture) to complement your verbal message. Establish eye contact with your listeners. Try to use regular and sustained eye contact.

4. Vary vocal characteristics, such as rate or tone of voice, to add variety and interest to your delivery.

5. Vary your arguments, sources of information, and types of evidence to add variety and interest to your message.

Developing Identification

In developing credibility, it is helpful to have audience members identify with you, your message, or both. They may find you to be a more believable, trustworthy person if they can identify with you. Sometimes, speakers try to establish identification between themselves and listeners by citing material that they believe they all can identify with. This is precisely what President Reagan did in an address on the problem of government waste and excess. To illustrate the point, he cited a story about San Francisco 49ers quarterback Joe Montana. Montana, argued Reagan, once acted in ways similar to the way the federal government acted— seeking the path of excess and waste. By tying his argument to the Montana example, Reagan attempted to have his listeners identify with the problem of excess and waste. Reagan explained:

> You know, I think the American people know what the 49ers quarterback, Joe Montana, found out the hard way. When he was making the transition from college to pro football, there were those who thought he was too thin. So Joe ate pizza and drank milk shakes at 2 o'clock in the morning, thinking the extra weight would be like extra padding, but it was all in the wrong place. And being the bright fellow that he is, he went back to doing what had gotten him into pro football to begin with. He found out that detours are rarely the road to excellence, and excess never leads to strength.[5]

There are several methods you can use to create identification between yourself and the members of your audience. For example:

1. Display qualities (honesty, virtue, openness) with which your listeners seek to identify. If they appreciate frankness, then you need to be frank with them.

2. Present material with which listeners can identify. Use stories or examples that are familiar to them. For instance, you may cite a recent incident with which they are familiar. Use this incident to illustrate a point in your message (as Reagan did in the previous example).

3. Present credible sources of information with which listeners can identify. Identify the sources (the names of experts, books, journals, or magazines) that you use. Try to use sources that your listeners will recognize and respect.

4. Show how you and your audience share similar concerns and possibly similar positions on the issues. "I share your concerns" is a statement sometimes heard from a speaker who is trying to establish a common position with the audience. Use such phrases or statements to point out any similarities that exist.

5. Show that you and your audience identify with a common goal or goals. Do this by pointing out the goal that you and members of your audience are seeking. For instance, you might say, "All of us are seeking the important goal of world peace."

Introduction of a Speaker

There may be occasions on which you are formally introduced to an audience. The introduction can establish a climate that enhances your initial credibility. You may have little control over what the person making the introduction says about you. However, if you are able to provide input, keep in mind the following suggestions for ways to develop credibility through an introduction:

1. Introductory remarks should be as brief and to the point as possible.
2. Your qualifications and expertise should be highlighted.
3. Previous experience, if any, in the subject should be noted briefly.
4. Any humorous remarks about you should be minimized as much as possible, especially if your speech will address a serious topic. You don't want your credibility undercut by remarks that make light of your experience and knowledge.
5. The final part of the introductory remarks should emphasize the belief that the announcer is happy and pleased to introduce you to the audience.

We will discuss speeches of introduction in more detail in Chapter 13, "Evocative Speaking." The brief suggestions presented here indicate ways in which the introduction of a speaker can contribute to the speaker's credibility.

SUMMARY

Speaker's credibility is an essential component of effective public speaking. Credibility is defined as the amount of belief a person has in someone or something, such as an institution. At the core of credibility rests the concept of belief. Belief suggests trust or confidence that someone is honest or something is true.

There are several advantages to having credibility; among them are the audience's perception of the speaker as being competent, confident, and trustworthy and as having goodwill. These advantages can help a speaker be more respected and persuasive.

To develop a high level of credibility, public speakers should work to develop the qualities of competence, trustworthiness, goodwill toward the audience, dynamism, and identification. An introduction can also have a great effect on a speaker's credibility. An introduction that establishes a high level of credibility is brief and to the point, emphasizing the speaker's qualifications, expertise, knowledge, and previous experience in the subject.

1. Choose a subject. Then select a person whom you believe to be a highly credible source on that subject. Write an essay explaining why you believe this person to be credible.

2. Select any three national political figures. Who of these three do you believe to be the most credible? Who is the least credible? Write an essay explaining the reasons for your decisions.

3. Provide your own definition of credibility. What factors do you believe are important in the study of credibility? Share your views with other class members in a small group setting. Each group will select a spokesperson to represent the group's views. Each spokesperson will present a brief speech, summarizing the views of the group and demonstrating the qualities contained in your definition of credibility.

4. Introduce one of your classmates to the members of the class as if he or she were going to speak to the class on a topic of his or her choice. In your introduction highlight your classmate's strengths, qualifications, expertise, experience, and competence to speak on the chosen topic.

NOTES

1. Murray Hewgill and Gerald Miller, "Source Credibility and Response to Fear-Arousing Communications," *Speech Monographs* 36 (1965), 95–101.

2. George Breitman, ed., *Malcolm X Speaks* (New York: Grove Press, 1968), p. 45.

3. Lane Cooper, trans., *The Rhetoric of Aristotle* (New York: Appleton-Century-Crofts, 1960), pp. 91–92.

4. Hewgill and Miller, "Source Credibility," pp. 95–101.

5. *Weekly Compilation of Presidential Documents* (Washington, DC: Government Printing Office, 1982), xviii, 55.

7

Delivery: Bodily Action and Audiovisual Aids

OBJECTIVES

When you finish reading this chapter, you should be able to:

1. differentiate between bodily language and bodily expression;
2. point out the values of bodily action for public speakers and their listeners;
3. tell how to get your body to talk when you are giving a speech;
4. list and explain the seven techniques of bodily action used in public speaking;
5. observe and interpret listeners' bodily actions; and
6. use audiovisual aids efficiently in delivering a demonstration speech.

7 Delivery: Bodily Action and Audiovisual Aids

When Carl Rix was elected president of the American Bar Association, he knew that he would be touring the country, making many speeches. His first step in preparing for the tour was seeking professional help from a speech coach. The instructor listened to the veteran attorney's speech and was full of praise for the content, organization, and interesting development of ideas. And yet there was something missing. Carl Rix was not taking full advantage of visual communication. He was not using enough bodily action, dramatization, and showmanship.

The instructor pointed out that Rix could be more effective if he would let go, use more gestures, and have a good time speaking before his audiences. Rix was a good student, and it wasn't long before he began using bodily action, dramatization, and showmanship to excellent advantage in his speeches.

Several months later, the instructor was pleased to receive a letter from Rix who stated, "I can see now what you were getting at when you drilled me on the visuals. I noticed on my tour that the good speakers are lively, and their listeners appreciate their enthusiasm. I've tried to be more animated, and I believe I'm getting better at it. Thank you for your help."

"What you see is what you get" was a line frequently used by comedian Flip Wilson. For the public speaker this line describes the visual message you communicate. The question is, "What do you want your audience to get?" Surely, you want them to get your message in a clear, interesting, motivating manner and you want them to identify with you, a speaker who is poised, alive, energetic, and stimulating.

Remember that your audience receives many visual impressions from you. Your clothing, stature, girth, weight, looks, hair style, muscle tone, posture, movement, gestures, facial expression, and eye contact all play a part in making you a visual statement.

In this chapter we will focus on two visual considerations, bodily action and audiovisual aids. The discussion of bodily action will focus on the public speaker's body movements, and the section on audiovisual aids will include discussions of mechanical aids outside the human body.

BODILY ACTION

What is bodily action? It is *visual communication in the form of bodily language or bodily expression*. Bodily language is visual communication that follows predetermined procedures. Examples include the finger signs used in the manual alphabet of the deaf, the arm signs used with flags in semaphore signaling, and the bodily signs and pantomime of referees and umpires. These predetermined procedures are set, and all persons using them are expected to make them alike.

Bodily expression, on the other hand, is visual communication that is *not* predetermined but individual and spontaneous. Bodily expression includes the excited gestures of children at play, the enthusiastic physical demonstrations of spectators at an athletic contest, or the irate gesticulations of someone in an argument. These visual indications are the personalized expressions of thought and emotion.

Distinguish, therefore, between the rigid, objective formality of bodily language and the creative, subjective spontaneity of bodily expression. Remember that bodily language is mechanical and built up from the outside in, whereas bodily expression is motivated and generated from the inside out.

What does all of this have to do with public speaking? As a public speaker, you should concentrate mainly on *what* you are saying, but you should also give some thought to *how* you are saying it. You cannot merely do what comes naturally or you may engage in meaningless and distracting movement, such as leaning, swaying, or aimless walking back and forth. On the other hand, if you give too much attention to how you are performing, you may develop an undue concern for the mechanics of speaking and make your listeners more aware of your technique and less attentive to what you are saying.

Bodily expression can nonverbally communicate the content and tone of your speech. For example, gestures and facial expression enliven your presentation and motivate listeners to give their full attention to your message. You can respond to such favorable feedback by putting forth an even greater effort to communicate.

In general, let your bodily action spring from within you in a motivated manner: pound your fist on the table when you are angry; throw your arms in the air in wide arcs when you express amazement with the vast expanse of the universe. Occasionally, at least, you ought to think of how you look to the audience and, if necessary, make some modifications. Avoid meaningless movement. Instead, let your body move for a reason.

Values of Bodily Action in Public Speaking

Why is bodily action important? Bodily action relieves tension. Nervous energy comes in through the nerves and goes out through the muscles. If you concentrate on what you are saying and let your body help you talk, your anxiety will lessen and your confidence will strengthen. Bodily action helps you break through the fear barrier.

Bodily action stirs up enthusiasm. Once you begin to *act* animated, you tend to *feel* animated. While the best sources of animation are internal motivation and desire to communicate, it is also true that external activity can start your internal machinery. Unlock your bodily response and you unlock your feeling and thinking.

Bodily action can help your listeners, too, because movement stimulates interest and sustains attention. A cake revolving on a pedestal in a bakery window gets more attention than a stationary one, and so it is with speaking. Some material almost *requires* bodily action. Discussions of a spiral staircase, pinking shears, or the snakelike movement of a winding road are examples that need the reinforcement of bodily action, not only to make them clear but also to make them interesting. Listeners enjoy speakers who dramatize ideas and have a good time speaking.

Getting Your Body to Help You Talk

Knowing what bodily action is and recognizing its values in public speaking are not enough. You as a speaker need to know *how* to engage in effective bodily communication. Four steps can prove helpful: vitalizing your attitude, using concrete illustrations, letting your imagination respond, and rehearsing your physical involvement.

Vitalizing Your Attitude.
Are you interested in your subject matter and your listeners? Think of reasons why you should be. For example, what can you do for your listeners to compensate for the time they are giving you? Would you like to finish with a feeling of accomplishment? Would you like a good grade? By asking yourself these kinds of questions, you strengthen your desire to communicate, to share eagerly, to speak energetically for a person, principle, cause, or institution. You'll need to get your mind off yourself and focus your attention on what you are saying and on your audience. In this situation of speaker, subject, listener, and

occasion, your motivation to communicate prompts your body to respond. Vitalizing your attitude contributes to effective bodily action.

Filling Your Speech with Illustrations. A good speech is not merely a concentration of ideas but a selection of good ideas amplified and developed by examples. Don't just talk about food or meat or beef. Talk about a New York strip steak on the grill oozing juices on the hot coals below and getting ready for a crisp toasted bun with a slice of sweet Bermuda onion and seasoned with barbecue sauce. Try saying that sentence in your speech without using bodily action!

Letting Your Imagination Respond. Mere thinking about your subject is usually not enough to generate bodily action. Your imagination must come into play. Visualize the strip steak. Hear the sizzle. Smell the hickory smoke. Taste the salted succulence of the slightly charred steak. Now, using the responses of your senses and imagination, you are ready to use descriptive gestures and facial expressions to describe this tasty treat.

Rehearsing Your Physical Involvement. If you think only about the bodily action you want to use in your speech, you may not use bodily expression to greatest advantage when you make your presentation. To make sure that your gestures and expressions contribute to your message, you must rehearse your physical delivery. Plan the bodily movements you will use and practice them as you rehearse. Don't make your movements so studied that they become rigid and mechanical, but don't neglect the physical aspects of your message. Decide where a certain gesture or movement will be most effective and incorporate that action into your rehearsal. Then, when you make your actual presentation, your movements and gestures will flow as naturally as the points of your speech.

Basic Techniques of Bodily Action for Public Speaking

In general, if you are eager to share your ideas with your listeners, if you are animated and enthusiastic, if you strengthen your desire to communicate, if you use demonstration and showmanship, your bodily action will be effective. There are several areas, however, in which you should be alert to possible problems that can threaten the effectiveness of bodily action. In this section we will describe these areas and make some suggestions about how to avoid problems and use effective bodily action.

Walking. A speech begins before the first word is spoken and continues after the last is uttered. Speakers tell their listeners something about themselves by the way they walk to the front of the room and later by the way they return to their seats. Project a positive and self-assured attitude as you walk. Avoid "walking on eggs," lumbering, plodding, or moving in a way that suggests insecurity. Don't begin speaking until you are poised in front of the audience. If through your walk and bearing you suggest a positive emotional state and an eagerness to communicate, your listeners are likely to find you less distracting and more credible. They will be likely to listen more attentively to what you have to say.

Finish your speech before you begin returning to your seat. Don't suggest discomfort or nervousness by hurrying back to your seat, and don't damage the effectiveness of your conclusion by returning to your seat while you are making your final remarks.

Sitting.   You may be sitting before an audience while you wait to be introduced. Be aware of the impression you are creating. Be comfortable but don't slouch. Be alert but don't be rigid.

Posture.   There is no one correct posture for all occasions. In general, good posture creates the favorable impression that the speaker wishes to create. An overly formal posture with hands hanging straight at one's sides, suggesting the orator in contest perfection, is usually not the best stance for an extemporaneous speech. On the other hand, leaning, swaying, frequent foot-shifting, and similar distracting mannerisms are equally bad. Let your posture be a balanced blend of relaxation and control. Be comfortable but look alive.

Movement.   Distinguish between meaningful and meaningless movement. Like an actor on a stage, move with a purpose. Apply the analogy of football. Avoid being offside. Don't let your backfield be in motion until the ball is snapped. For example, move when you take up a new point. Avoid foot-crossing. In going to the right, start with your right foot. Foot-crossing looks awkward and may make you appear less competent and less confident.

Gesture.   Gesture is the movement of the hands and arms coordinated with the entire body. Gestures in public speaking should be less mechanical than the bodily language of a referee giving signs to spectators and more constrained than the explosive bodily expression of an angry motorist. Beware of mechanical gestures. Let your gestures come from your ideas, attitudes, and desire to communicate. Let them be spontaneous and refined. Work for a graceful blend of ease and strength.

In making gestures, try to avoid faults that can distract listeners from your message: keeping your elbows glued to your ribs; making very small gestures that seem to sneak out from your hands and arms; making very broad, meat-cleaver-like gestures that overpower your message; using the same gestures too often; keeping your wrists stiff; failing to vitalize your arm gestures all the way down to your fingertips; gesturing simply for the sake of gesturing; using too many two-handed gestures; enumerating on the fingertips; and making gestures that are too studied, too sweeping, too grand, or that come too soon or too late. In short, avoid gestures that draw attention to themselves and distract your listeners from the point of your speech.

Facial Expression.   Your face is the most expressive part of your body and is capable of expressing more subtle feelings and emotions than you probably realize. Experiment in front of a mirror, conveying through your facial expressions the emotions of joy, sadness, love, hate, confusion, disappointment, disgust, anger, satisfaction, and so on. Notice the almost limitless variations that are possible. But what do many speakers do in front of an audience? They suggest the face of a poker player or a court defendant trying to hide guilt. If you as a speaker identify with your thoughts and emotions and live them while you are speaking, your listeners will be able to identify with you, and their attention level will be considerably higher.

Eye Contact.   See your listeners as individuals, not as a mass of humanity. Look into the eyes of as many listeners as you can. In the beginning, this attempt can be an ordeal because as you meet the eyes of someone who is looking into your eyes, you may become embarrassed and forget what you want to say. Of all the skills in public speaking, direct eye contact is one of the most difficult. Grow into it gradually, looking at more individuals as your speech progresses and as you gain experience. Remember, however, that listeners expect you to look at them and enjoy the personal contact you make. At first, your eyes may seem to have a glassy stare, but with experience you will find yourself looking into someone's responsive eyes and enjoying the total communication.

Avoid looking over the listeners' heads or at the spaces between them. Avoid looking at the back door, out the window, or on the floor. These are escapes. Look into some of your listeners' eyes. They feed so much back to you: agreement, disagreement, boredom, hostility, enjoyment, understanding, confusion, or inspiration. Seeing and recognizing your listeners' responses to your message can help you adjust your speech to them.

Reading Listeners' Bodily Expressions

Once you develop self-confidence and observe and analyze your audience, you can begin to notice the bodily expressions of the listeners. Notice whether they sit erect or slouch or shift positions; notice their restless movements, yawning, looking away, or scowling. These are ways your listeners talk back to you without words.

Audience and speaker interaction is usually accomplished through nonverbal communication. Visual feedback is only one form of nonverbal communication. All of the senses—sight, hearing, smell, taste, and touch—can be involved in nonverbal communication. In the next chapter, we will analyze vocal technique, such as tone of voice, and what it conveys over and above the word itself as a form of nonverbal communication. Here we will concentrate on reading listeners' bodily expressions as a form of nonverbal communication.

Circuit Judge Ronald Dreschler once remarked to a breakfast club audience that twitching toes, facial contortions, lip movements, and nervous hand and foot movements may be a tip off that a witness is covering up the truth. Sigmund Freud once wrote that "no mortal can keep a secret. If his lips are silent, he chatters with his fingertips. Betrayal oozes out of him at every pore." Frequently, through their nonverbal communication, listeners tell the speaker that hearing and understanding are difficult. Lifting or tilting the head, leaning forward, or cupping the hand to the ear are some obvious signs of hearing difficulty.

The story is told of a student talking to her instructor about a book she had read. The professor asked her what she thought of the book, and the student, rubbing her nose, replied that she had liked it. The professor concluded the opposite, because nose rubbing is a gesture associated with dislike.

New York's famous former mayor, Fiorello La Guardia, campaigned in English, Italian, and Yiddish. When films of his speeches are run without sound, it's easy to observe from his bodily action what language he was speaking. Have you ever watched a foreign film dubbed in English? Frequently, the words do not match the action, and the presentation is not satisfying or even believable.

When you make a speech, observe how many listeners are looking at you and into your eyes. What are they saying to you? If they look down or away from you, you can conclude, usually correctly, that they are bored or dislike what you are saying. Bodily expression, indeed, does say something, and the shrewd public speaker learns how to interpret it.

As we have seen, bodily action, including both bodily language and bodily expression, can contribute to the effectiveness of a public speech. Sometimes, however, a speaker needs more than bodily action to convey a message. In these instances the speaker may turn to the use of audiovisual aids in order to deliver a convincing message.

AUDIOVISUAL AIDS

As we mentioned earlier, a speaker communicates through all five senses: sight, hearing, smell, taste, and touch. A cosmetic salesperson may pass perfume around for its unusual fragrance. A cooking expert may ask you to smell shakers of various spices, or a demonstrator in the supermarket may offer you a sample of sausage. A clothing salesperson may ask you to differentiate by touch between flannel and sharkskin. Most of the time, however, a speaker communicates through the senses of sight and hearing.

A public speaker always uses the conventional techniques of voice and body, but sometimes the speaker needs to use extraordinary vocal and visual methods. The subject matter may be complex. In this situation, the wise speaker turns to the use of audiovisual aids, which bring listeners' attention to a high peak and maintain it to produce clarity, vividness, evidence, and memorability.

Because audiovisual aids can be very effective, speakers who use them may feel stronger in their presentation and develop more self-confidence. Listeners are satisfied because they learn and retain more from the speaker's message.

Audio Aids

Audio aids are used for amplification and playback. Amplification aids include the microphone, loudspeaker, and bullhorn. Playback aids include audiotapes and records. In this section we will examine how each of these aids can be used to good advantage. We will also consider some of the disadvantages associated with each.

Microphone.   The microphone has the obvious advantage of amplifying the human voice so that all listeners can hear easily. The disadvantage

Speaking effectively into a microphone is a skill that demands practice. Remember to keep the microphone at a workable distance from your mouth— far enough away to avoid "popping" on certain words and close enough for you to be heard. Also remember that some microphones have limited "live" areas—they pick up sound only in a certain pattern or direction.

is that use of a microphone, particularly a floor-standing model, confines the speaker to standing in one spot, thus limiting the effectiveness of bodily action and visual communication.

When, then, should a microphone be used? Normally, it need not be used for groups of less than a hundred listeners unless they are spread out in a very large room. Before larger audiences, of course, the microphone is such a helpful aid that one wonders what speakers before large assemblies did before microphones were available.

Beginning speakers frequently ask, "How should the microphone be used?" Although there is no adequate substitute for practice with the microphone, the following points provide a helpful guide:

1. More than thirty different types of microphones are available for every communication requirement from small pin-on lavalier microphones to those on a floor stand. Each type is slightly different in makeup and use. If an engineer is available, ask questions. If not, experiment through trial and error before you use the microphone to deliver your speech.

2. How far should your mouth be from the microphone? About eight to twelve inches is a good general rule, but each situation varies. The kind of microphone, the acoustics of the room, the amount of force and projection the speaker employs, and the volume level of the amplifier all affect delivery. Rehearsal in new situations will help you develop self-confidence with use of the microphone.

3. Don't get too close to the microphone. The sounds *p, t, k, f, th, s,* and *ch* will produce a sharpened, sputtering, irritating consonant effect if you are too close.

4. If you stand farther than eight to twelve inches away from the microphone, you must project your voice more.

5. Be sure to stay on the beam as you use the microphone. Do not turn too far to either side. Ideally, each speaker's stand should have two microphones, one to the left and one to the right. When there is only one, do not turn to the side unless you step back slightly first. Then you can turn a bit, but if you do, be sure to project. After all, you want your listeners to hear and understand easily.

6. Generally, as people grow older, their hearing deteriorates. Keep this in mind when you use a microphone. According to the United States Public Health Service, young persons (ten to nineteen years of age) show no deterioration in hearing, while slightly older persons (thirty to thirty-nine years of age) begin to show impairment in receiving higher frequencies, such as the sounds of *s, th,* and *f.* Persons fifty to fifty-nine years of age show marked deterioration in hearing, and deterioration is usually higher among men. Keeping in mind these facts about hearing impairment, you as a speaker should take care to enunciate clearly, speak slowly,

and articulate the consonant sounds distinctly.

There is one final point to remember. If you can, avoid too much bass in the amplifier and speaker. A reasonable amount of treble must be used to sharpen the consonant sounds, especially the higher frequency sounds of *s, th,* and *f.*

Loudspeaker. Whenever a microphone is used, a loudspeaker is necessary to project the speaker's voice amplified by the microphone. In a normal-sized room, the loudspeaker should be mounted about ten to fifteen inches high, higher in very large rooms. Do not set the loudspeaker on the floor. At least put it on a chair if it can't be placed any higher. Experiment to find the proper volume level. If the level is too low, listeners will have difficulty in hearing. If it is too high, the sound may become painful and listeners may become irritated.

A microphone including amplifier and loudspeaker built into the speaker's stand is a useful device. Another helpful device is the wireless lavalier microphone that transmits to an amplifier and loudspeaker on an FM-radio frequency. The wireless lavalier permits the speaker more freedom of movement than does the microphone built into the speaker's stand or mounted on a floor stand.

Bullhorn. The bullhorn is a battery-powered, one-hand megaphone often used for crowd control or for general announcements. This portable public address system does not pick up surrounding noises. You can speak into the bullhorn from a distance as close as two inches.

Audiotapes and Records. Sometimes during a speech you may find it helpful to play a passage on a tape or record. Audiotapes are mainly of two kinds: the larger reel, which has a higher fidelity response and is used with what is commonly called the reel-to-reel tape recorder, and the small cassette with a lower fidelity response, which is used with the cassette recorder. Because of its size and weight, the cassette recorder is much handier and more widely used. Records are useful if the equipment is light and portable. Material on records can also be put on tape.

Sometimes you will want your listeners not only to listen to what you have to say; you will also want them to see what you have to show them. A visual presentation is an important part of your message.

Visual Aids

We know from the experiments of many researchers that learning is strongest when acquired by means of the eye rather than the ear. However, when both the eye and ear are used, we learn more quickly and remember best of all. In this section, we will describe two kinds of visual aids: ordinary and electronic. Finally, we will offer some suggestions for using visual aids.

Ordinary Visual Aids. Ordinary visual aids are yourself, boards, models, pictures and charts, flash cards, and graphs.

1. *Yourself.* You can be a perfect visual aid. One young woman, a cheerleader, gave a speech on cheerleading in which she demonstrated some of the routines she had used in her audition. Her costume helped, but her effectiveness as a speaker derived mainly from her bodily action, demonstration, and showmanship.

2. *Boards.* Boards may be chalk, flannel, easel, or magnetic. Flannel, easel, and magnetic boards are frequently employed in the business world, but the most widely used is the chalkboard. Teachers would be lost without it, and speakers, too, can learn to use it properly. To make effective use of the chalkboard, follow these procedures:

   a. Plan in advance how you will use the board. Leave nothing to chance. If you have a complicated drawing, put it on the board before you speak.

   b. Talk to the audience, not to the board. If you are right-handed, turn your left shoulder toward the audience and your right shoulder toward the board. Doing so will help you talk to the audience rather than to the board. Step back occasionally so all listeners can see the board. Don't block the view. Use a pointer if necessary.

   c. When you are finished with the board, erase what is there. Do not let it compete with what you are about to say. When you are finally finished, clean the board for the person who will follow you.

3. *Objects and Models.* Any object or model you use should be large enough for all to see and easy enough for you to handle. A ring is too small to be a good visual aid. A large picture or drawing would be better. A large, wide automobile tire is not a good visual aid. It's too big, unwieldy, and not worth the effort. Sometimes public speakers spend too much time, effort, and expense in producing visual aids that are neither helpful nor necessary. On the other hand, objects and models can be an effective means of making ideas clear and interesting. Ultimately, you will have to be the judge as you weigh the advantages and disadvantages of using them. If you use a hand-held object or model, be sure to hold it high enough for all to see, but do not hold it directly in front of your face as you speak.

4. *Pictures and Charts.* Pictures, charts, maps, diagrams, and posters can be affixed up high with wall clips, thumb tacks, or adhesive tape. Be sure the aids are large enough to be seen easily by all members of the audience. When you are finished with the aid, take it down. Avoid passing visual aids around the room to members of the audience. You don't want your listeners focusing their attention on the charts instead of listening to your message.

5. *Flash Cards.* If you use flash cards, hold them up high and down front center and to the left and right if necessary. As with other aids, avoid passing the cards around. Make sure they are in good condition and easily legible to all in the audience.

6. *Graphs.* Graphs compare parts to a whole. For example, the frequently used pie graph shows various-sized pieces to indicate comparative relationships. Choose the type of graph that best fits your needs for a visual aid.

Electronic Visual Aids.

In addition to the ordinary visual aids that we have just discussed are the electronic aids that can further enhance a presentation. Before you decide to use electronic visual aids, ask yourself two questions: Are they really necessary? Will the time, effort, and expense involved justify their use? Electronic visual aids include projectors, motion pictures, and videotapes.

1. *Projectors.* The slide projector is a favorite for showing pictures. In addition, commercial slides are available on many subjects. Film strips can also be used.

The opaque projector can convert printed copy into screen images. The room must be dark, and the speaker must be behind at least part of the

FIGURE 7.1   **Graphs Used as Visual Aids**

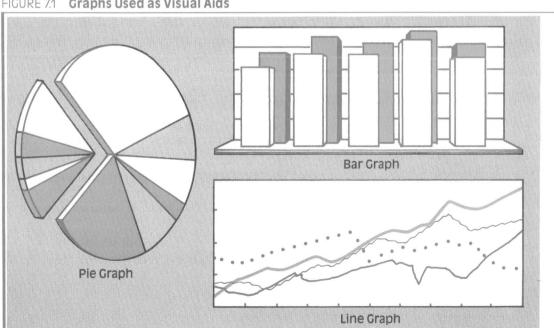

Pie Graph

Bar Graph

Line Graph

audience because the light from the speaker's stand illuminating the speaker's script or notes will interfere with the sharpness of the image on the screen.

The overhead projector can be used in a normally lighted room. The speaker can write or sketch on the machine's writing platform. The material used for showing must be transparent. Prepared transparencies can be used in overlaid combinations. These overlays are similar to those frequently found in anatomy and physiology books.

2. *Motion Pictures.* Motion pictures, both silent and sound, are available from commercial, public, and school libraries. If you decide to use a motion picture, you may need the help of a projectionist and some preparation time. Properly executed, motion pictures can enhance the effectiveness of your speech. Of course, more time in the speaking situation must be allowed if a film or parts of a film are to be shown.

3. *Videotapes.* Portable color videotape equipment is available for public speakers who wish to present videotaped excerpts in their speeches. Although videotape can be very effective, for some, the cost may be prohibitive. A speaker could videotape an event that happened shortly before the giving of a speech and use that tape to help listeners visually recall the event. One student gave a talk on listening to lectures. She made a videotape of the previous class, showing student inattention in a large lecture hall. Her video presentation, although rough and unedited, effectively made the point that many students were not listening very intently.

Some Suggestions for Using Visual Aids. Visual aids can often be tricky to use. Don't place yourself in the embarrassing situation of being unable to use your visual aid. Consider the following suggestions:

1. Let the visual aid be a supplement to your speech. It should not become more important than the speech. The visual aid is, after all, merely an aid.

2. Choose a visual aid that is suited to your abilities and skills. Know how to handle the aid, or if you can't handle it yourself, get help.

3. Remain calm and take adequate time to set up your visual aid. Don't rush. On the other hand, avoid the use of visual aids that take too much time to set up. Taking too much time will make both you and your listeners nervous and edgy.

4. Bring out your visual aids at the right moment when they can be harmonized with your presentation. Put them aside or remove them when you are finished.

5. Keep your visual aids simple, large but not unwieldy, and clearly legible. They should be presented in heavy contrast, in color, and in sufficient light.

6. While using visual aids, remember to talk to the audience as much as possible.

7. If you plan to use visual aids in your speech, rehearse with the use of the aids. This point also applies to the use of audio aids. You cannot use audio or visual aids for the first time during your actual presentation and still expect your speech to go smoothly. The use of audiovisual aids must be integrated into the rehearsal of your speech.

Audiovisual aids can make a presentation more effective. It is easier for a speaker to get and maintain listeners' attention. Thus, proper use of mechanical aids adds interest and variety to a public speech.

SUMMARY

Two ways in which public speakers can make their speeches more interesting, effective, and lively are through bodily action and the use of audiovisual aids. Bodily action encompasses both the rigid formality of bodily language and the creative spontaneity of bodily expression. In public speaking, effective bodily action includes both aspects; it is creative and spontaneous yet also disciplined, motivated, and meaningful.

Bodily action energizes the speaker and enlivens the listener. A speaker can generate effective bodily action by vitalizing an attitude, using concrete illustrations, letting the imagination respond, and rehearsing the physical involvement. In public speaking, applying effective bodily action occurs in a number of areas: walking, sitting, posture, movement, gesture, facial expression, and eye contact. In addition, the good speaker learns how to read and interpret listeners' bodily expressions.

Besides the ordinary techniques of voice and body, a speaker can use the extraordinary means of audiovisual aids to make an effective presentation. Audio aids include microphones, loudspeakers, bullhorns, and playback equipment, such as audiotapes and records. Frequently used visual aids are boards (flannel, easel, magnetic, and chalk), objects and models, pictures and charts, flash cards and graphs. Some speakers use electronic visual aids, such as projectors (slide, opaque, and overhead), motion pictures, and videotapes.

Before using an audio or visual aid, a speaker should know *how* to operate it or should enlist the help of someone who is familiar with its workings. Two important questions to consider before deciding to use an audio or visual aid are "Is this aid necessary?" and "Do the time, effort, and expense involved justify its use?" At all times, the speaker should keep in mind that bodily action and audiovisual aids are meant to contribute to the effectiveness of the speech not to distract from, undermine, or overpower the message.

ASSIGNMENTS

1. To generate audience participation, describe in detail a football, base-ball, basketball, tennis, hockey, or soccer maneuver. Role play your-self as the coach and the members of the class as the team.

2. Using bodily action, describe some unusual locations you visited on a vacation.

3. Prepare a one- to two-minute speech on a subject you feel very strongly about. One way to emphasize important points is to take a rolled-up, taped newspaper and pound it on the table. What are some other gestures you can use for emphasis? Incorporate them into your presentation.

4. Using one of your favorite, frequently run television commercials, analyze the audio and visual techniques used to make the message more effective. Write an essay describing your observations.

5. Using yourself as a visual aid, prepare a "how-to" talk on a subject such as changing a tire, putting a new filter in a vacuum cleaner, or giving directions for getting from your classroom to your home. Use gestures only—no chalkboard, map, or diagram.

6. Give a three- to five-minute demonstration speech on a subject that lends itself to a "how-to" explanation—for example, how to operate a certain type of camera, how to apply makeup, or how to manipulate puppets. Use any audiovisual aids that you think might be helpful. Be generous in your use of bodily action and try to generate some audience participation. Rehearse your presentation as you would a part in a play. Harmonize the use of your aids with what you are saying.

Determinants of Vocal Characteristics	Environmental Conditions	Home
		Neighborhood
		School
		Friends
		Place of Employment
Physiological Apparatus of Voice	Personality Factors	
	Generator	
	Vibrator	
	Resonator	
	Articulator	
	Evaluator	
Functional Vocal Skills	Force	Volume
		Emphasis
	Range	Pitch
		Inflection
		Melody Pattern
	Quality	Emotional Reaction
		Physical Mechanism
	Diction	Enunciation
		Pronunciation
	Pacing	Changes in Rate
		Use of Pause
The Manuscript Speech	Reading Aloud Your Manuscript Speech	Conversational Style
		Incorporating Quotations
	Reading Aloud Literary Passages	
	Literary Passages in Public Speaking	

8 Delivery: Vocal Technique in Speaking and Reading Aloud

OBJECTIVES

When you finish this chapter, you should be able to:

1. improve your vocal technique by
   a. understanding and compensating for the influence of your environment and
   b. recognizing and moderating the reflection of your personality in your voice;
2. explain the nature and operation of the generator, vibrator, resonator, articulator(s), and evaluator;
3. use your vocal mechanism more effectively by developing the functional skills of force, range, quality, diction, and pause; and
4. deliver a speech from manuscript, incorporating quotations and using effective vocal technique to interpret the manuscript.

8 Delivery: Vocal Technique in Speaking and Reading Aloud

Mike Klein was an eager student in Introduction to Broadcasting, a course with many vocal assignments: the reading of news, sports, commercials, interviews, and special events. Mike was so eager in his performance that the instructor often had to tone him down in front of the radio microphone.

One afternoon the manager of a local radio station called the instructor and asked him to send several students to the station for an audition. The station manager needed a part-time announcer. The instructor sent over half a dozen students including Mike Klein, even though he was not one of the best students in the class.

The next day the station manager called the instructor and said, "You're not doing very much teaching. The students are reticent, dull, and lack zip and zing. There's one young fellow, though, who has some potential, a guy by the name of Mike Klein."

What was it about Mike Klein that attracted the attention of the station manager? The station manager presumably was looking for someone with good vocal technique. It was his vocal skills that got Mike the job.

Although there are differences between public speaking and radio announcing, public speakers also must have good vocal technique to be effective communicators. Good vocal technique includes both the desire to communicate and the ability to use the vocal skills of force, range, quality, and pacing. By exercising good vocal technique, the public speaker gets and holds the attention of the listeners.

In this chapter we will discuss some of the environmental and personality factors that determine vocal characteristics. We will also examine the physiological apparatus of voice in order to give you an understanding of why you speak the way you do. We will then explore the ways in which you can learn how to use your voice more efficiently and effectively. Finally, we will discuss some methods for improving your vocal skills by reading a speech from manuscript. Although most of your speeches, both in and outside the classroom, will be delivered extemporaneously, there are good reasons for learning how to read a speech from manuscript. For example, there may be times when precise wording is required or strict time limits are necessary. In these instances you might find it necessary to read your speech from manuscript. Furthermore, reading a speech from manuscript enables you to focus on style—on writing the speech the way you would speak it—and can be an excellent vehicle for vocal training.

DETERMINANTS OF VOCAL CHARACTERISTICS

Have you ever heard a playback of your own voice? Were you surprised at the way you sounded? Perhaps you had the same reaction that many people have: "Do I really sound like that?" Sometimes they question the accuracy of the recorder.

This confusion is natural. You hear a playback of your own voice differently from the way you hear your voice when you speak. When you speak, you hear two kinds of vibrations: those inside your head and those outside your head. Others hear only those outside vibrations when they listen to you speak.

Another reason for confusion is familiarity. You are so familiar with the sound of your voice that most of the time you pay little attention to how you sound. In the playback, your voice is set apart from you. You hear yourself as others hear you. This revelation may be startling and even emotionally upsetting, but the recorder, like a sound mirror, reflects the vocal facts.

What determines these vocal facts? What factors contribute to making you sound the way you do? A combination of environmental conditions and personality factors determines your individual vocal characteristics. In this section, we will examine the influence of these determinants.

Environmental Conditions

Your voice reflects the influence of a number of environmental conditions. Your home life and the neighborhood in which you live affect the way you speak. So, too, do the school you attend, the friends you have, and the place where you work. We can present examples in each one of these areas to illustrate the influence of environmental conditions on vocal technique.

Home. Jim's father works in a noisy machine shop, where he uses excessive volume to be heard. He speaks loudly at home, too. Like his father, Jim speaks loudly.

Brenda's mother is an accountant. Both in her quiet office and at home, she speaks in a subdued voice. Brenda, too, has learned to speak softly.

Imogene is an only child. Her parents listen when she talks. She tends to be relaxed and confident when she speaks. Denny is the youngest of six children. Unless he speaks first, fast, and loudly, no one listens.

Neighborhood. Just as you can recognize speech differences among individuals from different parts of the country, so can you notice speech variations in different neighborhoods of a large city.

In one midwestern city, strong speech differences are discernible: German influence on the north side, Polish on the south, Italian on the east, and Irish on the west. In addition, there are suburban influences. One in particular, on the extreme north end, shows influences of the Eastern schools attended by many of the residents.

School.   One example is typical. Carol Ann attended a coeducational high school in a rough area of the city where hard work and the reality of hard knocks were apparent. She developed a bold, hard manner of speaking. After graduating from high school, she enrolled in a small, private college in a secluded rural area. The new environment soon began to take effect. One year later, Carol Ann's bold, hard manner of speaking had given way to a refined, carefully modulated vocal technique.

Friends.   The proverbs "Birds of a feather flock together" and "Tell me who your friends are, and I'll tell you what you are" can be reworded to read "Birds of a feather chirp alike" and "Tell me who your friends are, and I'll tell you what you sound like." One young woman spoke with a marked nasal twang that puzzled her speech instructor until he met her friend from another school whose voice also had a pronounced nasal twang.

Place of Employment.   Two brothers held part-time jobs. One worked as a busboy in an elite country club; the other hawked newspapers on a downtown street corner. The busboy developed a cultured, modulated voice; the newspaper hawker developed a powerful but overly loud voice.

One young woman was a long distance operator for the telephone company; her friend was a counter waitress in a large, noisy restaurant. After a year of working in these individual environments, each woman's voice differed noticeably from the other's.

As we have seen, a number of environmental conditions contribute to vocal characteristics. This does not mean, however, that the influence of environmental factors is inescapable. You can, in fact, learn to overcome the effects of environmental factors and change your voice. Before we turn to a discussion of how to accomplish this, let's examine another determinant of vocal characteristics, the influence of personality factors.

Personality Factors

"What you are thunders so loudly I cannot hear what you say," said Emerson. Think about that statement in terms of your voice and its effect on others. Your words may say one thing, but your entire vocal effect may suggest meanings you never intended. Your personality has been at work on your voice.

You reveal your true personality largely through your temperament, your emotional disposition toward a situation. When someone steps on your foot on the bus, do you push forward, fight back, move away, or feel sorry for yourself? When you see a bully picking on someone, do you step in between them, fight the bully, walk away, or get disgusted with human nature?

The emotional drives behind your actions are neither good nor bad. Their goodness or badness depends on your attitude as expressed by your personality. The mature speaker recognizes that voice reflects the influence of personality and understands that improving personality will help improve voice. In fact, radio writer and director Erik Barnouw once stated, "If you have an interesting personality, and your voice is a true expression of your personality, you probably have a good voice for broadcasting."

PHYSIOLOGICAL APPARATUS OF VOICE

The physiological components of voice production include the generator, vibrator, resonator, articulator, and evaluator. To understand how these physiological components affect vocal characteristics, we will first investigate the nature and function of each element.

Generator

When we speak of the generator, we are referring to the diaphragm and rib muscles that operate in the front, sides, and back of the rib cage. Consider the example of Mr. Smith sleeping peacefully in his bed. He lies there breathing easily. His stomach area rises and falls in an even pattern. His rib cage expands and contracts. This is normal breathing to sustain life.

Apply this observation in your own breathing. Lie down flat on your back. Place a book on your stomach area. Relax and breathe. Notice how the book is elevated and lowered. Feel your rib cage expand and contract. Now stand up but remain relaxed. Let your arms hang at your sides. Inhale just the way you did when you were flat on your back. Notice your stomach area protrude and feel your rib cage expand. Exhale. Notice your stomach return to its normal shape. Feel your rib cage contract. This, too, is normal breathing to sustain life.

Breathing for public speaking is basically the same with these exceptions: In ordinary breathing to sustain life you exhale rather quickly. In breathing for public speaking you control a slower output of air against the vibrating vocal cords.

In order to improve your breathing skills for public performance, you should understand, at least in general, how you control the intake and output of air in your lungs. Inside your stomach area is the diaphragm, a large muscle that looks like an upside-down mixing bowl. When you inhale, the diaphragm tends to flatten down. When you exhale, it returns to its bowl-like shape. If you inhale while you're lying down, the diaphragm tends to flatten out toward the walls of the room. If you inhale while you're standing, it tends to flatten down toward the floor.

Your rib muscles are also involved in the intake and output of air. When you inhale, the rib muscles in the front, sides, and back expand and pull the ribs out. When you exhale, the rib muscles contract and the ribs return to their original position.

The more the diaphragm pulls down and the more the rib muscles pull out, the more room there is for the lungs to expand for the in-rushing air. The more slowly you let the diaphragm and ribs return to their original position, the more effectively you can control the output of air against the vibrating vocal cords.

Vibrator

By the vibrator, we mean the vocal cords housed in the larynx, commonly called the voice box or Adam's apple, set in the front of the neck. To understand the function of the vibrator, blow up a balloon. Hold the neck of the balloon with the forefinger and thumb of each hand. Now stretch the neck of the balloon horizontally so that air escapes in a squealing sound. The balloon represents your lungs; the stretched neck of the balloon represents your vocal cords. The more you tense up, the higher the pitch. The more you relax, the lower the pitch.

The muscles around the vocal cords, unlike the powerful diaphragm and rib muscles, are small and delicate and can be strained easily by too much tension. They should, therefore, be used in as relaxed a manner as possible. Let pitch come from the vocal cords. Power should be controlled by the action of the diaphragm and rib muscles.

Resonator

The resonator in voice production includes three parts: throat, nose, and mouth. Each of these cavities resonates the fundamental tone produced by the vocal cords. Say the word "boom." Now say it into a metal wastebasket. Hear how much fuller the sound is. Something similar happens to the sound vibrated by your vocal cords when it passes into your throat, nose, and mouth. The sound is made bigger, richer, and fuller. The wider you open your mouth, the more the original vibration of the vocal cords will be enlarged into bigger, richer, fuller sounds.

Articulator

The articulator component of voice production includes the tongue, teeth, lips, lower jaw, and soft palate (the roof of the mouth near the throat). Say "this champion." Now say it again, feeling the movement of the tongue, teeth, lips, lower jaw, and soft palate. Use these articulators efficiently to produce full vowel sounds and crisp, clear consonant sounds.

Evaluator

The ear (along with the mind, of course) is the evaluator and ultimately the best judge of good vocal technique. If you don't listen critically to what you are saying, you can't change what needs to be changed. While you should not be so concerned about your voice that you forget what you want to say, you should give some conscious attention to *how* you sound. Only then can you listen to yourself critically and measure your improvement. Figure 8.1 shows the elements of the vocal apparatus and explains how voice quality is determined.

FUNCTIONAL VOCAL SKILLS

We have examined both the determinants of vocal characteristics and the physiological apparatus of voice. There are, in addition, a number of vocal skills that you can learn to develop to improve your vocal technique. These skills include force, range, quality, diction, and pacing. Like the skills involved in bowling, playing the piano, or singing, vocal skills are developed through much practice under the direction of an instructor. In this section we will explore vocal skills and suggest ways in which you can use each to improve your vocal technique.

Force

Force is concerned with volume and emphasis. If members of your audience are leaning toward you, cupping their ears with their hands, and showing evident strain as they try to listen, you probably have a problem with the vocal skill of force.

Volume.   The first vocal rule in public speaking is to fill the room with your voice. Breathe deeply and fully. Get your voice out on the air. Make it easy for your listeners to hear you. If at first you feel self-conscious when you hear your voice rolling out with authority, do not be embarrassed. Concentrate, rather, on your message and satisfied listeners who can hear you without straining.

How do you achieve volume? By breathing deeply and fully, opening your throat, and directing the sound out front forward. Try holding your nose shut and projecting your voice with the words "ho-ho-ho." Notice how your voice gets out on the air.

Emphasis.   Emphasis has two purposes: to stress certain words and to build to a climax. Some words are more important than others. The meaning you wish to convey will tell you which are most important. Read the

FIGURE 8.1 **Vocal Apparatus and the Quality of Speech**

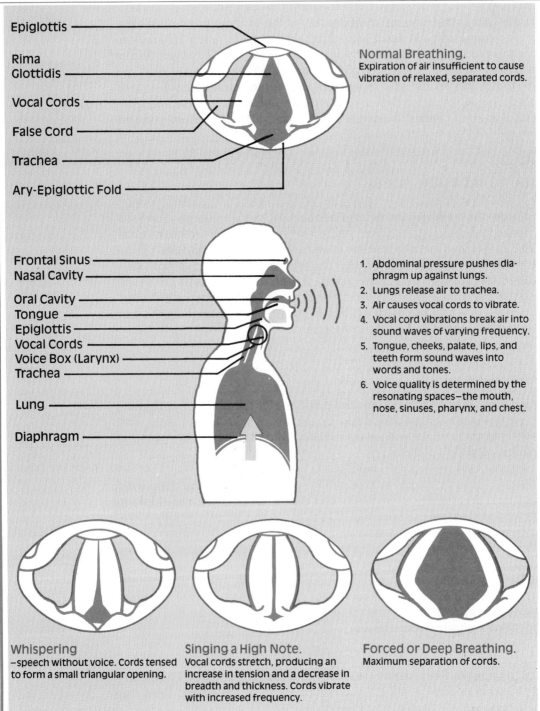

Epiglottis

Rima Glottidis

Vocal Cords

False Cord

Trachea

Ary-Epiglottic Fold

Normal Breathing.
Expiration of air insufficient to cause vibration of relaxed, separated cords.

Frontal Sinus
Nasal Cavity
Oral Cavity
Tongue
Epiglottis
Vocal Cords
Voice Box (Larynx)
Trachea
Lung
Diaphragm

1. Abdominal pressure pushes diaphragm up against lungs.
2. Lungs release air to trachea.
3. Air causes vocal cords to vibrate.
4. Vocal cord vibrations break air into sound waves of varying frequency.
5. Tongue, cheeks, palate, lips, and teeth form sound waves into words and tones.
6. Voice quality is determined by the resonating spaces—the mouth, nose, sinuses, pharynx, and chest.

Whispering
—speech without voice. Cords tensed to form a small triangular opening.

Singing a High Note.
Vocal cords stretch, producing an increase in tension and a decrease in breadth and thickness. Cords vibrate with increased frequency.

Forced or Deep Breathing.
Maximum separation of cords.

following sentence seven times. Stress the first word the first time, the second word the second time, and so on:

I never said he stole your money.

Notice in the following sentence how the word "one" must be stressed to bring out the meaning:

There were seven men in the group; only *one* of the men was an athlete.

If, instead of stressing the word "one" in the second part of the sentence, you stress the word "men," you fail to communicate a fine shade of meaning. One word of warning. Avoid stressing too many words. All light and no shadow results in no picture.

As you speak you will often find that your material builds to a high moment. Take advantage of this situation. Build to a climax. Doing so will strengthen your meaning and add variety to your delivery. Notice how the following paragraph of President John F. Kennedy's inaugural address builds to a climax:

> Let every nation know, whether it wish us well or ill, that we shall pay any price, bear any burden, meet any hardship, support any friends or oppose any foe to assure the survival and success of liberty.[1]

Range

Range is the full extent of pitch from highest to lowest tones. You're probably familiar with soprano and bass voices, each with its individual range of tones.

Pitch.   Your voice is capable of many pitches. How high or low you can go depends on the size and shape of your vocal cords. The longer and thicker your vocal cords, the lower will be your range; the shorter and thinner your cords, the higher will be your range. You cannot change the basic size and shape of the cords, but you can learn to use well what you have. You can learn to pitch your voice properly in your natural range by considering your middle pitch, your best pitch, and your habitual pitch.

Your best pitch, around which you build your rising and falling inflections, should be slightly below your middle pitch. This best pitch should become your habitual pitch. If your habitual pitch is too high, however, your upper range will sound strained on a rising inflection and tend to be nasal. If your habitual pitch is too low, your lower range will sound tight on a falling inflection and tend to be throaty.

If you call very loudly to someone from a great distance, increase your volume but do not use your upper range. When you are engaging in highly emotional communication, use a more intense quality, but do not use the upper range too much.

Inflection.

Inflection, which is a vocal glide on a word or syllable, can be falling, rising, or a combination of the two. A falling inflection is normally used to make a statement. It suggests confidence, assurance, and authority. Too many falling inflections can suggest an egotistical or overbearing personality. A rising inflection is normally used to ask a question. It suggests doubt, uncertainty, and indecision. Too many rising inflections can suggest a lack of self-confidence.

An occasional fault among some speakers is the use of a rising inflection when making a statement. It is as though the speaker is trying to elicit a "yes-yes" nod of the head from the listeners. For example, someone might say, "Yesterday we went on a picnic. George and Jane came. We played volleyball." At the end of each sentence, the speaker uses a rising inflection as though asking a question. Try to avoid this misuse of the rising inflection. It sounds juvenile.

Combinations can be either rising-falling or falling-rising. They can be used to suggest subtle meaning. The combination technique can be helpful in preparing material for oral reading. For example, when Mark Antony in *Julius Caesar* says, "Brutus is an honorable man," the rising-falling inflection suggests that Brutus is less than honorable. When Shylock in *The Merchant of Venice* asks, "Hath a dog money?" the falling-rising inflection indicates something more than a dog.

Melody Pattern.

Melody pattern refers to a succession and mixture of all kinds of vocal inflection. If the pattern sounds conversational, we say the speaker is natural. If it doesn't, we say the speaker sounds artificial or mechanical.

Listen to Tim Barnett evaluate the coach's basketball strategy in last night's game. Walking to class with a small group around him, Tim explains, demonstrates, evaluates, and advocates. His body and voice are true expressions of his ideas and emotions. He is highly persuasive. He is so effective, in fact, that someone suggests, "Tim, you ought to make a speech on that in class."

Tim decides to give a speech on the basketball game for his next assignment and spends the next week organizing the speech, developing his ideas, and choosing his words. Then he memorizes his speech word for word. When he delivers the speech in class, he fails to generate any interest or enthusiasm among his listeners. True, he is better organized than he was when he discussed the game with his friends; his ideas are developed more clearly, and his choice of words is better. But something has happened to his delivery, particularly to his melody pattern. Tim is reciting and his speech sounds artificial and mechanical; he has lost much of his natural effectiveness. The lesson here is clear. Memorization of speeches can have negative effects on the naturalness of your delivery.

Quality

Quality, resonance, and timbre are synonomous terms referring to the properties of a tone determined by its overtones. For example, when a child says, "Ho-ho-ho," imitating Santa Claus, the tone is probably weak and thin. Contrast the child's tone with that of an older, energetic actor with a rich baritone voice. His "ho-ho-ho" is big, rich, strong, and hearty.

The quality of your voice depends on two factors: your emotional reaction to what you are saying and the way your physical mechanism functions.

Emotional Reaction.   If you are in a relaxed emotional state with a minimum of fear and a maximum of enthusiasm, the emotional quality of your voice will be good. Fear tenses and constricts the muscles, and all the knowledge in the world of vocal anatomy and its operation helps little until you have acquired a reasonable amount of self-confidence. A lack of enthusiasm is equally disastrous. An unenthusiastic speaker, without motivation or desire to communicate, is little more than a physical robot.

Physical Mechanism.   There are several physical means you can use to improve your voice quality. These include full, deep breathing; relaxing the larynx; keeping an open throat; and using front forward placement. Full, deep breathing is essential to good voice quality. A generous supply of air is necessary to support the tone initiated by the vocal cords. If you want your vocal motor to hum, you've got to give it some gas.

Relax your larynx to avoid a pinched tone that may produce hoarseness, but tense your vocal cords sufficiently to produce a pure tone that lends itself to better resonance. Overly relaxed vocal cords permit air to escape into the overall tone, which results in a breathy quality.

To keep an open throat, yawn. Relax the tensed muscles. Make room for the vibrations coming up from your vocal cords to become bigger, richer, and fuller. Think of your voice as being poured from a pitcher, not squirted from a hose.

The only sounds in American speech that should go through the nose are *m, n,* and *ng.* All other sounds should be directed front forward as though they were hitting just above your upper front teeth. As an experiment, say "ho." Now say it again, holding your nose shut. If part of the sound is coming through your nose, you have not achieved complete front forward placement. Try it again until all the "o" sound is directed out front forward.

Diction

The word "diction" is used in the field of composition and literature to designate choice of words. The same word in the field of speech is used to indicate distinct enunciation and acceptable pronunciation.

If someone articulates the word re*mark* distinctly as *re*mork, the enunciation may be perfect, but the pronunciation is unacceptable for two reasons:

1. The accent is misplaced: *re*mark for re*mark*;
2. *ork* is substituted for *ark*.

Enunciation is concerned with distinctness and audibility of sounds, and pronunciation concentrates on the acceptable selection of sounds and accents.

Enunciation.   Enunciation is the articulation of vowel and consonant sounds distinctly by means of the tongue, teeth, lips, lower jaw, and soft palate. If your articulators are active, your vowel sounds will be full and consonant sounds crisp. If your articulators are overly active, your enunciation will be exaggerated.

Some speakers look like ventriloquists when they talk. They seldom move their lips. Others speak with such exaggeration that they make their listeners overly aware of their enunciation. Avoid extremes. Let your vowels be full and consonants crisp, but let the process appear effortless.

Take the circumstances into account. What is acceptable on a picnic may not be well received at a meeting. What may be adequate for a discussion in a small room may not be sufficient for a public speech in a large auditorium. What may be just right before a public address microphone may be too exaggerated before a radio microphone.

Much of good enunciation is a matter of ear training through trial and error. You speak. Someone listens, and tells you she can't understand easily parts of what you are saying. You try again. This time you learn that your enunciation is better in general but exaggerated in spots. You make adjustments. After much experience under varying circumstances in different sized rooms, you develop skill in producing enunciation that is effortless and suited to the situation. Through trial and error your ear becomes attuned to what is adequate and efficient.

Pronunciation.   Pronunciation is the expression of sounds and accents of words in connected speech in conformity with acceptable standards. There are four key elements in this definition: sounds, accents, connected speech, and acceptable standards. The basic sounds in words are vowels and consonants. Mispronunciations occur when vowels or consonants are added, omitted, or substituted. Words can be mispronounced when sounds are added:

arth*u*ritis for arthritis

*T*chicago for Chicago

idea*r* for idea

Words can be mispronounced when sounds are omitted:

alum*n*um for alum*i*num

li*b*ary for li*br*ary

honor*b*ul for honor*a*ble

Finally, words can be mispronounced when sounds are substituted:

Feb*y*uary for Feb*r*uary

*d*em for *th*em

le*n*th for le*ng*th (ng is considered one sound)

Accent refers to the amount of stress placed on a syllable. A word can be mispronounced by misplacing the accent:

*mu*seum for mu*se*um

*De*troit for De*troit*

the*a*tre for *the*atre

Connected speech refers to the pronunciation of words not as single units but as combinations with other words. The word "because" is usually pronounced bee-*cawz* as an individual word, but in connected speech, a speaker may correctly pronounce it bee-cuz. By virtue of the same principle of connected speech, *k'n* for *can* and *nd* for *and* are not only permissible but sensible. The purpose of speech is communication; speech should not call undue attention to itself. Speakers who pronounce every syllable of every word in connected speech the way they pronounce words singly fail to follow Hamlet's advice to the players:

Speak the speech, I pray you, as I pronounced it to you, trippingly on the tongue: but if you mouth it, as many of your players do, I had as lief the towncrier spoke my lines.[2]

Examples of other pronunciation variations in connected speech involve the simple words "a" and "the." Don't say "*ay* man." Say rather "*uh* man." Use *ay* only for emphasis, as for example, "I didn't ask all of you to help. I asked for *ay* (one) helper." Don't say "*thee* man." Say "*thuh* man" or better yet, "*th'* man." Use *thee* for emphasis, as for example, "He is *thee* man of the hour." Use *thee* also before a vowel sound: "*thee* apple" or "*thee* F.H.A."

Connected speech also permits contractions. Unless emphasis is desired, *it's, you're,* and *they're* sound better than *it is, you are,* and *they are.* Connected speech, then, combines acceptable pronunciation with clear enunciation, whether the circumstance involves a private conversation, use of a broadcast microphone, or use of a public address microphone in a large arena. To perform well in these widely different circumstances, remember these guidelines:

1. Don't overdo your diction in conversation or before a broadcast microphone.
2. Don't underplay your diction too much in public performance before a large gathering or before a public address microphone.

The last element in our definition of pronunciation is acceptable standards. An acceptable standard is a model, agreed upon by experts, for imitation. Language experts agree that there is no one pronunciation standard, acceptable for all words in American speech. Generally, they recognize three broad areas: eastern, southern, and general American, and even in these broad areas they recognize acceptable variations.

Generally, your pronunciation will be acceptable if you follow this rule: *Speak the language the way the majority of the better educated persons in your general area speak it.* To determine the pronunciation used by the better educated persons in your general area, listen to the clergy, teachers, political speakers, announcers, and other professional persons well versed in language. Even among these speakers, you will hear some variations. Choose for your own those pronunciations that sound most general.

Pacing

Pacing is the amount of vocal movement in given periods of time. A good speaker develops variety in pacing. Two ways in which you can develop this skill are through changes in rate and the use of pause.

Changes in Rate.
Rate, the number of words spoken in a given period of time, is determined by your personality, your material, your listeners, and the acoustical situation.

1. *Your personality.* By nature you may be quick or slow. If you're the racehorse type, you need to slow down. If your rate is that of a plowhorse, you need a greater zest for communication. Runaway speech leaves listeners behind, but plodding speech puts them to sleep.

2. *Your material.* You deliver upbeat or simple material at a faster pace than dignified or complex material, but in either case, to ensure variety, look for opportunities to slow down or speed up.

3. *Your listeners.* How much do your listeners know about your material? What do you want them to get out of it? You recite a quote from the Gettysburg Address more quickly to a group of adults than you do to a group of sixth-graders hearing the speech for the first time.

4. *The acoustical situation.* The larger the listening area, the more slowly you need to speak. Typical is the announcer in the football stadium, ball park, or large auditorium. The beginning speaker almost always talks too fast. The first rule, of course, is to make sure that you are understood. When you are confident that your listeners can understand you, you can begin to think about varying your rate for interest, effect, and meaning.

Use of Pause.   As a speaker you use the technique of pause for five reasons: to breathe, to collect your thoughts, to ensure meaning, to create dramatic effect, and to clarify organization by underscoring transitions.

1. *Pausing for breathing.* Confident public speakers, who have learned to fill a room with their voices, give little thought to the breathing pauses they take, and that is the way it should be. In reading aloud, however, unless they make a conscious effort to breathe deeply at certain points, they may run out of breath at the end of a long passage. Pausing for breath before completing the passage would weaken the meaning or dramatic effect. Deep breathing before long passages should be planned.

2. *Pausing to collect thoughts.* Audiences do not mind if occasionally the speaker stops to remember, rethink an idea, or look for a better word. This type of pausing, of course, should not take place too frequently or the pacing will suffer. An occasional pause can show that the speaker is thinking and not just rattling off ideas mechanically. To be truly effective, these pauses should be silent. Do not vocalize them with such verbal fillers as "er," "ah," or "um."

3. *Pausing for meaning.* The more complicated the meaning, the more are pauses necessary. Experienced speakers use this type of pause generously. They know how important it is to help listeners understand and remember.

The most effective way to pause for meaning is to divide longer sentences into thought-groups. A thought-group may be a word, phrase, or clause. Sometimes a thought-group can even be short sentences. For example, "Look out! The car!! Your baby!!!" Any pause between these sentences might result in tragedy.

4. *Pausing for dramatic effect.* There are many ways to highlight an idea or emotion. It can be done by stressing a particular word, by changing inflection, or by pausing before or after the expression of the idea or emotion.

5. *Pausing to mark transitions.* To make clear the organization of your speech, pause before you take up each new subtopic. In this way you let your listeners know that you are moving on to a new thought.

We have discussed the determinants of vocal characteristics, the physiological apparatus of voice, and the functional vocal skills that you can use to make your vocal technique efficient and effective. We turn now to the topic of applying these skills, using the specific assignment of reading a speech from manuscript. You may not often read your speeches from manuscript; nevertheless, there are specific skills involved in reading from manuscript that you can learn to put to good use in extemporaneous or impromptu situations.

THE MANUSCRIPT SPEECH

The Wisconsin Speaker's Association is an organization composed of professional speakers who attract large fees for their talented services. A member of that group, Lynn Surles, was asked to address the organization on the subject, "How to Read Aloud the Manuscript Speech, Especially Literary Quotations."

Why did these professional speakers want to hear a speech on reading aloud? Most likely because most of them needed training in using the technique. Not everyone who speaks well in conversation or extemporizes well in public speaking is able to read aloud effectively. Sometimes the difference in a performer's style of speaking and reading shocks the critical listener. Two basic skills are involved in reading the manuscript speech: (a) reading aloud your own prose manuscript and (b) reading aloud quotations from others whether they are ordinary prose, literary prose, or poetry.

Reading Aloud Your Manuscript Speech

Before you can read aloud well, you need a good script. If you write your speech well, you have won more than half of the battle. The effective manuscript speech is written in a conversational style, incorporating quotations in appropriate places to enliven and strengthen the presentation.

Conversational Style. A conversational style includes these elements:

1. personal pronouns: *I, you,* and *we;*
2. simple, short sentences;

3. sentence variety, perhaps sentence fragments;

4. questions;

5. contractions: *it's, we'll, there's*;

6. active rather than passive voice: "I want to say" not "Let it be said";

7. repetition: "Government of the *people,* by the *people,* for the *people*";

8. familiar words and expressions but not clichés (overworked expressions such as "time and again," "between the devil and the deep blue sea," "out of the frying pan and into the fire"); and

9. careful adaptation to the audience and the occasion.

Incorporating Quotations.   To ensure proper use of quotations in a speech, follow these guidelines:

1. Identify and give credit to the author. For example, say "George Reedy, former press secretary to President Lyndon Johnson, has this to say about answering questions in a press interview." Then quote Reedy.

2. Make sure the author you are quoting is really an authority. Determine the person's credentials, training, and experience.

3. Let the listeners know when the quotation begins and ends. Sometimes in very important matters you may use the expression, "Quote-unquote," but this technique should be used very sparingly. Find other ways to indicate the end of a quote by communicating visually or vocally, such as looking up or pausing.

4. Make sure there is a need for the quote; know why you're using it. Is it to inform, explain, prove, motivate, inspire, entertain, or solve a problem? Don't use quotes to pad or inflate your speech.

5. Don't let the quote get too long. It's your speech, not the quoted author's.

Reading Aloud Literary Passages

A literary quotation is a portion of a piece of literature, a work of universal value expressed in beautiful form and language. This definition includes five important elements. *Universal* is that which pertains to all or many. *Value* is that which is considered good by many individuals. *Beautiful* is that which is pleasing to the beholder. In prose, *form* refers to the short story, novel, drama, essay, or oration. *Form* in poetry is the didactic, lyrical, narrative, or dramatic poem. *Language* expresses worthwhile content with emotion and imagination.

Once you are aware that the passage you have chosen has literary merit, you are ready to plan how to read it aloud effectively. Through your reading you want to evoke listener response through visual, vocal, and verbal communication. If there is no response, the cycle is incomplete. While the listener has some responsibility, the main burden is on the reader.

Visual communication is revealed through bodily expression, including gesture and muscle tone. (Recall the discussion of bodily action in Chapter 7.) *Vocal* communication is revealed through the techniques of voice and diction. *Verbal* communication refers to the meaning of the passage and why the author selected those particular words to convey that particular meaning.

Literary Passages in Public Speaking

When you decide to use a literary passage in your speech, three kinds of understanding are involved: the understanding that the author of the passage intended, your understanding of the passage that you attempt to communicate, and the meaning evoked in the listener. Perfect understanding takes place when all three of these meanings are the same, but this ideal is seldom reached. Sometimes the author's meaning is not immediately clear. Sometimes you do not comprehend all of the meaning or you fail to communicate the full meaning. Sometimes the listener is beset with distractions.

It may not be possible for you to make the author's meaning any clearer or to remove all the distractions that interfere with the listener's understanding, but you can attempt to improve your own comprehension of the quotation by looking for three kinds of content: intellectual, emotional, and aesthetic.

Intellectual content appeals to reason. Facts, expert opinion, and logical conclusions are the raw material of the mind. They form the base, the bedrock foundation of meaning. For example, consider the First Amendment to the U.S. Constitution:

> *Congress shall make no law respecting an establishment of religion, or prohibiting the free exercise thereof; or abridging the freedom of speech, or of the press; or the right of the people peaceably to assemble, and to petition the Government for a redress of grievances.*

What does the First Amendment mean? Read the amendment aloud, trying to express its intellectual meaning. Which words will you stress? Where will you pause? Will you use vocal inflections? Ask yourself another question. Are you irritated by hecklers who disrupt speakers and make it impossible for them to carry on? Will your attitude toward hecklers change the way you read and orally interpret the phrase "peaceably to assemble"?

The emotional content appeals to feelings, needs, wants, and desires. A person is more than a rational animal. A person is an emotional being with the power of laughter and tears. If the intellectual content can be compared to a skeleton, then the emotional content can be compared to muscles, nerves, flesh, and blood. Read aloud the following selection from Paul's Epistle to the Corinthians. What emotions and needs of the human heart do you discover? Which words will you say with special warmth, strength, or contrast? Will your pace vary? Where will you pause?

> If I had the gift of being able to speak in other languages without learning them, and could speak in every language there is in all of heaven and earth, but didn't love others, I would only be making noise. If I had the gift of prophecy and knew all about what is going to happen in the future, knew everything about everything, but didn't love others, what good would it do? Even if I had the gift of faith so that I could speak to a mountain and make it move I would still be worth nothing at all without love. If I gave everything I have to poor people, and if I were burned alive for preaching the Gospel but didn't love others, it would be of no value whatever.[3]

A writer, in addition to appealing to a reader's intelligence and emotions, decorates the message with the elements of aesthetic content: figures of speech, poetic devices, and beautiful allusions. It is the speaker's function to make this aesthetic content vivid to the listener by making the voice sound like the meaning of the word. For example, the word "lullaby" sounds soft, while the word "thunder" sounds loud. In his poem "Ulalume," Edgar Allan Poe creates the mood of a scary swamp:

The skies they were ashen and sober;
  The leaves they were crisped and sere—
  The leaves they were withering and sere;

It was hard by the dim lake of Auber,
  In the misty mid region of Weir:—
It was down by the dank tarn of Auber,
  In the ghoul-haunted woodland of Weir.[4]

Do you have a favorite poem that includes vivid figures of speech? If you do, try reading passages aloud over and over until your ear tells you that you've captured the mood and the subtle changes within the mood.

In addition to getting the meaning, the public speaker who uses a literary passage must be able to *give* the meaning of the selection. To give the meaning effectively, follow these five guidelines:

1. *Identify with the author.* When you quote a literary passage, let yourself respond to and identify with the writer's thoughts, feelings, and beautiful language. Through this identification, you can communicate the author's thoughts, feelings, and appreciation for beauty.

2. *Be yourself.* All of us have different backgrounds, and we speak in

different ways. As long as you do not distort the essential meaning of a passage, capitalize on your individuality and learn to be yourself in your reading. In their interpretations of Hamlet, actors Maurice Evans, Laurence Olivier, and John Gielgud have shown their individual styles, yet each man has conveyed the essential meaning of the character.

3. *Be aware of the meaning as you speak.* You must live each moment of your speech. The moment you read a literary passage is one of re-creation, the re-creation of the author's original creation. This is possible only if you project yourself into the selection and let your imagination respond keenly to its ideas, feelings, sounds, melody, rhythm, and emphasis. In re-creating, use your mind, imagination, and all your senses: see, hear, feel, smell, and taste.

4. *Let your desire to communicate be evident.* Knowledge and scholarship, although essential and basic, are not enough. Action, communication, and listener response must also be present. You must desire to communicate.

The best kind of motivation for effective reading aloud of literary passages comes from within. Ask yourself these basic questions: Who wrote the passage? What does it mean? How can the message enrich the listeners' lives? Your answers should increase your motivation and desire to communicate.

5. *Be an artist but don't be artificial.* In general, three kinds of performance are possible: underdone, overdone, and just right. A performance that is underdone fails to take advantage of the author's work, the art of oral reading, and the human nature of the listener. An author's work is full of ideas, emotion, and beautiful language. A reader is a person with intelligence, imagination, and appreciation of the beautiful. Listeners have minds, hearts, and wills that can be moved in the right direction. If a performance is poor, the author, reader, and listener all suffer.

A performance that is overdone calls more attention to the performance than to the message. Listeners are quick to detect the insincerity of an artificial ring in the voice or a pseudomajestic tone. They know instinctively what they like or dislike, even though they may not know why. A poor performer fails to consider the natural judgment of the audience and focuses more attention on pompous technique than on the material and the listeners.

On the other hand, in the just right performance, the speaker uses the techniques of body and voice to bring attention to a high peak, but in a disarming and seemingly effortless manner. The speaker accepts Quintilian's advice that "great art conceals art." By that statement, Quintilian did not mean that good oral reading is reserved. He saw it rather as alive and creative. The speaker is certainly interested in the logical and intellectual content, but he or she is also inspired by the emotional and aesthetic content and remembers that to ensure communication the listener's total being must be reached.

Thus we see that the public speaker who reads a speech from a manuscript must, first of all, prepare a script written in a conversational style. If literary quotations are included, these suggestions are helpful: identify with the author, be yourself, be aware of the meaning as you read, let your desire to communicate be evident, and be an artist but don't be artificial.

SUMMARY

Before they can develop good vocal technique, speakers should have some understanding of why they speak the way they do. The determinants of vocal characteristics include both environmental conditions and personality factors. Environmental conditions include the influences of home, neighborhood, school, friends, and place of employment. The influence of personality factors on vocal characteristics is revealed through temperament and emotional drive. Speakers should recognize that just as voice reflects personality, so, too, does personality affect voice. Whatever is done to improve personality, then, can also improve vocal technique. The physiological apparatus of voice includes five elements: the generator, vibrator, resonator, articulator, and evaluator. Knowing the elements of the physiological apparatus of voice and understanding how each element functions can help speakers learn how to use the voice more efficiently and improve vocal technique.

Besides understanding the determinants of vocal characteristics and the physiological apparatus of voice, speakers should also be aware of the functional skills involved in developing an effective and efficient vocal technique. These functional vocal skills are force, range, quality, diction, and pacing. Force is concerned with volume and emphasis; range with pitch, inflection, and melody pattern. The quality of vocal technique depends on the speaker's emotional reaction and physical mechanism. Skill in diction includes both audible enunciation and acceptable pronunciation of sounds and accents. The good speaker develops the skill of pacing through changes in rate and the use of pause.

One specific application of the skills of vocal technique involves reading a speech from manuscript and reading literary passages within the speech. The effective manuscript speech is written in a conversational style and incorporates appropriate quotations that enliven and strengthen the message. A public speaker often uses literary quotations to enhance a presentation. To use such quotations effectively, the speaker must *get* the meaning of the selection by investigating its intellectual, emotional, and aesthetic content. The speaker must then be able to *give* the meaning of the quotation. Giving the meaning involves identifying with the author, being yourself, being aware of the meaning, letting the desire to communicate be evident, and being an artist without being artificial.

ASSIGNMENTS

1. Write and read a one-minute TV editorial. Create the illusion that you are conversing with your listeners.

2. Write a one-minute patriotic speech for one of the government holidays. Read it aloud, using a variety of emotion and tone. Use colorful images and vivid descriptions.

3. Write a short speech in which you vary the mood. When you read the speech, vary the pace to indicate the changes in mood.

4. Give a one-minute synopsis of a famous speech up to the climax. Then, in one to two minutes, read from the climax through to the end of the speech.

5. Write a speech of less than 300 words and read it from manuscript. Write the speech in a conversational style and include several literary passages. Try to communicate the intellectual and emotional meaning through conversational directness; adequate volume; proper emphasis; pleasing quality; appropriate pacing and pausing; acceptable pronunciation; and clear, crisp enunciation. Choose a subject you are already interested in, know something about, can research, and is worth your listeners' time. Write out your speech in a conversational style. Weave appropriate, supporting quotations into your speech, and then practice by reading it aloud several times. In preparing your manuscript, underline the words you want to stress. Make vertical lines where you want to pause.

NOTES

1. *Public Papers of the Presidents of the United States: John F. Kennedy* (Washington, DC: Government Printing Office, 1961).

2. *Hamlet,* act 3, scene 2, lines 1–4.

3. I Corin. 13:1–3.

4. Edgar Allan Poe, "Ulalume," in *The Complete Tales and Poems of Edgar Allan Poe* (New York: The Modern Library, 1938), pp. 951–54.

Importance of Language	Symbol Makers	
	Human Survival	
Language and Meaning	Meanings Are in People	
	Cultural Context	
Building Walls or Bridges	Building Walls: Barriers to Communication	Sexist Language
		Racist Language
		Technical Language
	Building Bridges: Highways to Communication	Affective Language
		Clear Language
		Concise Language
		Correct Language
		Active Language

Language and Meaning

OBJECTIVES

When you finish reading this chapter, you should be able to:

1. explain the importance of language;
2. define the triangle of meaning;
3. explain how language can help build walls between people;
4. explain how language can help build bridges between people; and
5. present a speech that uses affective, clear, concise, correct, and active language.

9 Language and Meaning

Note what happened to Tom who addressed a group of older people. In his opening remarks, he stated:

Uh, I want to talk about the art of truckin'. It's a great way to see the country. Uh, at times, it can be a heavy trip. But it's, um, worth the time and effort to cruise down the highway and catch the rays. Yeah, truckin' is quite an experience. I enjoy the heavy sounds from my tunes while waiting for a lift. They keep me floatin'. Yeah, uh, I can't wait to grab some tunes and catch a ride.

Most members of Tom's audience thought that he was talking about truck driving. They didn't realize that Tom was referring to hitchhiking. They became increasingly confused and frustrated as they listened to Tom. He neglected to adjust his message to his listeners by using terms that were understandable to *them*. And why did he have to? For Tom, "truckin'" is a common term, one he and his friends use all the time.

Commenting on the important difference between British citizens and United States citizens, Winston Churchill observed that the only thing separating the two groups is a common language. This explains what happened to Tom. He spoke English but in terms unfamiliar to his audience. If Tom had spoken in a foreign language, his listeners probably would not have understood much less of his message. In a sense, Tom's slang terms were a foreign language to his audience.

Important differences exist between an oral and a written message. A reader has the opportunity to reread a written message; a listener in a speech setting has only one chance to grasp the meaning (unless the speech is videotaped for replay). A speaker's oral language often contains incomplete sentences that suggest incomplete thoughts, which can cause confusion. Oral language is frequently sprinkled with "ahs," "ums," and "ers." Such verbal interruptions can help speakers collect their thoughts but can also become noise elements that distract listeners.

Yo, Chief! Get a clue. Hip-speak, punk talk, even Valley Girl lingo is out. Modern teen jargon from Harlem to Long Beach has shoved the words "far out" and "totally awesome" into ancient history. "Splitting the scene" is a lost art; now you "peel off" or "blaze." "My man" has turned into "homeboy" or "cuz." To be "superfine" is to be "super bad."[1]

A further problem, as illustrated in the previous quote, is that language changes. Pop expressions, technical terms, professional jargon, idiomatic expressions, and de-sexed terminology have brought about vast changes in today's language. Rapid changes in language place a serious burden on speakers who must select a language appropriate for their immediate audience. However, speakers should not consider this an insurmountable problem. When a speaker's language is clear and adapted to a particular audience, chances are that the listeners, for the most part, will understand the message.

THE IMPORTANCE OF LANGUAGE

Tom's experience is not uncommon. As a speaker, your language can excite audience members emotionally and intellectually; it can also help listeners think logically. But, your language can also confuse listeners. It is your responsibility to choose words wisely.

In this chapter, we will explore both the importance of language and its role in public speaking. We will discuss ways in which speakers can use language to build bridges, rather than walls, between themselves and their listeners. First, however, we will consider how language enables us to communicate meaning and the importance of language to our very survival.

Symbol Makers

How are we able to share our thoughts and feelings with each other? This task is largely accomplished through the words we use. Words are symbols; symbols stand for things. Words can contain multiple meanings; for example, think about the words "love," "hate," "car," "experience," "shapely," and "class." How many definitions exist for each term? Words (symbols) help us share our thoughts with other people. Because words can have multiple meanings, they expand our ability to communicate our views of reality to ourselves and to others. We seek to understand the world around us through the language we use to define it.

While the flexibility of language is very useful, it can also create problems in communication. Sometimes our meaning is not clear to other people. Nevertheless, we should continue to select and use symbols we believe will be understandable to others. In short, we must be "symbol makers."

Think about your daily activities. Do the words you use to describe them play a significant role in defining them? As with most people, from your first waking moments until the time you close your eyes, you use words to convey your meaning. You may, at times, become frustrated when you cannot find the right word to express your meaning. Of course, you must select the symbols that best explain your ideas to others. Consider, for example, such terms as "heavy," "communication," "love," "listening," and "freedom." How would you explain the meaning of these terms to someone of a different culture who spoke limited English? At first, you may think the challenge overwhelming. But with a few moments of reflection, you'll discover how flexible your language can be. You may not find all the words necessary to invoke a precise understanding of the terms, but you'll probably find enough of them to convey *your* meaning.

This is essentially what occurs in public speaking. You choose words that attempt to convey your meaning. The listener may or may not understand your language. If misunderstanding or confusion arises, you need to choose different symbols to clarify your views. Quite simply, language symbolizes the speaker's views for the listeners.

Human Survival

Have you ever considered the possibility that without language, civilization as we know it would come to a standstill? Language helps us grow; it helps us erect societies, conquer diseases, and discover new technologies. None of this would be possible without language. As we have learned, language is the vehicle by which we can express our ideas, feelings, beliefs, values, and attitudes. From our basic survival needs to our needs for self-esteem or self-actualization, we routinely use the tool of language to develop.

In public speaking, language can help people satisfy human needs. For example, a speaker may suggest a course of action (for instance, a new diet plan) that audience members accept as wise and useful. Such acceptance may lead them to carry out the plan and eventually experience better health and higher self-esteem due to physical well-being.

Human survival depends on our ability to use symbols. This presupposes a general agreement on the meaning of the symbols we use. If we use language narrowly, assuming that only *one* meaning exists for each word, we may have difficulty communicating with other people who assign different meanings to our words. We may also have difficulty if we assume that everyone is familiar with the words we use. This is the difficulty that befell Tom in the opening example in this chapter. If Tom had explained that by "truckin'" he meant hitchhiking, he could have made his meaning much clearer for his audience.

The words of language allow us to understand and interpret one another's ideas, attitudes, beliefs, and values. This interpretative process unites us in a world where we can survive and grow as human beings.

LANGUAGE AND MEANING

Alice pointed to a map and said: "This is the state of Colorado. The Rocky Mountains are located here in the western part of the state. The state of Wyoming is located north of Colorado."

Did Alice in fact point to the state of Colorado, to the Rocky Mountains, or to the bordering state of Wyoming? Her language seems to suggest that she did. Or did she merely point to their symbols on a map? This next section examines the origin of meaning, the relationship between language and meaning, and the impact of culture on both. First, let's look at where meaning originates.

Meanings Are in People

When Alice points to the map, she is not really pointing to the state of Colorado, to the Rocky Mountains, or to the bordering state of Wyoming. She is pointing to a map that symbolizes these places. Likewise, her words are symbols. Quite simply, the map is *not* the state of Colorado, and Alice's word "Colorado" is not the thing of which she speaks. Alice just as easily could say, "This is the state of hot dog." She could use any symbol to represent the object. But, she uses the term "Colorado" because she wants to use a symbol that evokes the same meaning to all her listeners.

The meanings contained in ideas, events, places, or things are ultimately lodged in people. People decide what the symbol means and what it represents to them. You may choose a symbol that means one thing to you but means another to the listeners. Why? In their work, *The Meaning of Meaning,* psychologist Charles Ogden and literary theorist I. A. Richards devised the triangle of meaning to illustrate the communication process.[2] Ogden and Richards argue that meaning usually starts with a thought. You think of a bushy tail, long whiskers, floppy ears, hopping action, and a small animal eating carrots. Putting all these thoughts together, you uncover the symbol "rabbit" as the focus of your thoughts.

FIGURE 9.1   **The Triangle of Meaning**

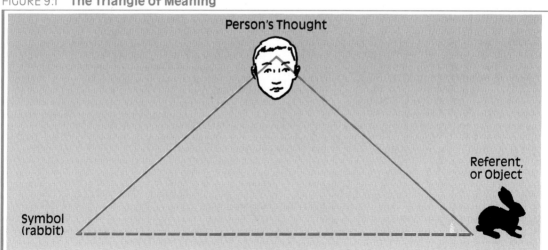

In the triangle of meaning, specific relationships exist between thought and object, and between thought and symbol. But the relationship between object (referent) and symbol is arbitrary. Any symbol can actually be used to stand for the referent. As a result, the relationship between symbol and referent may not be clear. The symbol represents the object; it is not the object. The word "rabbit" is not an actual rabbit. As a map is not the territory it represents, the word (symbol) is not the object (referent) it names.

In a public speaking situation, a number of triangles of meanings may exist. In his speech, Jamie says, "Computers are the way of the future," and he attempts to accentuate the positive features of the computer. Jill listens to Jamie, but she can only recall the problems she has experienced with the computer. Her bills are not paid on time because of computer error; she can't get the classes she wants because the computer is not working. Obviously, she shares neither Jamie's enthusiasm nor his meaning when he says, "Computers will make our lives easier." For Jamie, the word "computer" connotes advancement, convenience, and efficiency. For Jill, the same word connotes inefficiency, inconvenience, and trouble.

People's experiences and background weigh heavily on the manner in which their triangles of meaning are constructed. You, as a speaker, can not take for granted that audience members will construct their triangles

FIGURE 9.2 **Differences in Triangles of Meaning**

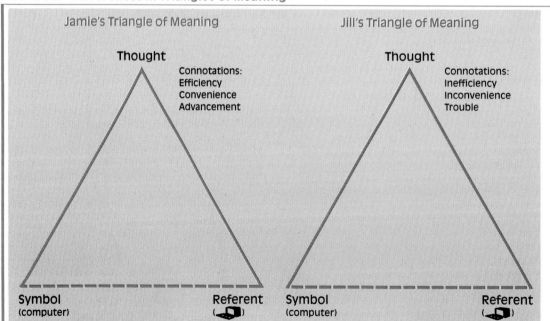

of meaning in a manner similar to yours. If audience members appear confused, angry, or bored, they are sending you an important message about their triangle of meaning during the communication process. To counter this difficulty, you can use one or more of the following methods to clarify meaning:

1. Give the audience the dictionary meaning of words that cause confusion and identify the source of the definition.

2. Define confusing words in subjective terms. For example, you may use the word "exam." To convey your meaning of the word, you can say, "I view the word 'exam' as more than a simple test. I view it as the opportunity to communicate my ideas in written form in response to statements made by my instructor."

3. Cite stories, analogies, or examples to help clarify meaning. For instance, you may wish to convey both the meaning and emotion you feel when using a particular word. Suppose you want to convey the meaning and emotion of the word "frustration." You can illustrate with an example, saying "Frustration to me is that feeling of rage that comes over me when I need a course that I can't get during registration."

4. Use a visual aid to illustrate meaning. For example, if you want to convey the meaning of the word "serenity," you may want to supplement a verbal description with a photograph (large enough to be seen by the audience) of a peaceful forest scene.

The science of semantics attempts to describe the way meaning is perceived. Noted linguist Mario Pei defines semantics:

The science of meaning and its transfer, semantics naturally includes all of the compartments of language, spoken, written, gestural or symbolic. Semantics is "language" in its broadest, most inclusive aspect. Sounds, words, grammatical forms, syntactical constructions are the tools of language. Semantics is language's avowed purpose.[3]

Simply put, semantics deals with the study of meaning. As Pei suggests, it is more than just the word alone that imparts meaning. Many elements combine to influence meaning. The point to remember is that meaning is *inside* us. Even as we are assisted by someone else's language, we ultimately decide what the symbol (word) means to us.

The meaning we attach to a word may be either *denotative* or *connotative*. Denotative meaning is the literal, or dictionary, meaning of a word. For example, "having great weight" is the denotative meaning for the word "heavy." Connotative meaning is the special, personalized meaning given to an object. For example, to say, "This is a *heavy* thought," may imply connotatively that the thought is significant.

A quick glance at a dictionary reveals that many words contain multiple definitions. A listener might apply a definition different from the one intended by the speaker, and sometimes cultural factors create different meanings for the same words. Semanticist S. I. Hayakawa reports:

> *The names of birds, animals, and plants are an interesting example of confusion about denotations. The English "robin" is an entirely different species from the American bird of that name. Many different and unrelated kinds of fish are denoted by the word "bream" (pronounced "brim" in the South). Belgian hares, we are told, are "really rabbits," while the American jackrabbit is "really a hare." The term "crocus," as popularly used, refers in different parts of the country to different flowers.*[4]

Meaning is created by people. As semanticists have suggested, the same words can have different meanings to different people. In public speaking, you need to be aware that the words you use have both connotative and denotative meanings. For example, the word "birth" denotatively means the beginning of life, but for many people the word carries a more connotative meaning, such as a blessed event or the fruits of shared love.

As we have seen, you, as a speaker may have to take extra steps to clarify the meanings of the words you use. You can cite dictionary definitions, definitions from credible sources, or examples to clarify meaning. For instance, to clarify the meaning of the term "child abuse," you can refer to specific examples illustrating child abuse, cite testimony from authorities defining acts of child abuse, or show pictures of child abuse that help complement the meaning of the term. In these ways, you can share the meaning of your language with your audience. However, it is the audience members who ultimately interpret the meaning of the symbols you use.

Cultural Context

> *Bill was invited to Linda's home for dinner. Linda, an Italian-American, informed Bill that her mother was preparing them an Italian dinner. Bill looked forward to the dinner invitation and wanted to make a good impression on Linda's parents. Finally, the night arrived. Flowers in hand, Bill knocked firmly on the door. Linda's father, Donato, opened it and said hello in Italian: "Ciao (pronounced chow), Bill." Thinking it an early invitation to eat, Bill responded immediately, "Show me the way!" To Bill's embarrassment, the smile on Donato's face turned into a look of bewilderment at Bill's response to his greeting.*

Unfortunately, Bill's first impression on Linda's father was not the one he had wanted to make. But is Bill completely at fault? Perhaps not. Rather, Bill is a victim of culture. Culture plays a significant role in the way we use and interpret words. The word *ciao* clearly carries a different meaning for Bill than it does for Linda's father. Bill, not being Italian, defines *ciao* from his cultural perspective. Bill's triangle of meaning for the word, as he heard it, relates to food. Donato views the word quite differently and uses it as a greeting within his cultural context.

As a public speaker, you need to be sensitive to the cultural make-up of your audience. When dealing with a culturally mixed audience, avoid using language that stereotypes people. Define confusing words using the methods mentioned earlier in this chapter.

BUILDING WALLS OR BRIDGES

Have you ever said something to someone and then later regretted it? Have you ever had the opposite experience—you said something to someone that heightened your feelings of trust and admiration for each other? Probably you have experienced both situations. The language you use can build either walls or bridges between you and others. Language that builds walls includes sexist language, racist language, and sometimes technical language. Language that is affective, clear, concise, correct, and active helps build bridges between people.

Building Walls: Barriers to Communication

Sometimes, language creates walls between people. We may not consciously realize this, but these barriers can diminish your chances of establishing effective communication. In public speaking, some of the more common wall-builders are sexist language, racist language, and technical language.

Sexist Language.   Sexist language discriminates against one gender. What effects can language that emphasizes one gender over another have on your ability to communicate effectively? In his work *Telling It Like It Isn't*, Dan Rothwell listed some common descriptions for men and women, which illustrate the connotative power of words.[5] These descriptions show how personal traits perceived in men can be translated into quite different traits when they are perceived in women.

Men	*Women*
He's inquisitive.	She's nosy.
He shares information.	She gossips.
He discusses.	She chatters.
He explains.	She complains.
He's cool.	She's frigid.
He's reflective.	She's moody.
He's a lover.	She's a tramp.

Male-linked words are those with the suffix "man." Differing views exist on the definition of such words. Some argue that male-linked words refer just to males. Others argue that the terms are generic, that they refer to both males and females. Studies in the wording of job descriptions, however, show that male-linked words affect people's perceptions of appropriateness. Based partly on their gender and the sex-bias wording of the description, people tend to shy away from "opposite-sex jobs."[6] Similar results concerning male-linked words were discovered in other studies.[7]

Judy Cornelia Pearson, author of *Gender and Communication*, offers this astute observation concerning gender and language.

> *We learned that while man-linked words and traditional generic pronouns [he, him, himself, her, herself] are both widely used, they do not refer with equal precision to women and men. They may, in fact, be limiting the behavioral options of women. We determined that women are denigrated in humor more frequently than men, that people find jokes in which women are denigrated funnier than jokes which denigrate men, and that individuals will tell jokes which denigrate women to women. . . . We learned that the portrayal of women and men in newspapers, magazines, print advertisements, and on television is not accurate. Women are generally unrepresented, and both women and men are portrayed in narrow sex roles. . . . Aggressiveness or bias toward either sex is injurious to both sexes. Stereotyping, or oversimplifying the roles which women and men play may have a variety of negative outcomes.*[8]

Pearson's observations are important for public speakers, who often will address both male and female audience members. Public speakers need to be sensitive to the type of language they use. Sexist language can build walls between people. Such words as "chick," "broad," or "career girl" distort perception. Speakers should try instead to build bridges of communication by using language that does not divide the sexes, language that recognizes the existence of *both* genders.

To avoid using sexist language, you, as a public speaker, should consider the following suggestions.

1. Eliminate, if possible, words containing the male suffix. For example, such words as chairman, policeman, and postman can be de-sexed and changed to chair or head, police officer, and postal carrier.

2. Avoid using language that stereotypes. For example, the word "girl" may be considered derogatory by an audience of college-aged women. They may view the use of such a word as an attempt to label them as immature, weak, or nonassertive.

3. If gender-based pronouns must be used, use both "he or she" or "him and her" when addressing the audience. However, use these pro-

nouns sparingly. Used too often, they sound stylistically awkward. A preferable alternative is to use plural pronouns, such as "you," "they," "their," or "them," which address both genders.

Racist Language.   Like sexist language, racist language, too, tends to divide people and construct walls between them. Racist language discriminates against a particular race. "Honky," "spic," and "jap," are some examples of racist language used to demean individuals. Such language places a group of people in an inferior position by labeling them in a derogatory manner. For example, the repetitive use of such language over a period of time has allowed the Ku Klux Klan, with partial success, to substitute "the words for the objects."[9] So successful are they with their racist language that some of their audiences, too, begin to perceive the word as the object. What does the following folk lyric suggest to you?

White, you're right.
Left, you can fight.
Brown, stand around.
Black, stand back, stand back.[10]

Words can be powerful factors in shaping messages and perceptions. Comparing the words "black" and "white," Dr. Martin Luther King, Jr., noted:

In Roget's Thesaurus, *there are some 120 synonyms for blackness, and at least 60 percent of them are offensive—such words as "blot," "soot," "grime," "devil," and "foul." There are some 134 synonyms for "whiteness," and all are favorable, expressed in such words as "purity," "cleanliness," "chastity," and "innocence." A white lie is better than a black lie. The most degenerate member of the family is the "black sheep," not the "white sheep."*[11]

There are, of course, some negative connotations to the term "white" (such as white flag, white wash), but they are few when compared to negative terms associated with such words as "black," "red," "brown," or "yellow."

The following guidelines suggest ways in which public speakers can counteract racist language.

1. Do not use terms that demean or belittle a race of people.

2. Use the correct term to refer to a specific race. For example, such terms as native Americans, blacks or black Americans, and Asians are currently considered accurate terminology for describing particular racial groups.

3. Avoid telling racial jokes. In public speaking, it is not humorous to tell a racial joke. Such jokes build walls.

These suggestions may seem like small steps, but they are consequential, if speakers truly seek to tear down walls created by racist language. Once you, as a public speaker adjust your language, you can overcome racial discomfort. You can feel more comfortable in communication settings containing listeners from different races.

Technical Language.   Are your teachers going to "hardwire" (give without thinking) their next lecture? Do you hope to "debug" a relationship that is causing you problems? Is it possible that we are starting to relate to people in the same way we relate to machines? With the advent of the computer revolution, experts believe that such technology does influence the way we think about and relate to the world around us. In her research on computers and the human spirit, sociologist Sherry Turkle notes:

> *"The something new" takes many forms. A relationship with a computer can influence people's conceptions of themselves, their jobs, their relationships with other people, and their ways of thinking about social processes.*[12]

Technical language, of course, encompasses more than just computer language. Every profession has its own jargon. The field of communication is no different. The technical vocabulary has grown enormously in

Skillful speakers choose their words carefully. Like all great speakers, Dr. Martin Luther King, Jr., was sensitive to the emotional components of language. He knew that words have the power to offend or to uplift.

this field in the last two decades. But are those who use technical language becoming overwhelmed with "techno-speak"? Are they using symbols (technical words) that create walls between them and the people who are unfamiliar with such terminology?

Suppose you were listening to a speech in which the speaker used such terms as "metacommunication," "proxemics," "kinesics," and "paralinguistics." Although these terms may be familiar to communication scholars, nevertheless they are technical terms that can create barriers to communication. What happens if such terms, or others unfamiliar to you, appear in a speech? The symbol is in the English language, yet you fail to understand it. Any triangle of meaning from your past experiences probably supplies limited assistance.

This does not mean that speakers should never use technical terminology. As a speaker, you should, however, consider the possibility that your listeners may be unfamiliar with these particular language symbols. You don't want to erect unnecessary walls between you and your listeners. There are a number of techniques you can use to clarify the meaning of technical terms: examples, analogies, stories, denotative definitions, and connotative definitions. You may also want to use visual aids to help explain the meaning of the technical terms. These efforts should help you build bridges between you and your listeners.

Building Bridges: Highways to Communication

You should be sensitive to your listeners' feelings, beliefs, and attitudes. This is not always easy. Language cannot be all things to all people, but you must try to be sensitive to the beliefs and feelings of others in order to establish a genuine dialogue with your listeners. Language that is

FIGURE 9.3 **The Technical Language Wall**

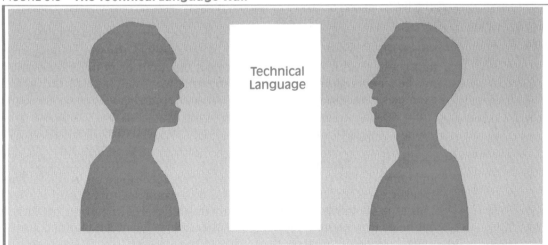

affective, clear, concise, correct, and active is language that helps build bridges.

Affective Language.   This type of language helps arouse emotions. You should avoid using sexist or racist language that arouses hostility. Instead, you should choose language that helps stir feelings of pride, fellowship, trust, and honesty.

For instance, suppose you want to develop a feeling of family unity with your listeners on a topic on which most of them disagree with you. You can tap their emotional ties to the symbol "family" by using affective language. You might say:

> We are part of the same academic family. As with any family, we will disagree with each other from time to time. We'll also share a laugh or tear. Yet, we trust each other enough to respect our rights to disagree. I am here today to state a position disagreeable to many in this family. I hope that as you would respect any of your biological family members' rights to speak freely, you will be of like mind, in this, our academic family.

You should avoid sounding emotionally detached from your listeners. Affective language can reduce the emotional and psychological distance between listeners and speakers.

Clear Language.   You, as a speaker, must be clear. If you use technical language, you should define terms, especially if the listeners are not trained or skilled in the areas that use this terminology. Vocabulary level should be appropriate for the listeners. If it is too high, listeners may fail to understand; if too low, listeners may feel insulted.

On the other hand, sometimes, "planned ambiguity" creates interest in a message. Occasionally, speakers purposely use terms that are unfamiliar to listeners. Speakers may even tell the listeners that few people are aware of the term's meaning. They eventually explain or define the term within the context of the speech. For example, the word "metacommunication," which means communication about communication, may not be immediately defined by a speaker, who may instead introduce examples of metacommunication, such as slapping someone on the back while saying, "How are you?" or smiling while saying, "How are you doing?" The speaker uses these examples to clarify the meaning of the term "metacommunication." Then the speaker can define the term by verbally explaining that metacommunication is communication, verbal and nonverbal, that gives clues to how a message is to be interpreted. The speaker can then tie the definition to the examples mentioned earlier. This type of planned ambiguity is not only effective in gaining attention but helps to demonstrate a speaker's flexibility. Too much planned ambiguity, however, can erode the clarity of the speaker's language—which, after all, is of primary importance.

Concise Language.   Have you ever heard someone lament, "I wish the speaker would get to the point"? This question highlights the speaker's need to be concise. This is especially true in public speaking where speakers often face time restrictions. One professor frequently comments to his class: "Almost everyone can hit the three main points of their speech in one hour. It indeed is the artist of communication who must adequately cover them within a much shorter period of time." Concise language aids in this process.

Conjunctions, terminology that does not have to be defined, and shorter sentences are devices speakers can use to reduce a breezy, long-winded style to a clear, concise, and effective method of communication. A speaker who says, "Today I'm glad to be able to present for your listening pleasure a message of significance on the topic of nuclear defense," is indeed verbose. A speaker who says, "Today I want to discuss nuclear defense," clarifies the message by being concise and direct. At times speakers may need to be more detailed in their explanations, but if this becomes their predominant language style, they may find it difficult to hold their listeners' attention. You will discover that concise, direct language promotes the clarity and strength of your message.

Correct Language.   Public speakers are on display. Listeners expect them to *sound* educated; they expect speakers to use grammatically correct language. As a result, a speaker's credibility may rise or fall based on the perceived correctness of his or her language.

Incorrect language draws attention away from the meaning of a message. Listeners may begin to focus more on the speaker's grammatical errors than on the purpose of the presentation or the meaning of the message. At times, a speaker may elect to use ungrammatical phrases to gain the listeners' attention. However, as with planned ambiguity, the speaker should use this technique sparingly. Overuse of ungrammatical phrases as an attention-getting device can prove counterproductive.

Active Language.   Active voice produces active language; active voice sounds bolder, more direct. As professors Flesch and Lass explain, "The active voice, which shows who is doing something—as in 'I hit Johnnie'—makes a sentence strong; the passive voice, which shows who is being acted on—as in 'Johnnie is being hit by me'—makes a sentence weak."[13] A public speaker who says, "Air pollution limits the quality of life," uses the active voice. The statement shows that the subject is acting. A speaker who says, "The quality of life is being limited by air pollution," shows what is being acted on. Active voice usually suggests more concise communication in both speaking and writing.

As we have seen, there are a number of language pitfalls that speakers should attempt to avoid. These include sexist, racist, and technical language. These types of language build walls between speakers and listeners. On the other hand, language can build bridges between speakers and their audience. Language that builds bridges is affective, clear, concise, correct, and active. In the language that you use in your public speeches, don't be a "wind-bag." Help your listeners experience the excitement and vitality of your ideas by using language that punctuates this excitement and vitality.

SUMMARY

Language plays a vital role in human life and in public speaking. We rely on language to communicate our thoughts and ideas to other people. Meaning in language stems from the individual; thus, a public speaker must be careful to use language that conveys his or her precise meaning. The triangle of meaning is a method used to express the relationship among people, words, and objects that gives rise to meaning in language. The triangle of meaning suggests that a specific relationship exists between a person's thought and an object, and between a thought and its symbol (word). There is, however, an arbitrary relationship between a symbol (word) and an object. Cultural differences also affect meaning, and the public speaker should be sensitive to the cultural make-up of an audience and adjust his or her language accordingly.

In public speaking, language can either construct walls or it can build bridges of communication between public speakers and their listeners. Barriers to communication—language that builds walls—include sexist, racist, and, at times, technical language. Such language can insult or confuse listeners. If technical language must be used, speakers can give examples, stories, analogies, denotative definitions, and connotative definitions to clarify technical terms. Highways to communication—language that builds bridges between public speakers and their listeners—is language that is affective, clear, concise, correct, and active.

ASSIGNMENTS

1. Recall the list of words presented in the chapter: "heavy," "communication," "love," "listening," "freedom." Write out your definitions for each of these words. Share your definitions with a group of three or four classmates, discussing both similarities and differences. Have one person in each group present a two-minute report on the discussion to the class.

2. Make a list of words that you believe fall into the category of sexist language. Explain why you believe such words to be sexist.

3. Complete the following sentences.

   I view a fireman as   I view a policeman as
   I view a girl as   I view a witch as
   I view a chairman as   I view a man as
   I view a woman as

Do some of your answers suggest a male-dominated description? Do some of your answers suggest opposite-gender equivalents that connote more positive or negative characteristics? Did your responses to such male-linked words as "chairman" suggest that you view them as exclusively male terms? In groups of three or four, discuss your responses to these sentences. Have one person in each group present a two-minute report on the discussion to the class.

4. Make a list of words that you believe fall under the heading of racist language. Explain why you consider such words to be racist.

5. Write down all the terms you associate with the two words "white" and "black." Compare your list with Dr. King's observations. Share your list with your classmates.

6. What would you add to the list of language that builds walls between people? Explain your list to your classmates.

7. Present a five-minute informative speech on a topic of your choice. See the appendix for suggestions of speech topics. Use language that builds bridges, not walls, between you and your audience. Use language that is affective, clear, concise, correct, and active.

NOTES

1. "Super Bad," *The Milwaukee Journal*, 2 September 1984, p. 1.

2. Charles K. Ogden and I. A. Richards, *The Meaning of Meaning* (New York: Harcourt, Brace, 1946), p. 11.

3. Mario Pei, *The Story of Language* (New York: Mentor Books, 1960), p. 118.

4. S. I. Hayakawa, *Language in Thought and Action* (New York: Harcourt, Brace and World, 1964), p. 84.

5. Dan Rothwell, *Telling It Like It Isn't* (Englewood Cliffs, NJ: Prentice-Hall, 1982), pp. 180–81.

6. Sandra L. Bem and Daryl J. Bem, "Does Sex-Biased Job Advertising 'Aid and Abet' Sex Discrimination?" *Journal of Applied Social Psychology* 3 (1973): 6–18.

7. For an excellent overview of these studies, see Judy Cornelia Pearson, *Gender and Communication* (Dubuque, IA: William C. Brown, 1985), pp. 70–72.

8. Pearson, *Gender and Communication*, p. 106.

9. Andrea L. Rich, *Interracial Communication* (New York: Harper & Row, 1974), p. 132.

10. Harold Isaacs, *The New World of Negro Americans* (New York: John Day, 1963), p. 84.

11. Haig Bosmajian, "The Language of White Racism," *College English* 31 (1969): 265.

12. Joseph Barbato, "Where Does the Computer Stop and Human Life Begin?" *Chronicle of Higher Education* 29 (14 November 1984): 6.

13. Rudolf Flesch and A. H. Lass, *A New Guide to Better Writing* (New York: Popular Library, 1963), p. 152.

Reporting	Definition of Reporting	
	Uses of Reporting	
	Tools of Reporting	
	Methods of Reporting	Narration
		Description
		Simple Explanation
Complex Explanation	Definition of Explanation	
	Purpose of Explanation	
	Effective Methods of Explanation	Going from the Known to the Unknown
		Illustrating
Organizing the Informative Speech	Standard Divisions	
	Patterns of Organization	Chronological
		Spatial
		Topical
		Logical
		Psychological
		Pro and Con
		Problem and Solution
	Principles of Outlining	Consistency in Using Symbols
		Coordination and Subordination
		Overlapping
		Single Idea Per Main Point
Developing an Oral Style	Simplify	
	Personalize Your Style	
	Be Concrete and Specific	
	Keep It Simple	
	Be Accurate	
	Avoid Redundancy	
	Avoid Excess	
	Bridge the Gaps	
Presenting the Informative Speech		

10 Informative Speaking

OBJECTIVES

When you finish this chapter, you should be able to

1. define reporting, discuss the uses of reporting, and identify the tools of reporting;
2. use the methods of narration, description, and simple explanation in reporting;
3. present a report;
4. define complex explanation;
5. develop an informative speech by going from the known to the unknown and by using illustrations;
6. explain a complex process;
7. identify the patterns of organization and choose an appropriate pattern to develop your informative speech;
8. identify the characteristics of a good outline; and
9. list the characteristics of an oral style and present an informative speech that uses an oral style.

10 Informative Speaking

> You're on vacation, driving the winding, hilly roads of western Wisconsin on your way to Minneapolis. Suddenly you realize that you may have taken the wrong road a few miles back. You turn into the next farmyard to ask the farmer for directions. After determining that you are bound for Minneapolis, the farmer says, "Turn around here in the driveway and go back in the direction you came from. Go back to the next road and turn left." (Notice he didn't say turn north.) "Follow Highway 93 until you hit I-94. Take the west exit." (He said "west" because that's the way the freeway entrances are marked.) You turn around, follow his clear directions, and soon you are on the right road once again.

It seems so simple when directions are given correctly. The tasks of giving information accurately and relating the known to the unknown, however, are not as simple as they might seem.

This chapter has two purposes: (1) to discuss the characteristics of reporting and give you experience in reporting information accurately and (2) to discuss the characteristics of complex explanation and give you experience in explaining a complex process.

Both of these kinds of speaking are called informative speaking, which is defined as the relating of factual data or personal opinion. Informative speaking covers many kinds of communication: the storyteller who entertains a group of children, the teacher who instructs a class, the vacuum cleaner salesperson who demonstrates before a group in a department store, the coach who explains a football play on the chalkboard, the instructor who trains ballet dancers through drills, the military officer who gives briefings on maneuvers, the professor who lectures on historical movements, and the television reporter who reviews a crime. All these are engaging in informative speaking, and they all share two essential traits:

1. They *report* information accurately.

2. They explain complex information by relating known information to unknown information and by using illustrations.

REPORTING

Reporting is done regularly in academic situations when a dean, for example, reports to the faculty. Reports are also made in professional associations, unions, clubs, societies, and classrooms, including public speaking classrooms.

In the first part of this chapter, we will define reporting, describe its uses, list the tools of reporting, and explain the methods and patterns of organization used in reporting.

Definition of Reporting

Reporting is the presentation of information. Reporting should attempt to be neutral, objective, and unbiased, although this ideal is often difficult to achieve. Suppose, for example, a speaker presents an oral report on Lourdes, a Roman Catholic shrine in France. If the report is neutral, unbiased, and objective, the listener should not be able to tell whether the speaker is Roman Catholic, Protestant, Islamic, Jewish, agnostic, or atheist.

If the report on Lourdes states, "Mary, Mother of God, appeared to Bernadette at Lourdes and caused many miracles to happen," the report is not neutral because it contains words based on faith: "Mother of God," "appeared," and "miracles." A neutral report might state, "Lourdes is a town in France where a Christian shrine is dedicated to Mary, the mother of Jesus. Thousands of cures are alleged to have taken place there, and

Reporting is the objective, factual presentation of information. Organizations make decisions based on the information collected by specially appointed individuals or committees. Reporting is an essential part of an organization's operating procedure.

medical doctors of many religious persuasions can offer no scientific explanation for about sixty cases involving swift transformations from illness to health."

Reporting should be accurate and factual but also tactful. On matters when the feelings of an individual may be hurt, good judgment should be used. A speech instructor, for example, tries to build students' self-confidence, rather than self-consciousness. An objective report of a student's first presentation could do more harm than good. In the beginning of the speech class, it is good to look at the positive aspects of a student's presentation. After a base is built, there's time for stronger criticism, but even then the approach should be constructive. The result is a confidence-building message, rather than a completely objective report.

In the play *Nothing But the Truth* by James Montgomery, one of the characters bets that he can tell the truth for a specified period of time. He does so, but he lands in all kinds of trouble. We can't always tell all the truth about our neighbor's child's attempts to play the violin, but insofar as we can in our speechmaking, we should make our reports neutral, unbiased, objective, accurate, and factual.

Uses of Reporting

In associations, unions, clubs, and societies, reporting is an essential part of the regular procedure. Perhaps you belong to such a group. As a member, you are probably aware that these groups have standing committees on membership, finance, and entertainment, to name a few. Reports from these committees are presented by one of the members to the larger assembly for further discussion and disposition through voting.

Organized societies also regularly appoint special committees whenever the organization must deal with a proposal for which it believes additional information should be available before a vote is taken. Essentially, such a fact-finding committee's job is to gather information and present it to the organization in a formal report so that a wise decision can be made on the proposal. For example, a large national student association considering a proposal to hold its next annual convention at a certain university might appoint a special committee to investigate the housing facilities, meeting rooms, food services, and relative transportation costs involved.

Students contemplating careers in law, medicine, business, education, engineering, or any other profession may expect that, to the degree they achieve success and prominence in these fields, they will be called on to present reports. Furthermore, success in presenting reports can lead to further prominence and success. Legal investigators are commissioned to study and report on the effects of old laws and the problems of enforcing new ones. Medical personnel report on epidemics, new diseases, and new cures. Business analysts report on marketing trends. Professors and teachers, advised to "publish or perish," report on their research and teaching methods at state and national conventions. Consulting engineers report feasibility studies on freeway design, rocket manufacture, or hydroelectric plant operation. As we can see, then, reporting is used in a variety of situations. In order to make an effective report, however, a speaker must know the tools of reporting and understand how to use them.

Tools of Reporting

The basic tools of reporting are called the five W's and the one H: who, what, where, when, why and how. Answers to these questions provide factual, accurate information. The tools of reporting enable the speaker to give the listeners factual, accurate information in the report.

Consider the following example in terms of the tools of reporting. Notice the specific, concrete detail the speaker used in his speech on water safety.

The temperature had been in the nineties for several days that humid August, so there was nothing original about my asking Jim and George to go for a cool swim. The only trouble was I didn't know Jim couldn't swim.	When Who
We got to my aunt's summer home on Phantom Lake just before suppertime and immediately took a rowboat to a floating raft about twenty yards from shore. About halfway out I jumped in the water and asked Jim to follow. "I can't swim," was his answer.	Where When What Where
Interpreting his remark to mean, "I'm not a very good swimmer," I dared him to jump in anyway. Well, he took the dare and he was right—he couldn't swim. Splashing away, he went under about a foot, came up, and started to go under again. Confidently, I reached over to grab him, but suddenly his arms locked around my head. I never realized how strong a drowning man can be.	Who How
We both started to go down, and although I exerted all my strength to get free, by then he had me in a death grip that left me helpless. I started to gulp some water and for a moment thought I was going to get away. But just as I began to get free, I could feel the strength of his muscles as his arms tightened around me like a boa constrictor.	What How
At that moment, with both of us struggling—I hadn't given up but honestly thought that was the end—I felt something or someone pulling very hard at Jim. In a second, it seemed, all three of us—Jim, George, and I— were at the surface. Jim and I were splashing and coughing very hard. Once I got a decent breath of air, it wasn't so difficult for George and me to get Jim to the raft where he hung on desperately. Meanwhile, George went swimming after the drifting boat.	Who Where

The speaker in the example used the tools of reporting to answer the questions who, what, where, when, and how in his speech. When you use your own experience or the experiences of others to make a point in your informative report, be sure that you answer the questions who, what, where, when, why, and how. Using these tools will help you gather information, then use it to give a complete report.

Methods of Reporting

The methods of reporting are the ways you can use to present your material interestingly, accurately, and clearly. These methods are narration, description, and simple explanation.

Narration.   Narration is storytelling based on real experiences or fictional creations. An ordinary story using the basic tools of reporting is okay, but a dramatic story using conflict, suspense, climax, personalities, and unusual settings can make the speaker's report more interesting and dynamic.

Conflict can be of many kinds: individual versus self, individual versus individual, individual versus a group, or society versus society. Other possibilities are nature versus an individual or a group, individuals versus animals, animal versus animal, or animal versus nature. The possibilities and combinations seem endless Wherever we look there is conflict. Examine the stories on the front page of tonight's newspaper. Notice both the open and the underlying conflicts in headlines, such as "Night Watchman Killed," "Fire Guts Restaurant," or "Political Pot Boiling in Mideast."

If a television announcer opens a program by saying, "This is the story of the *Savannah*, the first steamship to cross the Atlantic," much of the dramatic effectiveness of the program is lost. Because you know that the ship made the crossing successfully, suspense is eliminated. A better introduction for the program might be, "This is the story of the steamship *Savannah* and its fight to cross the treacherous Atlantic." This type of introduction arouses suspense because it introduces conflict but does not reveal the outcome.

In every dramatic story there is a high moment when the "good guy" or the "bad guy" wins. We call this turning point the climax of the story. There may be a series of lesser moments, called subclimaxes, when either the hero or the villain scores a triumph, but ultimately one or the other has to be the victor. It's very important to prevent the climax of the story from taking place too soon; otherwise, whatever happens later lacks interest. Speakers should arrange their material so that the account builds to a high point, the climax.

Most stories have people in them. While animals or such forces of nature as wind, sea, or volcanoes, are often important elements in a narrative, in most cases real persons or persons who seem real are the major concern of the storyteller. As far as possible, persons in a story should speak their own words. Characters in a story develop mainly by the way they express themselves in various situations that occur. Their temperament reveals their character.

A circus, a sports stadium, a funeral home, Glacier National Park, a slaughterhouse, and the inside of a cave are all unusual locations. Using such an unusual location as the setting for a narration will help make the report more interesting.

Description.   Description, which may be either scientific or artistic, is giving a word picture. Scientific description accurately answers such questions as how high, how deep, how wide, how long, and how to put together. Scientific description attempts to explain what frequently is complicated to the average person. We will explore this topic in more detail in the second part of this chapter when we discuss complex explanation.

Artistic description is creative in its appeal to the senses of sight, hearing, touch, smell, and taste. Notice in the following passage how the speaker appeals carefully to more than just the sense of sight.

> The best way I know to watch autumn is to sit on a log in the middle of the forest. Squirrels are busy workers. Before storing hickory nuts, they hasten their fall by running along the tree limbs and *shaking* the branches. The steady falling nuts sound like *rain on the leaves* below. Down in the marsh, cattails stand like burned-out candles The sumac is rusting on the hills, and the maples are starting to blush. Crows fly by and taunt everything. A rabbit zigzags across the *crunchy* leaves. I feel a slight *chill* in the air as the sun sinks lower and the cool breeze brings the *smell* of pines. My *appetite* quickens for a *tasty* stew, and I head for home intent on enjoying the *crackle* of a log in the fireplace, the first of the season.

Description brings detail to reporting. Scientific description affords clarity through accuracy, and artistic description heightens attention and interest through its creativity and multisensory appeal.

Simple Explanation.   In order to explain something, even something simple, you need to follow the basic steps followed in almost any type of speech: starting point, specific purpose, arrangement and development of subpoints, and summary. For a clear, interesting starting point, begin with something common to both you and your listener. Don't begin with something foreign to your listeners, plunging them into the cold waters of your selfish interests. Warm the water, as it were, and then lead them from the charted, shallow shoreline to the deeper areas of unfamiliar ideas.

To make it easy for your listeners to understand and remember, present a clear, specific purpose. Don't tackle a subject that is too broad, such as a report of childhood diseases. Limit your report to a single childhood disease, perhaps measles. Then word your specific purpose according to the reaction you want from your listeners: "I want my listeners to understand how to care for someone who has measles."

Arrangement of subpoints depends first of all on clarity and secondly on interest. Arrange your subpoints in a sequence that is orderly, consistent, and easy to follow.

The summary is your last chance to reach your listeners. Restate your specific purpose and summarize your subpoints. Resist the temptation to start over parts of the speech while you are summarizing. A summary is not the place to introduce new material. If you forgot something in the body of your speech, don't bring it in at this point.

COMPLEX EXPLANATION

Just before commencement, a college senior approached his psychology professor and said, "Now that the course is over and the grades are in, I want to tell you that this is the best course I ever took. I found it easy to learn. You made every lecture clear. I always knew what you were talking about. What is the secret of your teaching?"

"Illustration," replied the professor. "Use stories, examples, analogies, cases, anecdotes, and dramatized statistics. Use anything that will help you get your ideas across."

Years of experience have proved that the psychology professor was right. Good teaching, of course, includes many qualities but one of the most important factors is using illustrations of many kinds. The same attribute applies to complex explanation in informative speaking.

A technical writer once said, "Something is clear only when it means the same thing to everyone who reads it." If this statement applies to *written* material, think how much more it applies to spoken material. Readers can go back and reread the written word, but how often can listeners play back a recording of someone's oral communication? Usually, listeners must understand something the first time it is spoken or they will not get it at all.

When training his officers in how to give directions, Napoleon used to warn them, "If you *can* be misunderstood, you *will* be." Experienced teachers frequently ask, "Are there any questions?" They know how challenging it is to be instantly clear and how easy it is to be misunderstood. Explanation is not adequate if it summarizes only for those who already understand. The speaker must go further and make the meaning clear for those who don't understand.

Definition of Explanation

Explanation is making a concept understandable. Its purpose is to give meaning or interpretation to something that is not known or understood. Explanation, simple as it sounds, has an underlying meaning—to flatten so that all may see. In everyday language it says, "Level with me. Lay your cards on the table. Let's get things out in the open."

Purpose of Explanation

Recall the example used in Chapter 3 in the section on specific purpose (p. 42). *How* to throw a curve ball is different from *why* a baseball curves. Explaining how to throw a curve involves a demonstration of the skills involved: gripping the ball on the seams, snapping the wrist, and releasing the ball at the desired angle. Explaining why a baseball curves involves a consideration of certain principles of physics related to speed, spin, atmosphere, wind, and gravity. Explaining how to throw a curve requires at least a partial physical demonstration. Explaining why the ball curves requires more use of visual aids to show cause-and-effect relationships.

In order to determine clearly what you are explaining, write down in one carefully worded sentence exactly what you want to explain. This procedure helps you determine exactly what you want your listeners to understand and remember. Unless you determine specifically what you want your listeners to understand, you will have difficulty in finding a starting point, organizing your subpoints and arriving at a clear-cut conclusion. Instead of having neat individual servings of meat, potatoes, and vegetables, you wind up with hash.

Effective Methods of Explanation

Going from the known to the unknown is one way to explain material effectively. Illustrating through stories, examples, analogies, anecdotes, and dramatized statistics is another time-proven technique of effective explanation. Both these methods build bridges of communication between the speaker and the listeners.

Going from the Known to the Unknown.   Presenting complex material can be easy if you learn to hang new ideas on the pegs of old ideas. The purpose of a peg is to hold up and support the garment that hangs on it. Drawing your listeners' attention to the way students balance textbooks against the hip as they walk down the hall is a good peg to support an explanation of a recommended way to hold a baby if you have only one free hand. Because they involve common experiences, both of these pegs present a clear, familiar picture to your listeners.

In going from the known to the unknown, from the easy to the hard, from the simple to the complex, the speaker follows the most fundamental principle in teaching and learning. Suppose, for example, you are trying to explain to a man born blind what the colors red and blue are like. You say, "Blue and red are two of the three primary colors. If you mix them together, you get purple." Now that wouldn't help very much, would it? The man was born blind. Suppose instead you applied the principle of going from the known to the unknown and came up with this approach:

> Here, let me take this butter knife and press it against your cheek. Cool, isn't it? Well, that's what the color blue is like. It's a cool color. Now let me take my father's old briar pipe, which he's been smoking, and let me press the bowl of the pipe against your cheek. Warm, isn't it? Well, that's what the color red is like. It's a warm color.

Now you may argue, correctly, that the blind man still doesn't know what the colors red and blue really are. But he does have some idea, and you did the best you could under the circumstances.

Consider another example. You are trying to explain to a seven-year-old child what is meant by "renting a house." You tell the child, "In order to protect ourselves against the weather, we enter into an agreement with Mr. Miller, the landlord, who owns this house. We agree to pay him $400 a month, and he agrees to let us live in the lower flat." This approach is not likely to be very successful. Another approach might have greater appeal to the comprehension level of the seven-year-old.

> You don't have a bicycle, do you, Lynn? And you don't have a vegetable bowl full of nickels, dimes, and quarters to buy a bicycle, do you? But you do have two quarters that Grandma gave you, don't you? Well, those two quarters aren't enough to pay for a bicycle, but if you give those quarters to Sharon next door, she'll let you ride her bicycle all afternoon. You won't buy her bicycle; you'll just rent it.
>
> Now that's what Mommy and Daddy do when they rent our house from Mr. Miller. Daddy and Mommy give Mr. Miller some money, and Mr. Miller lets us live here. We don't buy the house with the money we give him. We just rent it.

Explaining the unknown in terms of what is already known is most often used as a starting point for a speech, but you will find it effective whenever a new idea calls for clarification. Whenever you introduce a new idea, hang it on an old idea, one familiar to your listeners. Go from the known to the unknown.

Illustrating.   Another effective method of explanation is illustration. You can illustrate your explanation with stories, examples, analogies, anecdotes, and statistics. Telling stories is often the easiest way of getting through to your listeners. Abraham Lincoln made frequent and effective use of this technique. Once, when he was asked if he thought a civil war was possible, he told the following story.

> When I was a young lawyer, and Illinois was little settled, I with other lawyers, used to ride the circuit. Once a long spell of pouring rain flooded the whole country. Ahead of us was Fox River, larger than all the rest, and we could not help saying to each other, "If these small streams give us so much trouble, how shall we get over Fox River?" Darkness fell before we had reached that stream, and we all stopped at a log tavern, had our horses put up and resolved to pass the night. Here we were right glad to fall in with the Methodist Presiding Elder of the circuit, who rode it in all weather, knew all its ways, and could tell us all about Fox River. So we all gathered around him and asked him if he knew about the crossing of Fox River. "Oh yes," he replied, "I know all about Fox River. I have crossed it often and understand it well. But I have one fixed rule with regard to Fox River: I never cross it till I reach it."[1]

Using an example, especially if it tells a story, is another way to illustrate. A life insurance company executive, in a speech on human relations, used an experience of his sister's to clarify what he meant by the question, "Did you give that needed pat on the back?"

> I distinctly remember an incident involving my sister. When she was learning to sew in grade school, she made the mistake of sewing the ends of the sleeve of a blouse together so that she couldn't get into it. That evening, between tears, she told us how the teacher, before the whole class, had said she would never be a seamstress. My sister was so embarrassed and humiliated that the memory of the incident has stayed with her always, and to this day she doesn't know how to sew. How much better it would have been if the teacher had begun with a verbal pat on the back by mentioning some of the better features of the blouse before offering criticisms. Let's give that needed pat on the back.

An analogy is a comparison of one thing with another. For example, astronomer Robert Jastrow asks his readers to imagine the individual atoms in a kitchen table as grains of sand. On this scale, the table would be 2000 miles long. Or if the outer shell of the electron in the atom were the size of the Astrodome, the nucleus of the atom would be a ping-pong ball in the center of the Astrodome.[2] An apt analogy is a rhetorical picture worth a thousand words.

An anecdote is a usually short narrative of an interesting and often amusing incident. Anecdotes are frequently used to explain the personality of an individual. In the following anecdote notice how the personality of the rebellious student and that of the professor are contrasted.

> A history major at the University of Wisconsin-Madison, one in a class of 250 students, glanced through the midsemester examination for the course, rose before the class and said, "I refuse to take this exam. It's an insult to our intelligence and has about as much validity as a pile of sawdust. It was conceived in idiocy. It merely requires a regurgitation of the material we read in the course. I'm going out for some fresh air." And he stomped out amid a ripple of comment and applause. The history professor who taught the course was not present at the time. He commented later, "That was an extremely inconsiderate action. The student should have walked out quietly."

Statistics are facts expressed in numbers. Because of their concentrated nature, however, statistics sometimes come like a flash flood with most of their meaning running down into the storm sewer.

The way to present statistics clearly and understandably is to dramatize them. You can do that by using charts, pictures, and graphs. It's easy enough to say that 6 million people reside in metropolitan Chicago, but that numerical fact becomes more interesting and meaningful if you dramatize it.

> Six million people in Chicago means that if you stood in front of Tribune Tower eight hours a day, five days a week, and one person passed by each second, you'd stand in front of that tower for about ten months.

You may have to do some arithmetic to dramatize statistics, but the end result justifies the effort. Your listeners understand and remember the point you wished to make.

ORGANIZING THE INFORMATIVE SPEECH

To organize an informative speech, you, as a speaker, perform three tasks. You structure your speech according to the three standard divisions of introduction, body, and conclusion. You then choose a pattern of organization for your speech. Finally, you outline your speech, following the general guidelines for outlining.

Standard Divisions

The standard divisions of a speech are the introduction, the body, and the conclusion. The introduction, an invitation to listening, should create an interesting relationship between speaker, subject, audience, and occasion. The introduction is a means to get the audience to listen to the body, the main part, of the speech. In the body you should outline the main points and subpoints of your topic. In the conclusion, restate the specific purpose of your speech and briefly summarize its main points.

Patterns of Organization

In Chapter 3, "Speech Preparation," you learned that a pattern of organization is a method of putting parts together in a unified whole. You choose a pattern of organization as a method to order your material to create a preliminary, overall view. Some commonly used patterns of organization are the chronological, spatial, topical, logical, psychological, pro and con, and problem-solution patterns. You may want to review the discussion of these patterns in Chapter 3.

Chronological. The chronological pattern (in the order of time) follows the sequence of past, present, future. This pattern is used primarily in narration, which covers storytelling, sharing of anecdotes, and relating of personal experiences.

Spatial. The spatial pattern is used in scientific description: how long, how wide, how deep? This pattern may seem simple, but consider that it is often used by the major national powers in discussing strategic geographical locations for national defense installations.

Topical. Sometimes called the grocery list, the topical pattern sets out a series of steps needed to reach a goal. The "how-to" speech is typical of the topical pattern: "Three Ways to Get A's."

Logical. Using a logical pattern, a speaker defends one side of an issue: either the pro or the con.

Psychological. A speaker using the psychological pattern presents the report in terms of the listener's background, interests, abilities, and prejudices. Starting with the listener's interests, the speaker builds a bridge to his or her own interests.

Pro and Con. In pro and con reporting, the speaker points out the good and the bad, the true and the false, the advantages and the disadvantages—all in order to present a fair, balanced picture.

Problem-Solution. If speakers want to make a completely objective report using the problem-solution pattern, they present a factual account of the problem, analyze major causes, and present possible solutions. Then, without taking sides, they summarize the possible solutions, letting the listeners decide which solution is best.

Principles of Outlining

As you learned in Chapter 3, an outline is to a speech what an itinerary is to a traveler or a blueprint to the builder of a house. There are two main types of outlines: the key phrase outline and the complete sentence outline. Generally, for speeches of complex explanation, the complete sentence outline works best. The key phrase outline is usually too incomplete and, therefore, not immediately clear enough for complex explanation. An outline that contains complete sentences is much more helpful to the speaker.

In this section, we will review some of the guidelines for making an outline. Developing your outline according to these guidelines should prove helpful, especially when you must deliver your speech extemporaneously.

Consistency in Using Symbols.

As you have learned, a symbol is a sign used to represent something. In outlining, a symbol is a sign used to distinguish relationships between the points of your speech. The symbols most often used in outlining are Roman numerals to indicate main points, capital letters to indicate major subdivisions, Arabic numbers to indicate minor subdivisions, and lowercase letters to indicate further subdivisions. The symbols must always be in combinations of two or more. For example, for each Roman numeral I, there must be a II. For every capital A, there must be at least a B. An outline using these symbols might look like this:

I.
  A.
  B.
    1.
    2.
      a.
      b.
II.
  A.
    1.
    2.
    3.
  B.
  C.

Coordination and Subordination.

As you learned in Chapter 3, subordination means putting under. Coordination, on the other hand, means making equal.

In an outline the symbols indicate coordination and subordination.

- I, II, and III are coordinate—of equal value.
- A, B, and C are coordinate to one another, but subordinate to I, II, and III.
- 1, 2, and 3 are coordinate to one another but subordinate to A, B, and C.
- a, b, and c are coordinate to one another but subordinate to 1, 2, and 3.

The following example shows how to make an outline using the standard divisions and symbols to indicate coordination of main points and subordination of subpoints.

Introduction

I. Would you like to be able to explain complex concepts more easily?   Get attention

II. It's not as hard as it seems.   Break down prejudice

III. The title of my talk is "Am I Getting Through to You?"   Give title

IV. In my talk today I'd like to show you how to explain a complex process.   State specific purpose

V. I'd like to explain the techniques of going from the known to the unknown and the ways of using illustrations.   Enumerate subpoints of speech

Body

I. I will explain going from the known to the unknown.   State the first main point

   A. I will use the example of a blind man and the colors of red and blue.   State subpoints

   B. I will use the example of a little girl and renting a house.

II. I will explain illustrating.   State the second main point

   1. I will explain telling stories: swimming.

   2. I will explain using examples: Lincoln.

   3. I will explain using analogies: atoms and grains of sand.

   4. I will explain relating anecdotes: history professor.

   5. I will explain dramatizing statistics: people in Chicago.

Conclusion

I. In my talk today, I've tried to describe how to explain a complex process.   Restate specific purpose

II. As you will recall, there are two methods to use: going from the known to the unknown and illustrating.   Summarize main points

III. Now that you know how to explain, you know how to teach and can apply to the president of this university for a job.   End with something clever

Overlapping. As you may recall, perfect categories and classifications are difficult to determine. You should strive for as little overlap as possible in developing an outline.

Single Idea Per Main Point. Each item in the outline should contain only one point. For example, suppose the outline of the introduction read:

Introduction

I. Get attention and/or break down prejudice.

This outline violates the rule of using only one idea per main point. A solution to this problem might be:

Introduction

I. Get attention.
II. Break down prejudice.

Following these rules of outlining should help you develop a speech that is clear and effective, one that will get and hold your listeners' attention. By now you probably realize that knowing the methods and rules for giving a speech are not enough to make your speech effective; you must be able to apply the methods, tools, and rules in your presentation.

DEVELOPING AN ORAL STYLE

An oral style is a manner of speaking well informally. You're probably familiar with the written style of textbooks. They tend to be in the formal style of disciplined prose. Don't you wish that some textbooks talked to you, not at you? That's the way audiences feel when speakers talk to them in a stilted and formal manner.

Read the following two examples. The first illustrates a written, formal style.

> In view of the increased inflation that Americans have experienced during the past decade, it might be advantageous to ascertain the causes behind this inflation.

Here's the same idea expressed in an oral style:

> Your dollar today isn't worth as much as it was ten years ago. Ten years ago you could buy lunch for a lot less. That same lunch costs you about twice as much today. Do you know why?

The following list of suggestions recommends some methods you can use to develop a clear and effective oral style.

Personalize Your Style

Use personal pronouns such as "I," "you," and "we." In general, use contractions. "It's" flows better than "it is"; "we'll" sounds more conversational than "we will."

Be Concrete and Specific

Something concrete is real, factual, specific, and related to experience. If someone asked you, "What's to eat?" a concrete answer might be, "Chocolate cream pie." If you answered, "a pie," you would be going up one level of abstraction. If you said, "dessert," your answer would be even more abstract. By the time you reached the general category of "food," you would be still further removed from the original concrete answer, the chocolate cream pie.

To be specific, you search for words that express precisely what you mean. "The jet plane traveled faster than the speed of sound" is specific; "The plane traveled very fast" is general.

Keep It Simple

Lois and Selma De Rahey are professors of scientific communication at Baylor College of Medicine. Their term for excessive and stilted wordiness is *medicalese*. To combat it, they give seminars to doctors who would like to become more articulate. When is the last time you asked your physician, "What does that mean, Doctor?"

Avoid long, involved sentences and stilted language in your speech, especially if the subject matter is highly technical. The use of synonomous terms can improve clarity. Don't say, "When breathing, use your diaphragm and intercostal muscles." Say instead, "Breathe deeply and fully," if you are talking to a nonmedical audience.

Although technical language is precise language for experts, the average person may not understand unless you explain the language immediately. Instead of using the words "212 degrees Fahrenheit" or "100 degrees Celsius," you could say "the point at which water boils."

Be Accurate

There are roughly 5000 feet in a mile, but often it is better to state the precise measurement, 5280 feet. And so it is with ideas. It is clearer to say, "The Labour government in England passed some socialist measures," than to say, "England went socialistic." Remember, as far as listeners are concerned, the quality of ideas increases when they are stated in words that are accurate expressions of those ideas.

Avoid Redundancy

A radio announcer might announce the time, "At the sound of the tone, the correct Central Standard Time will be two o'clock P.M. in the afternoon." The announcer could avoid redundancy by saying, "At the tone, two P.M." To illustrate, someone once pointed out that Lincoln's Gettysburg Address contains 266 words, the Declaration of Independence has 300 words, and a certain government order on cabbage prices contains 26, 911 words.

Avoid Excess

A *Milwaukee Journal* editorial asks:

> *What has happened to the English language? Why can't sturdy words still carry the same punch that they had in the past? The answer is that many words—like a worn out flashlight battery—have been drained of their voltage by overuse. For example, take adjectives such as huge, tremendous, hilarious, fantastic, amazing, alarming, colossal, astounding, unbelievable. What do they really mean nowadays when a quiet luncheon meeting can be a "huge success," a flea circus can be "tremendous," and the mildest surprises can be "amazing"? When truly momentous events take place, how can anyone find words powerful enough to fit the need?*[3]

Bridge the Gaps

Phrases such as "in other words," "for instance," "let's put it another way," "that means," and the often used, always effective "for example" make the speaker's style more conversational. These phrases are useful devices when the speaker wants to clarify a point, introduce another example, or move on to a new subpoint.

PRESENTING THE INFORMATIVE SPEECH

Finding, organizing, developing, and directing ideas toward the goal of imparting information, whether in reporting or explaining, are the verbal means of presenting your speech. In addition to these verbal means, there are nonverbal means, both visual and vocal. It's almost impossible for you, as a speaker, to communicate effectively through words alone. You need to support your words with bodily action or, more specifically, with gestures. Let your body help you explain. Demonstrate. Use gestures. Your listeners will enjoy all the more what you have to say. Not only will your presentation be clearer, it will be more interesting.

Let your voice help you, too. Speak with enough volume so that all can hear easily. Stress the important words. Talk to, not at, your listeners. Avoid the tone of a reciter. Let the quality of your voice respond to subtle meanings. Pause for reflection and understanding. Enunciate clearly. By successfully applying these techniques, you will communicate and explain more effectively.

SUMMARY

Informative speaking, defined as the relating of data or personal opinion, is the basis of communication. Reporting and complex explanation are the two basic types of informative speaking. Reporting is the presentation of information. This type of speaking is often used in classrooms, business, industry, various professional fields, and organized groups, both social and political. The characteristics of reporting are neutrality, objectivity, fairness, and tact.

The basic tools of reporting are the five W's and the one H: who, what, where, when, why, and how. By answering these questions in your report, you give the audience accurate, concrete, factual information. You can use various methods of reporting to present information accurately, interestingly, and clearly. These methods are narration, description (both scientific and artistic), and simple explanation.

Complex explanation is the second major type of informative speaking. In complex explanation, your goal is to make a complicated concept clear, plain, and understandable to the audience. Two ways of explaining a complex subject are going from the known to the unknown and illustrating through the use of stories, examples, analogies, anecdotes, and dramatized statistics. To determine clearly what is to be explained, you should write down in one carefully worded sentence exactly what you wish to explain. A clear, complete sentence outline of the speech of complex explanation will help you when the speech must be delivered extemporaneously. Complex explanation in public speaking is best presented in an oral style. In an effective oral style, use simple sentence structure; personalize the information; be concrete, specific, and accurate; keep the use of technical language to a minimum by using simple, understandable terms; and avoid redundancy.

ASSIGNMENTS

1. The purpose of this assignment is to help you develop skill in reporting factually in an objective, unbiased, fair, and accurate manner. Deliver a four- to five-minute report on one phase of a larger problem. Try to be fair so that your listeners cannot tell what side you are on. See the list of speech topics in the appendix for suggestions.

2. The purpose of this assignment is to help you develop skill in explaining complex concepts, processes, or theories. Choose a subject on which to speak. Explain the central idea of your speech by defining terms and using stories, examples, analogies, anecdotes, dramatized statistics, and any visual aids that might be helpful. See the list of speech topics in the appendix for suggestions. (four to five minutes)

3. Read the following report on a problem. Does it follow the criteria for reporting set up in the chapter? Which ones? Write a one-page critical evaluation of the report.

TEEN SUICIDE AT ALL-TIME HIGH
BY KEN FRANCKLING
UNITED PRESS INTERNATIONAL

At times in the healthiest stage of their lives more and more American young people find little to live for, choosing death over life in a society shaped for them by adults.

Suicide, the second leading killer of teenagers in the United States, is at an all-time high. And experts predict it will continue to rise through the late 1980s.

Figures from the Centers for Disease Control in Atlanta show an increase of almost 300% in adolescent suicides, those age 15 to 24, in the past 30 years. It is the only age group in America whose death rate has risen consistently.

The adolescent suicide rate, reflected in death certificates, has grown from 4.5 per 100,000 population in 1950 to 12.3 per 100,000 in 1980, the CDC said. An estimated 6,000 teenagers committed suicide last year in the United States.

In fact, suicide recently passed homicide to become the No. 2 leading killer of adolescents in America, second only to accidents. Some experts believe suicide soon will become No. 1 because stiffer drunken driving laws are reducing accident levels.

Others suspect it already is the No. 1 cause of death among teens, because they know some traffic accidents and drownings were suicides but have been ruled otherwise.

Cross-section of America

The victims represent a cross-section of America, rich and poor, and middle class. From cities. From suburbs. From rural areas. There are no economic or social barriers. There is no limitation to "problem kids."

Experts are frustrated at the scope of the problem because they believe suicide is "the most preventable kind of death there is," as Andrew Slaby, psychiatrist in chief at Rhode Island Hospital in Providence, put it.

"Suicide is anger turned inward," Slaby said. "Suicide is something that's not talked about very much in society, even though other things like drugs and sex are discussed openly. Because no one talks about it, adolescents who kill themselves don't realize that other people feel depressed, too."

Psychiatrists and other health officials cite a number of factors that can lead to suicide. All represent the fundamental changes in American society over the past three decades.

Those include higher divorce rates and family disintegration, high mobility of households as executives move around the country frequently, the unrealistic expectations of achievement-oriented youngsters and peer pressure.

"There is a breakdown in the ability to lean on others for support," says Barry Garfinkel, director of child and adolescent psychiatry at the University of Minnesota and one of the nation's experts on suicide.

Clusters of teenage suicides, like those in the last year in Texas and Westchester County, N.Y., focus public attention on the problem. They also lead officials to question whether the power of suggestion is a factor.

"Contagion seems to do more with the method than the decision itself," said Garfinkel. "The predisposition is already there in most cases. Those are communities where people are high achievers, go-getters, where there is dislocation."

Cosmetic Response

The Centers for Disease Control report the rate of suicide attempts is 8 to 10 times higher than the death rate.

New York Lt. Gov. Alfred B. DelBello, cochairman of the National Committee on Youth Suicide Prevention, said the nation had done little to come to grips with the problem.

"So far, the response has been largely cosmetic and feeble," Del-Bello said. "Why? Are we so unable to overcome the stigma attached to suicide? Is the search for answers so threatening?

"Those who believe suicide is unstoppable are wrong—tragically wrong. We must look the problem straight in the eye and respond on behalf of those thousands of young people who will otherwise choose death over life."[4]

4. Read the following explanation of the solar system. Notice how the writer uses an extended analogy to explain the topic. Does this explanation follow the criteria for complex explanation set up in the chapter? Write a one-page evaluation.

The sun is only one among 100 billion stars that are bound together by gravity into a large cluster of stars called the Galaxy. The stars of the Galaxy revolve about its center as the planets revolve about the sun. The sun itself participates in this rotating motion, completing one circuit around the Galaxy in 200 million years.

The Galaxy is flattened by its rotating motion into the shape of a disk, whose thickness is roughly one-fiftieth of its diameter. Most of the stars in the Galaxy are in this disk, although some are located outside it. A relatively small, spherical cluster of stars, called the nucleus of the Galaxy, bulges out of the disk at the center. The entire structure resem-

bles a double sombrero with the galactic nucleus as the crown and the disk as the brim. The sun is located in the brim of the sombrero about three-fifths of the way out from the center to the edge. When we look into the sky in the direction of the disk we see so many stars that they are not visible as separate points of light, but blend together into a luminous band stretching across the sky. This band is called the Milky Way.

The stars within the Galaxy are separated from one another by a distance of 30 trillion miles. In order to avoid the frequent repetition of such awkwardly large numbers, astronomical distances are usually expressed in units of the light year. A light year is defined as the distance covered in one year by a ray of light, which travels at 186,000 miles per second. This distance turns out to be six trillion miles; hence in these units the average distance between stars in the Galaxy is five light years, and the diameter of the Galaxy is 100,000 light years.

In spite of the enormous size of our galaxy, its boundaries do not mark the edge of the observable universe The 200-inch telescope on Mount Palomar has within its range no less than 10 billion other galaxies, each comparable to our own in size and containing a similar number of stars. The average distance between these galaxies is one million light years. The extent of the visible universe, as it can be seen in the 200-inch telescope, is 10 billion light years.

An analogy will help to clarify the meaning of these enormous distances. Let the sun be the size of an orange; on that scale of sizes the earth is a grain of sand circling in orbit around the sun at a distance of 30 feet; the giant planet Jupiter, 11 times larger than the earth, is a cherry pit revolving at a distance of 200 feet or one city block; Saturn is another cherry pit two blocks from the sun; and Pluto, the outermost planet, is still another sand grain at a distance of ten city blocks from the sun.

On the same scale the average distance between the stars is 2000 miles. The sun's nearest neighbor, a star called Alpha Centauri, is 1300 miles away. In the space between the sun and its neighbors there is nothing but a thin distribution of hydrogen atoms, forming a vacuum far better than any ever achieved on earth. The Galaxy, on this scale, is a cluster of oranges separated by an average distance of 2000 miles, the entire cluster being 20 million miles in diameter.

An orange, a few grains of sand some feet away, and then some cherry pits circling slowly around the orange at a distance of a city block. Two thousand miles away is another orange, perhaps with a few specks of planetary matter circling around it. That is the void of space.[5]

5. Choose a speech topic. Using the guidelines presented in the chapter, develop an informative speech by going from the known to the unknown. Present your speech using an oral style.

NOTES

1. Carl Sandburg, *Abraham Lincoln: The Prairie Years and the War Years* (New York: Harcourt Brace and World, 1954), I, p. 57.

2. Robert Jastrow, *Red Giants and White Dwarfs* (New York: Harper and Row, 1967), p. 9.

3. Editorial, *Milwaukee Journal,* 25 Nov. 1978.

4. Ken Franckling, "Teen Suicide at All Time High," *Milwaukee Journal,* 30 Oct. 1984.

5. Jastrow, pp. 11–13.

Definition and Overview of Persuasive Speaking

Propositions	Propositions of Policy
	Propositions of Fact
	Propositions of Value

Issues	Stock Issue Analysis
	Analysis of Issues in Propositions of Fact
	Analysis of Issues in Propositions of Value

Proof	Evidence	Valid Assumptions
		Facts
		Statistics
		Testimony
	Reasoning	Data
		Warrant
		Conclusion
		Toulmin Model of Reasoning
	Types of Reasoning	Generalization
		Causation
		Analogy
		Sign
		Deductive Reasoning
	Fallacies of Reasoning	Begging the Question
		Pseudoauthority
		Irrelevant Appeals
		Overgeneralization
		Faulty Classification

Developing a Speech of Conviction

A Sample Speech of Conviction

11 Persuasion Through Argumentation

OBJECTIVES

When you finish this chapter, you should be able to:

1. define persuasive communication;
2. know the basic parts of arguments;
3. analyze issues and discover arguments in support of a specific proposition;
4. explain the fallacies of reasoning; and
5. develop and present a persuasive speech of conviction on a specific proposition.

11 Persuasion Through Argumentation

Tony walked to the front of the room. He wanted to convince his audience that the school's proposed policy to raise next year's tuition by 10 percent was harmful to both the school and the students. Because Tony knew that emotional appeals alone would not sway his listeners, he armed himself with sound, logical arguments as well. When addressing the audience, he said, "According to our school's financial aid officer, Mr. Ted Jones, 'A rise of 10 percent in your tuition will cause a third of our students to drop out of school. They simply will not be able to pay the higher tuition cost.' "

In his opening remarks, Tony presented a causal argument to convince his listeners that higher tuition costs would cause a number of students to quit school. (We will define causal argument later in this chapter.) He attempted to persuade them through argumentation.

To learn how to prepare this type of persuasive message, we must first examine the essential components found in speeches of persuasion through argumentation. These elements include propositions, issues, and proof. We will begin, however, with a definition of persuasion.

Persuasion is the art of reinforcing or changing an attitude or behavior. Effective persuasive speakers analyze the audience and develop strategies that appeal to listeners' wants, needs, values, and beliefs.

DEFINITION AND OVERVIEW OF PERSUASIVE SPEAKING

Communication professors Teri Gamble and Michael Gamble view persuasive speaking's main goal as seeking "to reinforce or change an audience's beliefs."[1] This view of persuasive speaking captures its essential purpose: to reinforce or to change a point of view. But, in reinforcing or changing a point of view, the persuasive speaker may also affect an audience member's attitudes, values, or behaviors. We can add to Gamble and Gamble's view of persuasive speaking by defining it as *the art of reinforcing or changing beliefs, attitudes, values, or behaviors on a particular subject.*

According to the definition, persuasive speaking is an art. The word "art" in the definition means *the flexible application of concepts.* To perform an art, you must apply certain theories, principles, or techniques in order to attain the goal of the art. In this case, your goal is giving an effective persuasive speech. In this chapter we will introduce the important concepts of persuasive speaking and show you how to apply them in an artistic manner. You'll discover that certain persuasive strategies work well with some audiences. In other situations, similar persuasive techniques may not work as well, which is why you'll need to be flexible. Flexibility in speaking in general, and in persuasive speaking in particular, implies adaptability. By being flexible in the application of persuasive strategies, you are learning to adapt your message to a specific audience and occasion.

Argumentation means the discovery of *proof* underlying a statement, or *proposition.* In persuasion through argumentation, you use arguments to support your particular proposition. The arguments may be logical, appealing mainly to the *cognitive* (thinking or reasoning) *component* of persuasion. Other types of arguments appeal to *emotional and ethical components* of persuasion. Together, these arguments make up the broad boundaries of persuasive speaking.

In the next two chapters, we provide a broad overview of persuasion in public speaking. Because of the scope of topic areas in persuasion, we will consider them in two chapters: persuasion through argumentation (this chapter) and persuasion through motivation (Chapter 12). We believe this approach is a manageable way to learn the major proofs of persuasion—logical proofs, ethical proofs, and emotional proofs. Although you will learn about persuasion in two separate chapters, in reality, the persuasive act often encompasses all three modes of proof simultaneously. This holistic nature of persuasion allows a speaker, for example, both to influence a listener's cognitive process and, at the same time, to motivate the listener. If you keep this view of persuasion in mind, you'll find the study of persuasion more rewarding when attempting to send or evaluate persuasive messages.

In this chapter, "Persuasion Through Argumentation," we first examine the major types of propositions. A proposition is a statement of the major point we want our listeners to believe. Propositions are built on the analysis of issues. An issue is a question that reveals a point of disagreement or conflict between arguments. We will explore the nature and analysis of issues that underlie specific topics. From this exploration, we will learn to discover and formulate arguments (which provide proof) necessary for defending propositions. We will look at ways to formulate specific types of arguments. Finally, we will examine some of the major types of fallacies of reasoning that can weaken argumentation.

TYPES OF PROPOSITIONS

Before you can change or reinforce listeners' beliefs, values, attitudes, or actions, you need to know exactly what you want to modify. Is it in the area of flying saucers, President Kennedy's assassination, heart transplants, speed limits, wage and price controls, abortion, national defense, or scholarship plans?

Determining the general area is a good place to get started, but you can't attempt to change or reinforce beliefs, values, attitudes, or actions unless you first form your statement into a complete sentence called a proposition. A proposition in persuasive speaking is a thesis statement that requires proof.[2] A proposition should be narrowed to a specific statement and worded clearly. For example, you can't argue about "basketball," but you can argue that "the NCAA ought to investigate more thoroughly those colleges suspected of recruiting violations." There are three major types of propositions: Propositions of policy, propositions of fact, and propositions of value.

Propositions of Policy

"We should increase Social Security benefits by 5 percent." "The United states government should adopt a national health care plan." These are propositions of policy. A proposition of policy is *a statement that calls for a specific plan to be adopted.* To prove that a proposition should be adopted, a speaker must answer basic questions or issues, which, in turn, need the support of evidence.

The success or failure of a proposition of policy depends on your analysis of issues. One useful set of issues for analyzing a proposition of policy is called stock issues. These are standard questions dealing with the criteria of need, plan, and advantages versus disadvantages. Stock issues, used in the analysis of a proposition of policy, ask these three questions:

Stock Issue I: *Is there a need for drastic change in the current system?*
If Jane tries to persuade her father to buy a new car because the tires are bald, the paint faded, and the engine sluggish, her father might ignore her request and argue that the car still runs. But his position to keep the

current system in effect does not take care of the needs: bald tires, faded paint, and sluggish engine. If Jane cannot prove the need for a complete change, she may have to continue driving the car in its current condition.

Stock Issue 2: Is there a plan presented to meet the need for this change of policy? Who is going to pay for the new car? Will the father pay half and each of the two older teenaged children pay one fourth? How will the car be financed? By a loan? At what percent interest?

Stock Issue 3: Do the advantages of the plan outweigh the disadvantages? Will the interest charged on the loan over a two-year period be so high that the interest fees could be used to buy new tires, repaint the old car, and tune it up?

These stock issues help you organize and analyze your material according to the criteria of need, plan, and advantages versus disadvantages. Developing a proposition of policy becomes far more manageable when stock issues are used to analyze the proposition.

Propositions of Fact

A proposition of fact is *a statement that attempts to prove the truth or falsehood of a statement or alleged fact.* A proposition of fact might be, "Flying saucers are an impossibility," or "More than one assassin was involved in President Kennedy's death."

The basic ideas of need, plan, and advantages do not apply to propositions of fact. You judge a proposition of fact by the truth or falsehood of the statement. In the case of the flying saucer proposition, you need to judge the truth or falsehood of the statement that "flying saucers are an impossibility." Your analysis might include these questions:

1. Does the concept of flying saucers violate the laws of physics?
2. Are other explanations possible for most sightings of unidentified flying objects?
3. Do most experts believe that flying saucers exist?

If your analysis of these questions suggests that flying saucers do not exist, you can then argue the probable truth of your statement. There are no standard questions for a proposition of fact. You must generate such questions based on the truth or falsehood of the situation in question.

Propositions of Value

A proposition of value is *a statement that attempts to persuade a listener that something is either praiseworthy or blameworthy.* "The dance at school last night was terrible" or "our football team is great" are value statements. In analyzing a proposition of value, you reveal your beliefs of right or wrong, good or bad, moral or immoral. A proposition of value often relies on facts (as standards of judgment) for support. For example, if you say, "Chemical warfare is morally wrong," your statement indicates that you view such an act as something blameworthy. In a persuasive speech, you will need to support this value statement with facts. To find such facts, you must first analyze your value statement to establish the criteria by which to judge it. You might ask questions such as these:

Definition
Use
Effects

1. What is meant by chemical warfare?
2. How has it been used in the past?
3. What are some of its effects?
4. Do experts on the subject want chemical warfare banned? Why?
5. How many countries have banned its use? Why?

Your answers to these questions can provide support for your conviction that "chemical warfare is morally wrong." Such an analysis defends you against charges of being too subjective in your persuasive message. As with propositions of fact, no standard questions exist for propositions of value. You must analyze your proposition of value by defining important terms in the statement and by establishing criteria by which to judge your value statement.

ISSUES

Pat seemed confused by the choices he needed to make in his freshman year. Should he major in computer science? Should he take public speaking in the fall semester? Should he live on or off campus? Should he look for a part-time job? How could he possibly answer all these questions?

Pat realized that he had a number of difficult issues to decide. He knew that both sides of each issue would have to be explored before he could make an intelligent decision. You, too, will be facing a number of issues when you deliver a persuasive message.

As previously mentioned, issues reveal points of conflict or disagreement between opposing sides. Should Pat major in computer science, for example, is an issue in question form. It reveals a choice. One choice is to major in computer science; the other choice is not to major in computer science. Under each choice rest reasons for and against majoring in computer science. These reasons for and against reveal the clash between arguments.

Analysis of issues can help a speaker identify the arguments that best support the proposition and appear most believable and persuasive to the audience.

Stock Issue Analysis

One way to analyze a proposition of policy is to use stock issue analysis. As previously noted, the analysis covers the following issues: (1) Is there a *need* for change in the present situation? (2) What is the *best plan* for bringing about the change? (3) Do the *advantages* of the plan *outweigh* the *disadvantages*? A simple and effective method to analyze the proposition is to diagram the stock issues. Write the first issue (need) at the top of the page. Then, draw a line down the middle of the page. On the left-hand side, write arguments that support the position "need for change." On the right-hand side, write arguments for the opposing view. After each point, cite briefly the source, if any, for the argument. This will help you remember where your material came from. Follow this procedure for each remaining issue. As an example, let's diagram the proposition of policy that "University X should increase next year's tuition by 5 percent." Stock issue 1 is "Is there a *need* for University X to increase tuition by 5 percent?" The diagram of this issue may look something like this:

Stock Issue 1
Is there a need for University X to increase its tuition by 5 percent?

Pro	*Con*
1. Need higher salaries to attract new faculty. (University X's President "State of the University" remarks August 28, 1987)	1. Salary levels are already competitive with other schools of comparable size and status. (Report from University X's *Newsletter*, April 10, 1986, p. 3)
2. Higher operating costs are projected for next year. (President's "State of the University" remark)	2. It's difficult to project with certainty next year's operating budget. (Interview with Tom Smith, Director of University Budgets, April 15, 1987)
3. There is an anticipated 3 percent drop in student enrollment for next year. (Interview with Redmond Haskins, Registrar, April 14, 1987)	3. Although an anticipated drop expected, it should not affect next year's budget significantly. (Interview with Tom Smith)

To make your analysis manageable, keep the number of arguments small (from three to six arguments for each side of the issue). To list large numbers of arguments may appear impressive, but you can easily overwhelm a listener. You'll notice that by listing arguments for both sides of the issue, you develop a wider view of the topic. You are then in a better position to analyze the strengths and weaknesses of the arguments. For instance, you may even want to mention a point raised against your position. You then can show the weakness in the argument (possibly the argument is based upon outdated material).

You can analyze stock issue 2 in the same way:

Stock Issue 2
What is the plan for raising tuition by 5 percent at University X?

Proposed Plan	*Current Policy*
1. President will ask board of trustees for approval of a 5 percent tuition increase.	1. Currently, the president must seek input from the faculty for the need to raise tuition cost. (University Procedures and Guidelines, fall 1986, p. 27)
2. President will present proposal for tuition increase to Committee on State Educational Institutions in state legislature.	2. Representative from the president's office presents proposal for tuition increase to Committee on State Educational Institutions in state legislature. (University Procedures and Guidelines, p. 31)
3. President will send notice of increased tuition cost to students and parents by spring term.	3. President sends notice of increased cost to parents of students at University X. (University Procedures and Guidelines, p. 32)

In your diagram list any important differences between the existing plan and the proposed plan. This is important for three reasons. First, you'll need to see the differences that exist between the proposed plan and the present plan for performing particular tasks. Second, you'll need to see if the proposed plan actually satisfies the proposed needs. What good is a plan if it does not solve the problems identified in the analysis? Third, you'll need to discover advantages that exist in your plan. You'll want to make certain that the advantages of your plan outweigh any disadvantages.

The analysis of the third stock issue may look as follows:

Stock Issue 3
Do the advantages of the plan outweigh its disadvantages?

Advantages	*Disadvantages*
1. Plan will raise necessary funding to increase faculty salaries. ("State of University" remarks, August 28, 1987)	1. Plan may cause additional expenses for the university, such as additional mailing cost of letters to students.
2. Plan will raise necessary funding for meeting increased operating costs. ("State of University" remarks)	2. Plan may irritate faculty who are now bypassed in the process concerning tuition increases. (Interview with Dr. Emily Pit, Chairperson of Faculty Committee, April 19, 1987)

3. Plan will increase amount of money in contingency fund if projected decrease in enrollment occurs ("State of University" remarks)
4. Plan speeds up the process of seeking tuition increase from state legislature.
5. Plan will appear more credible if the president, and not one of the representatives from the president's office, appears before the state legislature.
6. Plan involves notifying the students who may be the ones responsible for paying tuition costs.

3. If plan fails, president's credibility may be diminished.

You can add more advantages and disadvantages as you uncover them. Based on your analysis, ask yourself if the advantages outweigh the disadvantages. If so, then you are in a strong position to argue for acceptance of your proposition of policy.

Analysis of Issues in Propositions of Fact

The diagramming of issues is not limited to stock issues that underlie propositions of policy. Issues related to propositions of fact or value can also be diagrammed. Suppose your proposition of fact is the statement "The sun rises in the east and sets in the west." You might diagram the issues and arguments in that proposition in the following way:

Issue 1
Does the sun possess the property of rising?

Pro
1. Millions of people witness it rise each day.
2. Every time that I go fishing in the early morning, I see the sun rise.

Con
1. The sun does not possess the physical property of rising.
2. The rotation of the earth causes the illusion of the sun rising.

Issue 2
Does the sun possess the property of setting?

Pro
1. Millions of people witness it set each day.
2. Every time I go for a walk in the early evening, I see the sun set.

Con
1. The sun does not possess the physical property of setting.
2. The rotation of the earth causes the illusion of the sun setting.

From this brief analysis, you can uncover the important issues inherent in the proposition of fact. They focus on the falsehood or truth of the situation. In this case, the sun's ability to rise or set. Arguments both pro and con are identified under each issue. You need to weigh the arguments and evidence to determine the truth or falsehood of the proposition.

Analysis of Issues in Propositions of Value

Likewise, propositions of value can be diagrammed. Issues for propositions of value focus on the praiseworthiness or blameworthiness of the object in question. For instance, if you say, "This movie is beautiful," you are praising it as being a good movie. Some of the possible issues and arguments for analysis under this proposition may include the following:

Issue 1
Is the acting of high quality?

Pro	*Con*
1. Leading actors in the movie have the reputation for being among the best in their profession.	1. Reputations alone are not enough to guarantee that an actor will do a good job.
2. The leading actors were nominated for academy awards.	2. The actors did not win the academy awards.

Issue 2
Is the photography of high quality?

Pro	*Con*
1. *New York Times* review praised the photography in the movie.	1. Review in *Times* magazine said the photography lacked professionalism.
2. Photographer was nominated for an academy award.	2. Photographer did not win an academy award.

From the brief analysis, you can locate important issues inherent in the proposition. Other issues for analysis might involve the quality of the director, script, or costumes. Each issue contains arguments and evidence for analysis. Note that factual statements are often utilized in attempts to establish the value advanced in the proposition.

When possible, arguments under the analysis of issues for propositions of policy, fact, or value need to be documented. This documentation helps establish the credibility of your arguments and evidence. Diagramming of issues helps you locate the proofs necessary for presenting your position. In the next section, we will examine the elements that make up proof: evidence and reasoning.

PROOF

Rosemarie knew that the members of her public speaking class were becoming more critical each day. They were no longer unquestioning listeners. They challenged speakers' propositions; they wanted to hear reasons and evidence, not just their opinions. Rosemarie prepared for her audience. She included ample proof to support her position. Her audience responded favorably. They appreciated her effort to inform them of important evidence and arguments on the issues.

Have you ever been asked to prove your point? As a public speaker, you are being asked to defend yourself—with ideas supported by reasons and evidence. This task becomes increasingly important when you advance propositions for audiences who may be unfamiliar with or skeptical of your position.

Persuasive speeches that seek to convince others of a particular point must contain the essential element of proof. In this section, we'll see that *proof consists essentially of evidence and arguments in support of a proposition.* Speakers can offer a number of proofs in a persuasive speech. The audience ultimately accepts or rejects those proofs. Select your proofs wisely, then, if you wish to convince your listeners.

Evidence

Evidence is the raw material of proof found in valid assumptions, facts, statistics, and testimony. Evidence is the initial point on which proof is built. As Douglas Ehninger suggests, "the evidence . . . is the ground upon which the argument rests, the base from which it starts, the matters of fact or opinion to which it ultimately appeals."[3]

Valid Assumptions.

A valid assumption is a self-evident starting point that is acceptable to the listener. In our society we may make the following valid assumptions:

Democracy is good.

This is the land of opportunity.

Justice should prevail.

Parents should be respected.

Students have rights.

Valid assumptions can be used as evidence if listeners believe them to be inherently true. Such assumptions rarely require any additional supporting evidence.

Facts.   In general, a fact is something that has actually happened or is true. From a purely empirical viewpoint, a fact is an observable, verifiable phenomenon. It is not a judgment or evaluation. If you see a driver make a right-hand turn from the middle lane, you can designate this phenomenon as a fact. Physical facts can be observed by any of the senses, but they must be verified or tested. To test a fact, we ask these important questions to determine its truth:

a. Is the fact current? If it is not current, it may be inaccurate when compared to more current ones.

b. How was the fact gathered? By controlled experiment? By verifiable observation?

c. Is it consistent with other facts? If other facts in similar circumstances appear to be different, then your fact may be atypical. That is, it may not be consistent with other facts reported on the same subject.

d. Has the fact been reported by a reliable source? The source should be knowledgeable on the subject and have the necessary skills (writing, observing, and so forth) for reporting the fact accurately.

Facts are vital in speeches of conviction, as they help establish the truth of your arguments. Use facts that successfully answer the questions listed above, but avoid overwhelming your listeners with too many facts. Sometimes, only one or two are necessary to establish a point You'll need to exercise judgment and common sense in determining how many facts to use.

Statistics.   A statistic is a "descriptive measure of some characteristic of a sample."[4] Statistics are generalizations or comparisons expressed in numerical form. "Ninety percent of the students at school Y did better on the SAT exam than students at school Z" and "three out of five children this year will get the measles" are statements that contain statistical information.

When using statistics, you'll want to make sure of the following:

a. They need to be current. Statistics can change frequently, as in the case of federal unemployment statistics. Don't use outdated statistics.

b. Be sure you have a fair sample. For example, in the immediate innercity of Milwaukee, there is almost a complete saturation of television sets (99.85 percent), but only 74 percent of the homes have telephones. Suppose someone makes a telephone survey of homes in the city of Milwaukee to determine TV viewing habits. Can you see the problem? The sample would be incomplete because those without a phone could not be contacted.

c. Be sure that your statistics are consistent with other statistics reporting on the same populations (groups of people studied). If the statistics from one poll on voting preference suggest that 80 percent of the voters favor candidate X, the results of this poll should be consistent with other polls on the subject. If not, then you may want to question whether or not the statistics were accurately gathered and reported in the poll you're using.

d. Check the source of your statistics. The Gallup Poll and Harris Poll, for example, are considered reliable sources because of their reputation for gathering and reporting valid statistical information. Use only reputable sources.

Statistics can be a potent form of persuasive evidence, but make sure that you understand the meaning of the statistics that you use. If you have difficulty interpreting their meaning, ask for help from your instructor or from individuals trained in statistical analysis. You may find it helpful to use a visual aid (possibly a graph or chart) to present your statistics. Don't overuse statistics; don't overwhelm your audience with too many statistics. Careful audience analysis may help you determine how many statistics to use in a speech. For example, your listeners may possess strong views, which are opposite yours, on an issue. In this case, you may want to use several statistics to convince them of your views.

Testimony.   The fourth type of evidence is testimony. Testimony can come from three kinds of sources: the casual observer, the trained observer, and the expert. When using these types of testimony, consider the following:

1. The use of the casual observer as evidence may be a weak technique. The testimony of one person may or may not be accurate. As the number of persons giving testimony grows, however, credibility can increase. The testimony of three witnesses who report the same findings at the scene of an accident is probably more accurate than the testimony of just one witness.

2. The testimony of a trained observer, such as a professional journalist adept at finding and reporting factual information, is usually more highly regarded than is the testimony of a casual observer.

3. Experts are expected to possess sound judgment on their area of expertise. Their background often includes professional training and broad and varied experience. A psychiatrist, for example, is a person whose testimony can probably be believed in matters of hu-

man behavior, especially in the areas of abnormal or deviant behavior. Unfortunately, expert opinion is expert only to a degree in many cases.

Sometimes not all the facts are available, and human error is also a possibility. That is why it is good to consult more than one expert. Here are some guidelines to follow to test expert opinion:

1. Is the person really an expert? Is he or she recognized as an expert on the subject? Are the person's opinions expert or are they those of the casual observer?
2. How current is the expert's opinion?
3. Do other experts agree with your source's statement?
4. How biased is the expert's testimony?
5. Is the expert's testimony supported with evidence?
6. Is the expert's testimony verifiable?

In a persuasive speech, your use of testimony can add vital support to your proposition. Using expert testimony can provide the proof necessary to convince listeners of your position. When using testimony, however, attempt to select that which meets the criteria of effective testimony.

Your own credibility may depend on the strength of the testimony you use. Don't overuse testimony. Remember, your message should be based mainly on your thoughts. If the majority of your message consists of the testimony of others, you become a minor contributor to your own message. Finally, when you give testimony in your speech, do so with appropriate feeling. Allow the testimony to come alive. Your vocal delivery helps add persuasive force and meaning to the testimony, which, in turn, contributes to the persuasive impact of your message. (You may want to review Chapter 8 on vocal technique).

Reasoning

Reasoning is the process of developing arguments. Every argument contains at least three basic components (either stated or implied): data (evidence), warrant, and conclusion. Let's take a closer look at each of these elements.

Data.   Data are the evidence (fact, statistic, testimony) in an argument. Data are literally the building blocks on which conclusions are built.

Warrant.   The warrant is the reasoning process that explains the relationship between the data and the conclusion. Generally, the warrant is implied rather than stated. However, when testing arguments, you must state the warrant in order to identify it and to test the soundness of the reasoning process. For instance, if the evidence of the argument is "Crista was born in the United States" and the conclusion is "Crista is a United States citizen," then the warrant could be "a person born in the United States is a United States citizen." The warrant shows the connection between the evidence and the conclusion.

Conclusion.   The conclusion is the end point of an argument, the point that the speaker wants the listeners to accept. Conclusions may be implied. However, if you state self-evident conclusions, your listeners may be more inclined to remember them, especially if they had to put forth some effort to draw their own conclusion from the data.

Toulmin Model of Reasoning.   The components of data, warrant, and conclusion can be diagrammed in a manner that reveals the relationship among them. British philosopher and logician Stephen Toulmin provides a useful model for diagramming arguments.[5] The following example shows how the Toulmin model works:

Annette has a fever of 100. Her eyes are red. Her nose is stuffy. Annette infers (guesses) that she has the flu. Using the diagram you can plot the arguments as follows:

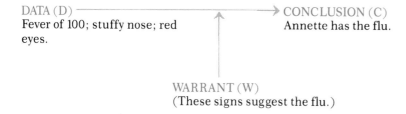

DATA (D)
Fever of 100; stuffy nose; red eyes.

CONCLUSION (C)
Annette has the flu.

WARRANT (W)
(These signs suggest the flu.)

Annette reasoned that she had the flu. However, she did not specifically state that "these signs suggest the flu." Rather, she implied this, which is her warrant and is stated here in parentheses.

The Toulmin diagram highlights the three basic components in an argument—data, warrant, and conclusion—and reveals the relationship among them. Although other components can be added to this model, we limit ourselves to these three, which are essential to any argument. In the next section, we will discuss the types of reasoning in persuasive speaking and see how the Toulmin model applies to each type.

Types of Reasoning

The two most common types of reasoning are deductive reasoning and inductive reasoning. Notice how these two forms work in the following example.

Suppose you go to a particular apple tree and take an apple from one of the branches. You bite into it and find the apple to be sour, dry, and woody. You try another apple from another branch. That one, too, is sour, dry, and woody. Just to be sure, you examine the tree to see if there are any grafted branches. There are none. You try one more apple on the other side, higher up. You get the same result: the apple is sour, dry, and woody. Using the evidence of these particular apples, you conclude that all the apples on the tree are sour, dry, and woody. This procedure of reasoning is called induction, reasoning from particular cases to a universal conclusion. Then, one of your friends comes along and starts to reach up to pick an apple from the same tree. Because you have reached a general conclusion about all the apples on the tree, you can say, "Don't bother with that apple. It's sour, dry, and woody." This procedure is called deduction, reasoning from a universal conclusion to a particular case.

In public speaking, you'll present arguments in both the inductive mode and the deductive mode of reasoning. In this part of the chapter, we will explore some types of arguments that exist under these two modes. We will see how the warrants in each type are tested in order to establish the soundness of the conclusion. We will examine four major types of inductive reasoning: generalization, causation, analogy, and sign.

Generalization.
An argument based on generalization reveals that a universal conclusion has been generalized from a fact or set of facts within the same class. For instance, Linda is an excellent speaker and is in the college speech club. In her first three years in the speech club, she won the state oratorical contest each year. This will be her fourth year in the club. An argument of generalization is diagrammed as follows:

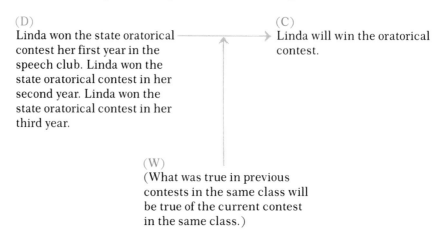

Testing the warrants in reasoning by generalization involves the following questions.

1. Do enough examples exist to warrant the conclusion? No magic number exists to tell you how many examples are enough. Your listeners may expect more than one example to warrant the generalization. Be prepared to supply more, if necessary, to convince listeners of your generalization.

2. Are the examples representative? For example, are the examples of Linda winning the oratorical contest typical of what she will experience this year at the contest? Were her previous wins atypical? Perhaps her competition this year will be much stronger than in years past.

3. Do any negative examples exist? Perhaps as a member of another speech club Linda lost a state oratorical contest. This one example may not be enough to weaken the generalization; however, if enough negative examples exist, listeners may begin to doubt the generalization.

Generalizations are never 100 percent accurate. Exceptions can usually be found. But generalizations are based on the concept of probability. That is, in inductive reasoning, you assume that the conclusion (in this case it is one of generalization) is probably correct. Warrants that are tested properly help establish the *probability* of the accuracy of the generalization in its relationship to the evidence. This is also true for the other types of inductive arguments.

Causation. A causal argument attempts to demonstrate a specific relationship between a cause and an effect. In an argument of cause and effect, the causal factors are the data and the effect is the conclusion. Suppose you need to establish a causal connection between Linda's oratorical talents and her winning state oratorical contests. Your diagram would look like this:

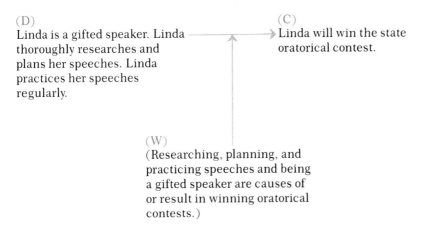

(D)
Linda is a gifted speaker. Linda thoroughly researches and plans her speeches. Linda practices her speeches regularly.

(C)
Linda will win the state oratorical contest.

(W)
(Researching, planning, and practicing speeches and being a gifted speaker are causes of or result in winning oratorical contests.)

Testing the warrant in an argument of causation involves asking these questions:

1. Is the cause strong enough to produce the particular effect? Is the evidence that Linda is a gifted speaker who researches, prepares, and practices regularly significant enough to cause her to win the state oratorical contest? One or more of the pieces of evidence, in the minds of the listeners, might not be significant enough to produce this effect. The evidence must be significant enough to produce the desired effect.

2. Are there some other factors that could have caused the effect? With Linda winning the state contest so often, the judges may have become unfairly biased in her favor. If this is the case, then another factor (other than the ones alleged to have caused her winning) is the true cause of her winning.

3. How consistent is the relationship between cause and effect? Linda has won the contest three times. The same causes that existed then exist now.

Analogy.   An analogy is a comparison of one thing with another. The argument of analogy is based on the assumption that if two things are alike in certain known aspects, then they are alike in other aspects.

There are two kinds of analogies, figurative and literal. A figurative analogy compares two things from different categories. In a figurative analogy, for example, you can compare public speaking to learning how to drive a car. At first, you may be nervous about driving. But once you "get the hang of it," you may enjoy driving. Similarly, you may be nervous giving your first speech. But, once you "get the hang of it," you may enjoy public speaking. Figurative analogy is used only for clarifying or illustrating your meaning. It doesn't establish a truth that can be generalized.

In a literal analogy, you compare items within the same class. Let's return to Linda's example and diagram the argument of analogy.

(D)
When he was in high school, ──────────→ (C)
Bill, a gifted speaker who   Linda will win the state high
researched, prepared and   school oratorical contest this
practiced his speeches, won   year.
the state oratorical contest four
years in a row.

(W)
(Linda is similar to Bill in
talent, dedication, and success
at winning state oratorical
contests for the past three
years.)

Testing the warrant of an argument of analogy involves asking the following questions:

1. Are the items being compared significantly similar to each other? Are Linda and Bill similar in talent? Preparedness? Research ability? Practice of speeches? Success at winning state oratorical contests? If not, then a comparison between them is suspect.

2. Are there a number of significant dissimilarities to outweigh any serious comparison between the items? Is the fact that Linda was trained by a different coach a factor? Is the fact that Linda enjoys practicing in front of an audience, while Bill did not, a factor? If there are enough dissimilarities to outweigh the similarities between them, then any valid conclusion drawn from the evidence appears difficult, if not impossible, to establish.

If done well, an analogy can produce an effective argument. One must keep in mind, however, the differences between a figurative analogy and a literal analogy. Failure to distinguish between them can create confusion and mistrust in the minds of the listeners.

Sign. Sign arguments are frequently confused with causal arguments. The key difference between the two is that a sign does not cause an effect to occur; a sign, instead, is an indicator that suggests that a condition or set of conditions exists. For instance, when you are ill, you may have a temperature, watery eyes, a cough, and a sore throat. These are signs that you are ill, but they do not *cause* your illness. In a sign argument, the warrant suggests that a particular sign indicates that a certain condition exists or may exist.

A sign argument for Linda winning the state oratorical contest might be diagrammed in this way:

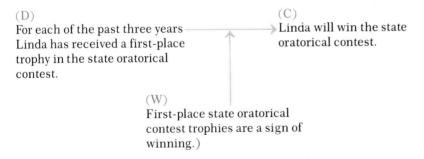

(D)
For each of the past three years Linda has received a first-place trophy in the state oratorical contest.

(C)
Linda will win the state oratorical contest.

(W)
First-place state oratorical contest trophies are a sign of winning.)

To test the warrant of an argument of sign, ask the following questions:

1. Do the signs indicate the presence of the conclusion? When Linda receives a first-place trophy in the state oratorical contest, does it mean that she is the winner? Perhaps, Linda was given this trophy

(for whatever reason) by the first-place winner. If this is the case, then the signs do not indicate the conclusion that Linda will win the state oratorical contest this year.

2. Are there enough signs to justify the conclusion? The fact that Linda has already won three state trophies may be a sufficient number of signs for your listeners to believe that she will win again.

3. Do a significant number of contradictory signs suggest another conclusion? If Linda has taken second or third place—or didn't place at all—in other oratorical contests, then there may be enough contradictory signs to invalidate the conclusion that she will win this year.

Sign arguments, then, suggest that certain conditions exist. This form of reasoning helps a speaker clarify his or her position that certain factors are present when a specific situation occurs. For the argument to be successful, however, listeners must be able to understand this relationship between signs and conclusions.

Deductive Reasoning.   Deductive arguments are another form of reasoning. A sound deductive argument is formed when a conclusion follows logically from true statements. For instance, consider these two statements: All men are mortal. Socrates is a man. If you assume these two statements to be true, then the logical conclusion to be drawn is: Socrates is mortal. This conclusion is true and follows logically from the two preceding statements. Note that the conclusion does not go beyond what is contained in the first two statements. The conclusion simply deduces information from what is given in the statements.

Let's use the Linda example and diagram it in deductive form:

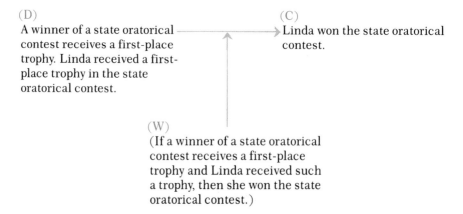

(D)
A winner of a state oratorical contest receives a first-place trophy. Linda received a first-place trophy in the state oratorical contest.

(C)
Linda won the state oratorical contest.

(W)
(If a winner of a state oratorical contest receives a first-place trophy and Linda received such a trophy, then she won the state oratorical contest.)

Testing the warrant of a deductive argument involves asking the following questions:

1. Are the first two statements (premises) true? If either or both of the premises are false, then the conclusion won't be true. If Linda did not get a trophy for winning the state oratorical contest, then the conclusion that she won the contest would not logically follow from the premise.

2. Does the conclusion relate only to the information contained in the premises? If not, the conclusion no longer follows logically from the stated premises.

Inductive and deductive forms of reasoning are important components in presenting persuasive speeches. Diagramming your arguments can help you see better the relationships among data, warrant, and conclusion. You can test the reasoning process by applying the appropriate test questions to the argument's warrant. If your listeners accept your arguments, they may be more likely to accept your message's major proposition. However, sometimes your arguments may be flawed by faulty reasoning. In the next section we'll examine some of the more common fallacies of reasoning.

Fallacies of Reasoning

In speeches of persuasion through argumentation, your arguments need to be sound. However, sometimes they may not be. Arguments may appear logical but, on closer inspection, reveal basic weaknesses. When this occurs, you may find it difficult, if not impossible, to influence listeners.

Numerous fallacies of reasoning can exist in arguments.[6] In this section we will discuss five common fallacies: begging the question, pseudoauthority, irrelevant appeals, overgeneralization, and faulty classification.

Begging the Question. Begging the question is assuming the truth or falsehood of a position without proving it. A speaker, for example, may say, "Canada is first in hydroelectric power. That country, therefore, leads the world in producing hydroelectric power." No evidence is given to support this conclusion. The speaker assumes the truth of the premise without proving it. He or she begs the question of why Canada leads the world in producing hydroelectric power. There are a number of types of begging-the-question fallacies, but, for now, you simply need to remember that begging the question occurs when people assume the truth or falsehood of a position without proving it.

Pseudoauthority. This is the fallacy of appealing to false authority. If a speaker says, "Dr. William Haskins claims that eating large quantities of red meat is unhealthy for humans," is the speaker quoting an authority on the subject? Is Dr. Haskins an expert in the field of medicine or nutrition? If he is not trained in one or both of these areas, he is not an authority on the subject. It may seem as though the speaker is using the evidence of expert opinion, but the doctor quoted is not one who is an authority on the subject. Expertise, then, is an important factor in identifying a bona fide authority. Simply because a person is an authority on one subject, he or she is not necessarily an authority on other subjects.

Irrelevant Appeals.

Irrelevant appeals occur in arguments when conclusions are established that have nothing to do with the issue or the premises of an argument are irrelevant to the point at issue. One common type of irrelevant appeal is the personal attack made by one person on another. If a speaker says that her opponent in a debate is "a greedy, dishonest pig," she has attacked the personality of the individual and not the issues her opponent stands for in the debate. Her attack is an irrelevant appeal because it asserts a conclusion that has no relevance to the issues of the debate. In its simplest form, the irrelevant appeal is "name calling." Often the opponent being attacked is slandered; his or her ideas are not at the center of this attack. For example, to call a person "stupid" or "a Communist sympathizer" establishes an irrelevant appeal.

Overgeneralization.

This type of fallacy establishes conclusions that go beyond the stated premises. The conclusion overgeneralizes from the evidence provided. For example, if a speaker relies on only one example and then claims, "I bet that they are all like that," the speaker is overgeneralizing. The speaker must supply evidence that the example is representative of the other examples within the same class.

Faulty Classification.

In faulty classification, inappropriate or false categories are used to establish arguments. For example, the "golden mean" fallacy suggests that there is a midpoint between two sides of an issue at which an appropriate answer lies. Suppose a speaker says, "We are confronted with three choices today. Let's ignore the extremes and take the second choice." The speaker advances the midpoint choice without any justification for its selection, other than that it is the midpoint. This is a false category based on the misperception that since it is "halfway between" it must be safe or correct.

Although there are other types of fallacies of reasoning, the ones discussed here are some of the most common "pitfalls" to sound reasoning. At first glance, they may appear reasonable, but on closer inspection it is evident that they do little to advance the truth or soundness of an argument. You can avoid these fallacies of reasoning by examining the evidence and arguments you use to support your propositions.

DEVELOPING A SPEECH OF CONVICTION

A speech of conviction is one that attempts to persuade through argumentation. In this type of speech, you use reasoning to support your proposition. The reasons that support your proposition will become clear as you analyze the issues (see pp. 202–206 on diagramming issues) related to your proposition.

Suppose that your topic is medical experimentation on prison inmates. You want to argue that medical experimentation is harmful to prison inmates. In an abridged version, let's see how the outline takes shape.

Main ideas

Assuming that you have analyzed the key issues, your major points for discussion in the body of the message might look like this:

    I. Medical research on prison inmates involves danger to them.

   II. Medical research on prison inmates may involve their contracting a disease.

  III. Medical research on prison inmates may not be conducted safely enough to protect prison subjects.

Each of the main points is a reason for proving that medical research on prison inmates is harmful to them. Each main point must be supported by additional reasons and evidence. With the additional support, the body of the outline looks like this:

    I. Medical research on prison inmates involves danger to them.

       A. The effects of the drugs are unknown.

       B. The amounts of drugs that can be harmful to subjects are unknown.

   II. Medical research on prison inmates may involve their contracting a disease.

       A. Inmate subjects in Ohio and Illinois were injected with live cancer cells.

       B. Inmate subjects in Iowa received experimentally induced scurvy.

  III. Medical research may not be conducted safely enough to protect prison subjects.

       A. Inmate subjects may not receive proper diets as required by experimental procedures.

       B. Prisoners may be injected with unsterilized needles.

Completed Outline

Once the body of the speech is developed, you develop the introduction and conclusion. You may need to add a bibliography of sources (on a separate page) to the outline. The completed outline (although here it is abbreviated in length and detail) might look something like this:

Proposition: To prove that medical experimentation on prison inmates is harmful to them.

Introduction

    I. Have you ever been given an injection of drugs and then felt deathly sick?

    II. This same experience is happening to prison inmate subjects who are involved in medical research experimentation.

    III. Medical experimentation on prison inmates is harmful to them.

Body

    I. Medical research on prison inmates involves danger to them.
       A. The effects of the drugs are unknown.
       B. The amounts of drugs that can be harmful to subjects are unknown.

    II. Medical research on prison inmates may involve their contracting a disease.
       A. Inmate subjects in Ohio and Illinois were injected with live cancer cells.
       B. Inmate subjects in Iowa received experimentally induced scurvy.

    III. Medical research may not be conducted safely enough to protect prison subjects.
       A. Inmate subjects may not receive proper diets as required by experimental procedures.
       B. Prisoners may be injected with unsterilized needles.

Conclusion

    I. How many more prison inmate subjects will suffer?

    II. Medical research on prison inmate subjects has been shown to be dangerous to them.

    III. I hope that you agree with this position.

While constructing your outline, examine your arguments and evidence. Are they clear? Do they relate to the problem? If any arguments appear vague or unsound, or if the evidence or warrants in the argument fail to pass the appropriate tests, leave them out of your outline.

The major proposition of the speech is your specific purpose, and it must be clearly worded. Arguments and evidence must support and develop the proposition. If they fail to do this, not only is your outline weakened, but any hope of convincing your listeners diminishes.

Once you are satisfied with your outline, it's time to practice your speech. As you practice, allow your confidence to grow. Exciting the minds of your listeners to new or different views on topics of consequence can be a stimulating experience for both you and your audience.

A SAMPLE SPEECH OF CONVICTION

The following address (quoted here in part) was made by Secretary of Defense Caspar Weinberger. He delivered it to the Foreign Press Center in Washington, D.C. His message seeks to establish the need for strategic defense. He offers a brief history of the decline of our defense system due to mistaken perceptions about the Soviets and the nuclear arms race. You'll notice that Weinberger offers examples and statistics to support his analysis. Sources of his material, however, are not mentioned. Do you think this hurts his credibility as a speaker?

THE RATIONALE FOR STRATEGIC DEFENSE

President Reagan has made it clear that he wants to reduce the threat of all nuclear weapons, particularly the most dangerous ones—the nuclear-tipped ballistic missiles. By strengthening conventional forces—through both traditional and new technologies—he has begun with our allies to restore a balanced deterrent and to reduce reliance on nuclear arms in Europe. And now, by initiating a research and technology program on defenses against ballistic missiles, he has opened the door to a future in which nuclear missiles will become less and less capable of their awful mission, until we could hope for the day when the threat of nuclear weapons could be removed entirely.

The American people have overwhelmingly endorsed these objectives. In the second Reagan administration, the president is determined to meet his commitment to [them] and to America's allies. . . .

This journey to a safer world will not be easy, nor short. The strategic defense research program will have to bear fruit before we will be in a position to make any decisions on deployment options. I am confident, though, that we can master the technical task before us, as we have accomplished so many other technical miracles in the past.

For 20 years now, the Soviet nuclear missile forces that threaten our nation and our allies have grown relentlessly. I am afraid they will continue to do so, unless we can convince the Soviet leadership that we can mutually agree to reduce the nuclear ballistic arsenals through negotiations. . . . The

Weinberger attempts to gain the attention of his audience by establishing the credibility of President Reagan as a man of peace. He then lists objectives that Reagan wants to accomplish.

He seeks to establish support for these objectives by claiming that the American people endorse them. However, he begs the question by failing to offer factual support to establish this conclusion.

The third and fourth paragraphs continue the introductory remarks.

He establishes the purpose of the speech, which provides the rationale for strategic defense research.

A chronology of events is given to explain our defense strategy built on acts of restraint.

He uses causal reasoning. He argues that the reduced number of U.S. warheads (cause) should provoke Russia to reduce its number of warheads (effect).

He argues that our policies have produced the exact opposite effect regarding Russia's production of nuclear warheads.

He offers an argument that leads to a generalization about American attitudes toward Soviet violations of treaty agreements. No evidence is given, however.

He presents a causal argument, which establishes the belief that no one feared a

president's strategic defense initiative can contribute to curbing strategic arms competition by devaluing nuclear missiles and thus imposing prohibitively high costs on the Soviets, if they continued in their quest for missile superiority.

In the 1960s and early 1970s, we had different expectations. . . . We thought our self-restraint in offensive nuclear forces, combined with a ban on missile defenses, would lead the Soviets also to restrain their offensive arms, abandon defenses and accept mutual nuclear deterrence between our countries for the indefinite future. The U.S. acted on this expectation.

Through the 1960s until the end of the 1970s, we cut the budget for nuclear forces every year. Today, the total megatonnage of the U.S. stockpile is only one fourth the size of our 1959 stockpile. Seventeen years ago, we had one-third more nuclear warheads than we do today. We thought this would induce the Soviets to restrain the growth of their nuclear forces.

We also thought we could reinforce Soviet restraint and facilitate limits on offensive arms by guaranteeing our own total vulnerability to a Soviet ballistic missile attack. We unilaterally gave up all defense, not only of our cities, but of our Minuteman silos as well. We did so even though the ABM treaty permitted each side one ABM site. Advocates of this policy reasoned that if the Soviets could easily strike American cities, they would have no incentive to deploy more missiles. . . .

Improvements and additions to the Soviet missile force continue at a frightening pace, even though we have added SALT II restraints on top of the SALT I agreements. The Soviet Union has now built more warheads capable of destroying our missiles silos than we had initially predicted they would build, even without any SALT agreement We now confront precisely the condition that the SALT process was intended to prevent. . . .

Moreover, as the President reported to Congress, the Soviet Union has violated several important SALT provisions, including a ban on concealing telemetry of missile tests. Since that provision was designed to allow verification of the SALT agreement, even President Carter stressed that "a violation of this part of the agreement—which we would quickly detect—would be just as serious as a violation on strategic weapons themselves."

The vast majority of Americans are deeply concerned about this pattern of Soviet violations. Yet some people who pride themselves on their expertise and concern for arms control have taken an upside-down view. Instead of recognizing the problem of Soviet violations, they have criticized President Reagan for informing Congress about those violations. They argue that this showed he was "not sincere" about arms control; as if sincerity required that we ignore Soviet violations. . . . During the first four years of the nuclear era, there was no mutual nuclear deterrence—we had a monopoly. Because the monopoly was ours, no one seriously feared nuclear war. Even Stalin—often described as defensive minded—violated the Yalta agreement on Poland, crushed democracy in Czechoslovakia, blockaded Berlin, and encouraged North Korea's attack on South Korea. He had no fear, paranoid or otherwise, that the U.S. would use its nuclear monopoly to maintain compliance with Yalta, much less to launch an unprovoked attack.

Later, when the Soviet Union also built nuclear weapons, there was still no mutual deterrence based on absolute vulnerability. For during the 1950s we spent some $100 billion (in current dollars) to defend against Soviet strategic bombers—then the only nuclear threat to the U.S. . . .

It was not until the Kennedy and Johnson administrations that we began to abandon our efforts to defend against nuclear attack, and instead base our entire security on the odd theory that you are safe only if you have no defense whatsoever. It came to be known as mutual-assured destruction, or MAD. It has played a central role in the U.S. approach to arms control for the past 20 years; even though for many years now, actual U.S. strategy has adjusted to the fact that the original MAD concept was flawed. Our strategy has moved well beyond this to the point that it now seeks to avoid the targeting of populations. . . .

True believers in the disproven MAD concept hold that the prime, if not the only, objective of the strategic nuclear forces of both the U.S. and the Soviet Union is the ability to destroy each other's cities. They believe that any U.S. defense against this threat is "destabilizing." It will, they say, inevitably provoke an overwhelming increase in Soviet forces and will increase Soviet incentives to strike pre-emptively in a crisis. They fail to appreciate the deterrent value of missile defenses, because they wrongly project upon the Soviet military their own irrational idea of the purpose of a Soviet attack. In fact, the Soviet military have designed their offensive forces to be capable of destroying allied and U.S. military forces, in particular our silo-based missiles and military targets in Europe. At the same time, the Soviet Union has never abandoned its objective of defending its homeland against nuclear attack.

The ABM treaty never blinded the Soviets to the need for effective defenses. They have continued to place great emphasis on air defense. They are now ready to deploy a defense system with capabilities against both aircraft and many ballistic missiles. They have a massive program of underground shelters. They have built five ABM radars, with another one under construction, that give them double coverage of all ICBM approaches to the Soviet Union; and they have exploited fully the provisions of the ABM treaty and—what is more—almost certainly violated it, as they advance their capacity for deployment of a widespread ballistic missile defense. Since [the ABM treaty], the Soviet Union has spent more on strategic defensive forces than on strategic offensive forces. Clearly, the Soviets do not share the MAD philosophy that defenses are bad.

So, it is quite wrong to argue that the president's initiative on strategic defense would "upset 35 years of mutual deterrence," and spoil a successful approach to arms control and stability. On the contrary, the President's initiative will finally correct the conventional wisdom, which is so often wrong.

He tries to reassure his listeners that the U.S. will not abandon its current offensive systems. But, he balances this view with one that suggests this policy is not enough and even dangerous to our security if an effective defense system is not developed.

This next section serves as an effective transition to the final part of his speech. It begins to preview the advantages of the President's military system.

He cites a significant advantage of the need for a strategic defense system.

He cites another advantage of the President's policy.

The major goal of the policy is clear.

He clearly summarizes the need and benefits of the plan. He concludes that the President's plan is far more credible, moral, and logical than the plan of those who advocate abandonment of our defenses. This conclusion tries to give added strength to the idea that a strategic defense system is in our best interest.

As we proceed, we will of course not give up our triad of deterrent offensive systems. Rather, we continue to maintain deterrence, and indeed strengthen and modernize all three elements of our triad, because we do not know when we will actually be in a position to put our strategic defense system in place. But reliance exclusively on these offensive systems, without pursuing effective defenses, condemns us to a future in which our safety is based only on the threat of avenging aggression.

. . . We all recognized from the outset that a complete system, or combination of systems, for strategic defenses could not be deployed overnight. There could be a transitional period when some defenses would be deployed and operating before others would be ready. . . . If properly planned and phased, the transitional capabilities would strengthen our present deterrent capability, which is one of President Reagan's high priorities. In fact, they could make a major contribution to the prevention of nuclear war, even before a fully effective system is deployed.

If the Soviet leaders ever contemplated initiating a nuclear attack, their purpose would be to destroy U.S. or NATO military forces that would be able to oppose the aggression. Defenses that could deny the Soviet missiles the military objectives of their attack, or deny the Soviets confidence in the achievement of those objectives, would discourage them from even considering such an attack, and thus be a highly effective deterrent.

But we would not want to let efforts towards a transitional defense exhaust our energies, or dilute our efforts to secure a thoroughly reliable, layered defense that would destroy incoming Soviet missiles at all phases of their flight. Such a system would be designed to destroy weapons not people. With such a system we do not even raise the question of whether we are trying to defend missiles or cities. We would be trying to destroy Soviet missiles by non-nuclear means. . . .

The choice is not between defending people or weapons. Even the early phases in deployment of missile defenses can protect people. Our goal is to destroy weapons that kill people.

Thus, based on a realistic view of Soviet military planning, the transition to strategic defense would not be destabilizing. In fact, initial defense capabilities would offer a combination of benefits. They would contribute to deterrence by denying Soviet attack goals. And should deterrence ever fail, they would save lives by reducing the scope of destruction that would result from a Soviet military attack. The more effective the defenses, the more effective this protection would be. This objective is far more idealistic, moral and practical than the position taken by those who still adhere to the mutual-assured destruction theory, namely that defenses must be totally abandoned.[7]

SUMMARY

Persuasive speaking is defined as *the art of reinforcing or changing beliefs, values, attitudes, or behaviors on a particular subject.* Persuasion through argumentation seeks the conviction of listeners' beliefs, values, or attitudes on a particular subject. The basic components of persuasive speaking through argumentation include propositions, issues, and proof. There are three types of propositions: propositions of policy, propositions of fact, and propositions of value. A proposition of policy calls for a specific plan to be adopted; a proposition of fact attempts to prove the truth or falsehood of a statement or alleged fact; a proposition of value attempts to persuade listeners that something is either praiseworthy or blameworthy.

An issue is a question that reveals a conflict between arguments. Issues can be diagrammed for each type of proposition. Diagramming the issues helps the speaker gain an overall view of the reasons both for and against a particular position. Stock issues are standard questions used for analyzing propositions of policy. These questions concern the areas of need, plan, and advantages versus disadvantages of the plan. Propositions of fact can be diagrammed according to questions of truth or falsehood of the alleged fact. Propositions of value can be diagrammed according to questions of praiseworthiness or blameworthiness.

The essential elements of proof are evidence and reasoning in support of a proposition. Evidence is the initial material on which proof is built. Evidence can be found in valid assumptions, facts, statistics, and testimony. Test questions of evidence can be applied in each of these areas. Answers to the questions help determine if the evidence is accurate.

Reasoning, the other essential element of proof, is the process of developing arguments. The three major components of reasoning are data, warrant, and conclusion. These components can be diagrammed using the Toulmin model of analysis. Data is the evidence in an argument. The warrant is the process that explains the relationship between the data and the conclusion. The conclusion is the end point of the argument.

Reasoning may be either inductive or deductive. Inductive reasoning is that which moves from a particular case to a universal conclusion. Deductive reasoning moves from a universal conclusion to a particular case. The types of inductive arguments are generalization, causation, analogy, and sign.

Fallacies of reasoning weaken the soundness of an argument. Five common fallacies of reasoning are begging the question, pseudoauthority, irrelevant appeals, overgeneralization, and faulty classification.

Public speaking students who seek to convince their listeners need to be aware of the components involved in speeches of persuasion through argumentation. A good grasp of these components can help speakers present stronger and more credible arguments to their audiences.

ASSIGNMENTS

1. Listen to a commercial on TV or radio. What types of arguments do the advertisers use to convince you to buy their products? How sound are their arguments? Write an essay describing your observations.

2. Construct a proposition of policy. Use stock issue analysis to analyze the proposition. Diagram each stock issue. Include the arguments, both pro and con, under each issue. Write an essay explaining your observations.

3. Apply the test of evidence to a speech that you will be giving in your next speech assignment. How does the evidence stack up? Does your evidence meet the tests for usability? If so, why? If not, why not? What evidence do you want to use in the speech? Why? Share your examples with members of the class.

4. Using the Toulmin model, construct an example of an inductive form of argument and a deductive form of argument. Test the warrant of each argument. Does each warrant pass the test? Why? Share your examples with members of the class.

5. The purpose of this assignment is to help you convince your listeners that a certain proposition of fact, value, or policy should be accepted. Select a specific proposition. Support it by using the proof of evidence and sound reasoning. You might choose one of the following suggestions for your proposition or consult the list of speech topics in the appendix.

   a. Propositions of fact: President Kennedy was killed by more than one assassin; wage and price controls will lead to a recession; the 55-mile-per-hour speed limit saves lives.

   b. Propositions of value: Sex discrimination is harmful to both men and women; television is a vast wasteland; public education is not succeeding.

   c. Propositions of policy: The U.S. Supreme Court should modify its stand on abortion; as a graduation requirement, students should demonstrate the ability to write an acceptable 1000-word paper; capital punishment should be abolished.

   Limit your speech to five to six minutes.

NOTES

1. Teri Gamble and Michael Gamble, *Communication Works* (New York: Random House, 1984), p. 312.

2. Jo Sprague and Douglas Stuart, *The Speaker's Handbook* (New York: Harcourt Brace Jovanovich, 1984), p. 19.

3. Douglas Ehninger, *Influence, Belief, and Argument: An Introduction to Responsible Persuasion* (Glenview, IL: Scott, Foresman, 1974), p. 11.

4. Charles T. Clark and Lawrence L. Schkade, *Statistical Analysis for Administrative Decisions,* 4th ed. (Cincinnati: South-Western Publishing Co., 1983), p. 10.

5. For a more detailed account, see Stephen Toulmin, *The Uses of Argument* (London: Cambridge University Press, 1980).

6. For an excellent overview of this subject, see W. Ward Fearnside and William B. Holther, *Fallacy: The Counterfeit of Argument* (Englewood Cliffs, NJ: Prentice-Hall, 1960) and Richard D. Ricke and Malcolm O. Sillars, *Argumentation and the Decision-Making Process,* 2nd ed. (Glenview, IL: Scott, Foresman, 1984), pp. 79–84.

7. Caspar Weinberger, "The Rationale for Strategic Defense," *Wall Street Journal,* 2 Jan. 1985, p. 12.

Overview of Persuasion	Motivation	
	Approaches to Motivation	Rewarded Behavior
		Hierarchy of Needs
		Group Identification
		Self-Image
	Applications of Persuasion Through Motivation	
	Formula for Organizing a Motivational Speech	
Sales: An Example of Persuasion Through Motivation	**Personal Qualities of Effective Salespersons**	Honesty
		Knowledge of the Product
		Belief in the Product
		Warmhearted Friendliness
		Enthusiasm
		Sense of Humor
		Emotional Stability
		Acceptance Appearance
A Sample Sales Talk to a Group	**Time-Tested Sales Steps**	Begin with the Listener's Interests
		Point Out the Benefits
		Present the Evidence
		Demonstrate
		Answer Objections
		Close the Sale

12 Persuasion Through Motivation

Objectives

When you finish this chapter, you should be able to:

1. define motivation;
2. explain the various theories of motivation;
3. determine how a persuasive speaker motivates you as a listener;
4. list the qualifications of a good salesperson;
5. make a sales talk to a group, selling a product or a service; and
6. make a persuasive speech in which you apply one or more of the approaches to motivation.

12 Persuasion Through Motivation

Seven-year-old Carrie wanted to go to the state fair one evening at seven o'clock, a little late for a little girl. She began her persuasive talk to her Grandpa with these words. "Grandpa, I know it's too late to go to the fair, but could we just ride over there and drive around the outside? All I want to do is see the Ferris wheel from the street. Could we go for just a half hour, Grandpa, could we?"

Whether it was too late or not, how could Grandpa turn down a little girl's request just to drive around the fair when all the time it would take would be half an hour? And at no cost?

On the way to the fair, watching Carrie's eyes sparkle and listening to the music in her voice, Grandpa began thinking, "This kid should be teaching a course in persuasion on the college level."

You've already guessed the rest of the story: cotton candy, a ride on the merry-go-round, an Italian sausage sandwich, and a cold cola drink.

How did Carrie persuade Grandpa? You might argue that grandfathers are easy prey for granddaughters, and you're probably right, but Grandpa could have been purely logical and insisted on Carrie's eight o'clock bedtime. Why didn't he? What interrupted his usual logic? What motivated him to succumb to the persuasive pleading of a seven-year-old child?

We'll seek the answer to these questions in this chapter. We will discuss how to persuade others to change their behavior as well as how to be aware of how others are trying to change our behavior. Speaking to persuade is one side of the coin, while listening to evaluate is the other.

As you study this chapter on persuasion through motivation remember that three main forces are usually at work in the persuasive process: the speaker's credibility, argumentation, and motivation. The credibility of a speaker is based on how we perceive him or her. If we see the person to be fair, honest, cheerful, friendly, intelligent, competent, and emotionally stable, then that speaker has a very good chance of being persuasive, provided the argumentation is sound and the motivation appealing.

OVERVIEW OF PERSUASION

The previous chapter, "Persuasion Through Argumentation," dealt mainly with an appeal to the listener's thinking process. In this chapter we deal with an appeal to the listener's emotional needs, wants, desires, and values.

In the preceding chapter we defined persuasion as the art of changing someone's beliefs, attitudes, values, or behaviors on a particular subject. Some examples can help illustrate these purposes of persuasive speaking.

Physics major Phil attempts to prove to his roommate that flying saucers are an impossibility. Logician Leona tries to convince her friends that more than one assassin was involved in President Kennedy's death. Pre-med student Martha contends in her speech that heart transplants involve more overall disadvantages than advantages. These speakers are trying to convince their listeners to modify their beliefs and to change their way of thinking. These speakers do not expect their listeners to do anything about the situation. Their purpose is merely to change beliefs, attitudes, or values.

Restless Robert supports the proposal that the maximum speed on the nation's highways should be 70 miles per hour. Economics major Ed warns that wage and price controls will lead to a recession. Theology student Thelma urges that the U.S. Supreme Court should declare abortion on demand unconstitutional. These students, too, are trying to convince their listeners to modify their beliefs and to change their way of thinking. There is one big difference, however. While there isn't much that listeners can actually do about flying saucers, President Kennedy's death, or heart transplants, the listeners to the propositions on speed limits, economic controls, and abortion can take action. They can join organized groups, sign petitions, and write their representatives in Congress.

Sophisticated Sally proposes to her sorority that their annual dinner be changed to a jazz party at the Blue Note. Senior Sam entreats his dorm council to sponsor a day of donating dollars for the famine victims in Ethiopia. Loyal grad Gloria asks the alumni board to work out scholarship plans for underprivileged Native Americans. These speakers are trying to motivate their listeners to modify their behavior.

In this chapter you will learn the techniques of changing behavior, getting the listener to do something. First, you must learn how to motivate.

Motivation

Motivation is the moving force behind a person's behavior. Why do we do things? What makes us tick? Other people try to sell us cars, books, or insurance; to get us to donate money for a charity; to enroll us at a certain college; to take a position with a certain company; or to join a union or service organization. Others spend large sums of money to persuade us to buy a particular toothpaste. In the 1985 Super Bowl broadcast, a one-minute commercial cost $1 million, because its potential audience of consumers was especially large. Why do we buy? How does the persuader induce the listener to respond? In order to understand these questions, we will examine some theories of motivation and then make some practical applications.

Approaches to Motivation

A number of theories, methods, and approaches have been advanced to explain motivation. We narrow the study of motivation to the basic approaches of rewarding behavior, hierarchy of needs, group identification, and self-image. Although these are not the only theories of motivation, they are the ones most often found in messages of persuasion through motivation.

Rewarded Behavior. Sociologist W. Phillips Davison states that "[t]he communicator can influence attitudes or behavior only when he is able to convey information that may be utilized by members of his audience to satisfy their wants or needs."[1] He theorizes that rewarded, or reinforced, behavior motivates people to act in certain desirable ways. This is the point made by psychologist George Homans in a summary of B. F. Skinner's work with pigeons:

> *The pigeon's behavior in pecking the target is an operant; the operant has been reinforced, grain is the reinforcer; and the pigeon has undergone operant conditioning. Should we prefer our language to be ordinary English, we may say that the pigeon has learned to peck the target by being rewarded for doing so.*[2]

Advertisements appeal to our wants and needs in an attempt to direct or change our behavior.

The speaker's task is to find the appropriate "grains" or rewards to motivate the audience. Note what Tom does to convince his listeners to join the college ski club. He admits that skiing is an expensive proposition, but he explains that by joining the club, students will experience a number of benefits. They will see beautiful country; establish good friendships; have a good time; and exercise in fresh, crisp air—benefits that far outweigh the costs. He shows pictures of some of the ski club's outings to his listeners. These pictures help reinforce the benefits (rewards) associated with membership. At the end of his presentation, he invites the audience members to meet with him after class if they desire more information. No doubt, Tom plans to suggest additional rewards that result from joining the club.

Rewarded behavior as a motivating mechanism appears in many aspects of your life. Consider the grades you receive. Do they motivate you to behave in certain ways?

Hierarchy of Needs.

Have you ever had an urge for a particular type of food? Have you ever wanted to belong to a specific club or organization? Have you ever felt the need to be recognized as being good at a particular sport? If so, you were experiencing needs that motivated you to do something. The hierarchy of needs approach helps you develop persuasive messages within the boundaries of satisfying an individual's needs. One classic approach to identifying motivational needs is provided by Abraham Maslow.[3] In Maslow's hierarchy, five categories of needs are arranged in a specific order of importance. No need in the hierarchy can be satisfied until preceding needs are at least partially satisfied. The order of needs from the most basic and important are basic physiological needs, security needs, social needs, self-esteem needs, and self-actualization needs. For example, a person's needs for food must be satisfied before he or she becomes concerned about self-esteem needs. Hunger is a more immediate, life-threatening concern than is job status, for example. Figure 12.1 illustrates the components of Maslow's hierarchy of needs.

1. *Basic Physiological Needs.* Humans have basic physiological needs that sustain life. These needs include oxygen, water, food, and the elimination of wastes. Unless these needs are satisfied, human life would end. Needs that go unsatisfied can become strong motivating forces that compel us to act in ways that help satisfy those unmet needs.

As a speaker, you can "plant a thought" that motivates listeners to want, for example, a particular type of food or drink in order to satisfy their physiological needs for nourishment. You might suggest how the brand of food tastes and smells. You can use visual aids to illustrate how the food looks. You can motivate the audience to seek this brand of food by presenting it to them as a desirable way to satisfy their needs.

2. *Security Needs.* We need to feel secure in our work, educational endeavors, and family relations—for that matter, in almost every facet of life. We want to believe that we will not be fired from our jobs; we want to believe that we have enough insurance coverage in case of an accident; we want to feel secure in our homes. The strength of these needs will in part depend on how insecure we feel about them.

You can, for example, demonstrate how the security need can be satisfied. This is most practically done by showing courses of action listeners can take. You can recommend a specific course of action (for instance, using seat belts in a car) for the listeners to implement. You then explain how this action satisfies the security need, the need to feel safe and protected.

3. *Social Needs.* Once people feel that the first two needs have been at least partially satisfied, then, suggests Maslow, the other levels of needs take on greater importance. Social needs make us want to "belong."

FIGURE 12.1 **Hierarchy of Needs**

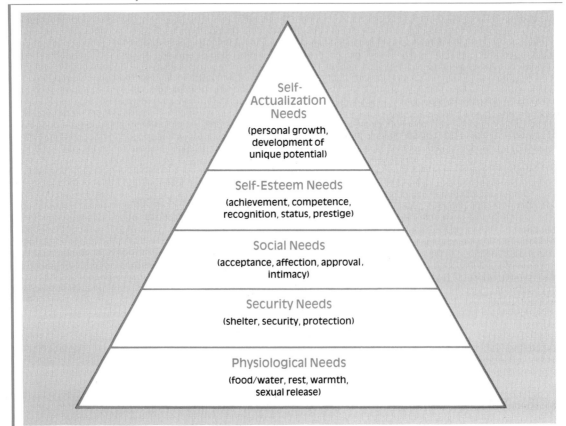

Self-
Actualization
Needs
(personal growth,
development of
unique potential)

Self-Esteem Needs
(achievement, competence,
recognition, status, prestige)

Social Needs
(acceptance, affection, approval,
intimacy)

Security Needs
(shelter, security, protection)

Physiological Needs
(food/water, rest, warmth,
sexual release)

To help satisfy social needs, you can suggest that "we need to work together in resolving a problem affecting all of us." You can emphasize collective personal pronouns such as "us," "we," and "ourselves," which unite the listeners with one another and with you. You can point out some of the social rewards of belonging to a particular group.

4. *Self-Esteem Needs*. Maslow predicts that once we satisfy our social needs, we then seek satisfaction of our self-esteem needs. Simply, these needs underscore our desire to be recognized by other people (especially by significant people in our lives) for doing well in school, on the job, in a sport, and so on. We want to feel valued and appreciated. The cry of a mother, for example, who laments that she is "just a baby-sitter" suggests that she lacks respect from other family members. Most people prefer to feel appreciated.

You can motivate listeners who seek satisfaction of this need by explaining how their action on an issue will bring them respect, praise, or honor. Consider recruiters in the military. They frequently encourage young people to join particular branches by appealing to self-esteem needs. If they join, the recruiters argue, they will gain self-respect, respect from others, and honor by serving their country.

5. *Self-Actualization*. At the top of Maslow's hierarchy is the need for self-actualization. People who seek self-actualization are beyond the need for wanting recognition. They take pleasure in succeeding at a task.

You can encourage listeners to self-actualize. Identify for them the internal feelings (for instance, joy, happiness, euphoria) that may occur from their action in the direction that you promote. Suggest ways that they can develop specific skills to help them prepare for achieving difficult goals. Show that the risks are worth taking in order to achieve this state of accomplishment and personal fulfillment. "Nothing ventured, nothing gained" is an appropriate statement when suggesting to other people the rewards that can accrue from satisfying the need for self-actualization.

Group Identification.   According to the group identification theory of motivation, audience members are less motivated by individual needs than by group needs. The focus of motivation shifts from the individual level to the group level. The group is made to appear attractive because of its status and its ability to reward or punish members. In a sense, the group dictates the attitudes and behaviors of its individual members. A public speaker, such as a politician who claims that "good Democrats" will vote for candidate X, is using the group identification approach.

Self-Image.   The self-image approach focuses primarily on the ego of the listener. Much advertising, for instance, appeals to a viewer's sense of pride, free spirit, or sensitivity. Appeals based on fear can also be used to influence a person's self-image. In this case, the suggestion is made that you should buy a specific car or risk being out of step with society. If the speaker effectively challenges the listener's self-image, he or she will act in a manner desired by the persuasive speaker.

Sometimes, to motivate listeners, advertisers (persuaders) develop an "ego-ideal," such as the "Marlboro man" as a sex symbol. The ego-ideal becomes the benchmark to which listeners compare themselves. Have you ever bought a product (one you probably didn't need) simply because a person who symbolized an "ego-ideal" used it? The self-image approach assumes that a person's personality and ego are important factors in the ways in which he or she will respond to a persuasive message.

Clearly, numerous approaches exist in the art of persuasion. No one approach appears superior to all others. In a persuasive speech, you must decide which approach or approaches will work best. You may need to use several approaches because of the diversity of your listeners, or you may use only one approach that plays on the audience's homogeneous nature.

Whatever the case, the final judges of a persuasive message are the listeners themselves, for they decide *if* they want to be motivated or *if* they will change their behavior. As a target of a persuasive message, the listener has a great deal to say about its effectiveness. A listener who is aware of the different approaches to persuasion is in a better position to

Various approaches are used to persuade. Sometimes persuaders present an ego-ideal to which we compare ourselves—if we find we don't "measure up," the advertised product or service is offered as a method for achieving the ideal. Or, sometimes we are told that a particular product or service will ensure our positions as valued members of society. Ultimately, however, the effectiveness of any one type of persuasive message depends on the needs, wants, and values of its intended receivers.

evaluate the message presented. A speaker who is aware of the different approaches to persuasion is in a better position to motivate the listeners. Both speaker and listener can profit from a shared experience.

Applications of Persuasion Through Motivation

"You can lead a horse to water but you can't make him drink." "A man convinced against his will is of his own opinion still." "What's in it for me?" These sayings are not without foundation. They are intimately associated with motivation—getting the listener to act.

In trying to motivate someone we must ask ourselves if we are appealing to the listener's needs, wants, desires, or values. For example, we stand a better chance of getting little Johnny to eat his oatmeal if we tell him it will make him big and strong like Daddy, or if we tell him it will help him beat Sandy next door in a tricycle race than if we tell him that oatmeal contains vitamin B_1 and is nutritious.

Many expensive automobiles are sold because some people hunger for prestige. Some teenagers smoke because it gives them a feeling of adulthood. Many college students wear blue jeans almost everywhere because this attire gives them a feeling of identification with their peers.

Consider the example of a clergyman who was delivering his sermon one Sunday. It was a nice day in April when everyone longs to get outside and go for a ride. The clergyman started the sermon by talking about "wheels"—automobiles and the feeling of power you get when you zoom down the road. From this motion of power, he made a transition to another kind of power, the power received when a person becomes filled with spiritual power. Members of the congregation listened attentively to the clergyman. He was talking in terms of their immediate interests, needs, wants, desires, and values.

As we have seen, there are many ways to motivate people. The following extended example shows how several appeals—security, knowledge, power, prestige, accomplishment, aesthetics, and love—can be used to motivate people.

Let's imagine that a young, successful business executive has been asked to address a group of incoming freshmen. Her proposal is "study hard and use your time well." Notice how she links the motives of security, knowledge, power, prestige, accomplishment, aesthetics, and love to the proposal at hand.

1. Security: If you study hard and use your time well, you'll have little fear of being put on probation or of being asked to leave the university.

2. Knowledge: Accumulate a wealth of knowledge and training, which no one can ever take from you.

3. Power: Gain better control over your own talents to be able to meet more confidently the growing competition.

4. Prestige: Increase your status in society by having your college degree.

5. Accomplishments: Prove to yourself that you have the determination and perseverance of which great leaders are made.

6. Aesthetics: Learn to appreciate the worthwhile things in life and all they have to offer.

7. Love: Make your loved ones happy by showing them that you are worthy of their concern and that you are making something of yourself.

Each one of the foregoing sentences is powerful, but you can't give a speech of motivation with a series of generalizations. Each generalization must be supported by evidence.

Let's look at the first motivational sentence appealing to security and add the evidence.

I. *You'll have little fear of being put on probation or of being asked to leave the university.*

    A. Poor study habits lead to these statistics, according to the College of Liberal Arts:
       1. Twenty percent of students are put on probation after the first year.
       2. Six percent are dropped from the university.
    B. Here's an example of poor study habits: the case of Playboy Joe.
       1. Out late almost every night.
       2. Failure to get up on time for early classes.
       3. Inability to understand assignments and follow through.
       4. The result is his getting dropped from the class and getting an *F* for the course.

Do you see how motivation works? You present evidence that appeals to the needs, wants, desires, and values of your listeners, and by sound reasoning you attempt to motivate them. This example used the basic motive of security. Try developing such an outline of evidence for the other motives (knowledge, power, prestige, accomplishments, aesthetics, and love).

One further suggestion will help you prepare your motivational speech. You need a formula for organization, a pattern for putting your package together. An easy way to organize your outline can be found in this six-step formula.

Formula for Organizing a Motivational Speech

1. *Get attention:* Relate a personal experience you had at the campus block party last year.
2. *State your point:* Ask the class to come to the party this year.
3. *Point out benefits:* Give a report on the music, refreshments, games, and meeting friends and new people.
4. *Give concrete examples:* By prearrangement have some of the members of your audience stand and relate how much fun they had in regard to one of the benefits you pointed out.
5. *Ask for specification:* Pass a sheet around urging those who plan to come to sign up.
6. *Answer questions:* Be cordial and helpful. This is your last chance to get listeners to attend.

Suppose your motivational speech dealt with encouraging students to attend this year's campus block party. Using the six-step formula, you might develop your speech in the following way.

1. Get attention by arousing interest.
2. State your point, proposal, or proposition at least in a general way. For psychological reasons you may want to withhold your specific proposal until later in the speech.
3. Point out the benefits that will come to the listener who follows your suggestions.
4. Give concrete examples. Demonstrate. Encourage listener participation if possible. Point out the benefits again.
5. Restate your proposal. Ask for specific action. Make your request easy to follow by giving such specific information as time, place, date, and price if practical.
6. Be cordial in answering questions of information or objections to your proposal.

Very closely allied to the speech of persuasion through motivation is the sales talk. Salespersons move the products and services of the nation. Some of the nation's highest salaries are paid to men and women in this field of persuasion. In the following section we will analyze and study the sales presentation and discover various techniques that can be used in a public speaking situation.

SALES: AN EXAMPLE OF PERSUASION THROUGH MOTIVATION

All of us are salespersons at times. We try to sell our ideas, emotions, attitudes, preferences, and even our way of living. The clergy in the pulpit, the politician behind the speaker's stand, the attorney in the courtroom, the businessperson in the marketplace, and many others are selling with one end in view: to motivate the listener to buy a product, subscribe to a service, change an attitude, and so on.

The art of selling consists of creating a desire to buy. This art is based on time-tested scientific principles. The salesperson must reach the needs, wants, and values of the listener. Although there is no one best way of selling, certain established procedures produce better results. You are on a safer course if you follow the time-tested methods.

Sales are usually conducted on a one-to-one basis. There are situations, however, when the basis of the sale is one-to-many—as in a public speaking situation. You have seen, for example, a cosmetics demonstration in a department store while a group gathers to watch, or you may have watched a pitchman at the state fair demonstrating a new gadget. Perhaps you have heard a presentation concerning lake lots, condominiums, vacation clubs, or solar heating. The following examination of how

Successful salespersons are persuasive speakers. They are perceptive analysts of prospective buyers' needs, wants, and values. They are able to develop a message that creates within each buyer a desire to make a purchase that appears to satisfy his or her needs, wants, and values.

a meeting for group sale is frequently conducted might give you some pointers on how to develop your public speaking skills in sales to groups.

First of all, listeners are motivated to come to a meeting with the promise of winning a prize. Once the audience is assembled, a public speaker introduces the program, which consists of a five- to ten-minute introduction (or even longer in some instances), a professionally produced movie with an effective commentator, and, finally, a return to the original speaker who invites the listeners to remain at their tables to fill out questionnaires and receive their prizes. Individual salespersons then move in to discuss the situation on a one-to-one basis and to close the sale or at least to get a down payment. Prizes are awarded to everyone, but only after the salesperson has completed the sale or exhausted every opportunity to do so. Sometimes if the prospects do not buy, they must ask for their prize to receive it.

Whatever we may think of these methods, we must admit that these meetings are conducted with professional finesse. If you aspire to professional sales, you will need to evaluate your personality and study some time-tested sales steps. The following section suggests some methods you can use to analyze your aptitude for the sales field.

Personal Qualities of Effective Salespersons

Sales is not the field for introverted or worrisome personalities. The salesperson is expected to be a model of outgoing enthusiasm for the product and the prospect. The personal qualities most expected in a salesperson are honesty, knowledge of the product, belief in the product, warmhearted friendliness, enthusiasm, a sense of humor, emotional stability, and an acceptable appearance.

Honesty.   "You can fool some of the people," but in the long run the honest person, not the distorter of facts, will be the credible one. Momentary success from misrepresentation is not worth the risk.

Knowledge of the Product.   It is the duty of the salesperson not only to know the product but also to continue to learn more about it and the new developments in the field.

Belief in the Product.   Sooner or later the telltale signs of lack of belief will show: lackadaisical attitude, daydreaming, and lack of enthusiasm. Very few of us are consummate performers in suggesting that we are sold on a product when we are not.

Warmhearted Friendliness.   A manager of a sales organization was once told, "The speaker treated our small group like a million dollars." The manager replied, "That's because you are a million dollars." A smile, warm voice, and firm handshake can do much to build credibility.

Enthusiasm. Insincere mannerisms are no substitute for the real thing. We have all met "the gusher" and have been turned off. The effective salesperson, whose main function is to be of service, displays genuine enthusiasm.

Sense of Humor. If you have been around enough salespersons, you have probably observed that many of them have jokes to share and entertaining stories to tell. Humor is often a helpful tool in building spirits and making sales.

Emotional Stability. The salesperson may weaken under the strain of long hours; little success; and ignorant, barbed objections. The more emotionally stable the salesperson is, the better are the chances of weathering disappointments.

Acceptable Appearance. You feel more comfortable in the presence of a salesperson with groomed hair, brushed teeth, clean fingernails, reserved attire, shined shoes, and courteous manners who is neither smoking nor chewing gum. As in any public speaking situation, these qualities reflect good breeding and promote poise and self-assurance, which in turn elicit credibility and trust. In addition to the personal qualities needed for success in sales, the prospective salesperson should also be familiar with the time-tested sales techniques.

Time-Tested Sales Steps

The traditional procedure in sales follows six steps: beginning with the listener's interests, pointing out the benefits, presenting the evidence, demonstrating the product, answering objections, and closing the sale.

Begin with the Listener's Interests. Sales presentations often focus on interpersonal relationships. You can gain more attention and establish more rapport by talking about your prospective buyer's interests, needs, wants, desires, and values for one minute than you can by talking about yourself for an hour. We tend to like those individuals who are interested in us and talk about our interests. Small talk is one way of getting started. "How do you like the weather?" "Did you get caught in the traffic jam tonight?" "I'd like to tell you how happy we are that so many of you were able to make the meeting."

It's a good idea to plan your opening remarks, especially the first sentence. If something unexpected happens, you can make an adjustment. Avoid a misleading opening that will let people down. Don't begin, "How many of you would like to win a thousand dollars tonight?" unless you have a thousand dollars to offer. Avoid an opening that calls too much attention to itself, such as smashing a water pitcher with a hammer.

What kind of a group do you have: a homogeneous one such as a university faculty being approached with a new life insurance plan or a heterogeneous one such as people coming from many different backgrounds to hear a presentation on buying lake lots? Perhaps you can take a brief survey using three to five questions. You will gain some information about your listeners and you will be using an attention-getting technique that centers on your specific purpose.

Point out the Benefits.   The second step is to point out the benefits of the product or service. People don't buy washing machines. They buy clean clothes washed with a minimum amount of effort. People don't buy refrigerators. They buy preserved food and easy-to-get ice cubes.

A philosophical axiom states that "no one wants what he or she does not understand." Stated another way, that axiom might say, "The more you understand the benefits of a product, the more you want it." By pointing out benefits to a listener, you can appeal to an innate or created need. For example, you might say, "With this new lake lot set in virgin timber, you will find relief from those hot, humid days in the city, and your children will love you for making the decision."

Present the Evidence.   A salesperson should have an abundance of evidence, but the evidence must appeal to the needs, wants, desires, and values of the prospect. For example, the car salesperson who notices a backpack and binoculars in the prospect's old car might stress the model car's advantages for camping trips. The testimony of satisfied customers is also an effective form of evidence, especially if names of satisfied persons are given for verification.

Demonstrate.   Demonstration is showing what the product is, how it works, and what it can do for the prospect. At meetings for selling lake lots, the movie tries to take the buyers to the lake lot and let them see the sunset through the pines, watch a fish being netted, and hear the campfire crackle. The demonstration of cosmetics in the department store appeals to the sense of sight with color and the sense of smell with the many fragrances that waft over the cosmetic counter.

A demonstration can be boring unless some creativity and showmanship are used. At the meeting promoting the sale of lake lots, how could you inject some showmanship? Have pine boughs decorating the room? Give each person a small fishing pole? Let someone be the lucky winner of a picnic basket?

Another way to enliven a demonstration is through audience participation. In the cosmetics department, someone from the group could be selected as a model for a makeup demonstration.

Answer Objections.   There are going to be objections, or at least questions, no matter how well the sales presentation is made. The first rule for the salesperson is never to become defensive and argumentative. You may win the argument but lose the sale. Try to keep the prospect in a positive frame of mind. Point out the benefits on both sides and let the prospect have the feeling of choice. As a salesperson, let the buyers feel they are making the decision. Avoid telling them what to do and how to think. The best salesperson does the job so well the customer feels that buying the product is a personal decision.

Sometimes you can answer an objection by turning a disadvantage into an advantage. If a prospect says the price is too high, you can reply, "Yes, the price is high but only because the quality and workmanship are so good. In the long run, you'll be better off because this product will last longer and be of better service to you than will an inferior product."

Finally, beware of overselling. Sometimes the prospect is already sold and indicates so with a smile, a genuine interest, and a desire to close the sale. All you have to do is be of service. Don't talk yourself out of a sale.

Close the Sale.   The prospective buyer may bring up some final objections. Answer them as they arise. Don't argue. Explain. Point out the advantages of your product. Watch for nonverbal cues such as muscle movements and tone of voice, and you will be able to read the clues to a forthcoming response.

Even if the situation looks like a lost cause, continue in a positive manner. If necessary, ask the prospects for three main reasons why they have decided not to buy. These reasons could give you one last chance to answer what the prospects consider strong objections.

If, despite all your efforts, your sales presentation is turned down, take consolation in the fact that you did your best. When you are successful, let the exuberance of accomplishment generate enthusiasm for the next sale.

A SAMPLE SALES TALK TO A GROUP

The following sample speech illustrates how to use the six time-tested sales techniques in a speech of persuasion through motivation.

The speaker begins with an appeal to the listeners' interests, needs, wants, desires, and values.

Ladies and gentlemen, I'd like to begin this afternoon by thanking the Plain County Small Business Association for allowing my staff and me to address you in hopes of making your jobs a little easier for you in the near future. I've enjoyed this afternoon's luncheon because I believe that each one of you has some need or concern in your business that can be met by the EASY Product Center. We are here today to help you find solutions that will make your business run more smoothly and more competitively. Later, you will have an opportunity to sit down at one of the many computer stations we have set up around the room. Furthermore, individual appointments can be set up with our marketing representatives. This is the only way that we can accurately meet your needs. No two businesses have the same problems or require the same solutions. I appeal to you: Don't be trapped into the notion that you have to have the same office equipment that your competitor has.

I've had the opportunity to speak with most of you today and in the process, compiled a healthy list of questions that are on your minds. Many of you are wondering if a computer is what you need. By being here today you've answered that question. You have acknowledged the fact that your business needs something and that, from what you have seen, read, or heard, a computer might be the answer. Many of you have even shopped around. Folks, the shopping stops today. If you had seen something out there that you knew was what you needed, you wouldn't be here now. No business professional can afford to shop around forever. The sooner you can install the proper business solution—an EASY Personal Computer in your office—the sooner you can start saving. Profits are the name of the game. EASY can help you earn those bigger profits. Some of you quickly find that the cost of your solution will become insignificant compared to the long-term savings you will reap.

Another concern that I've heard a lot about is in the area of support. Who's going to support this equipment if it fails or if my needs change? Who will train me how to use it? Your worries are over. When you decide to buy from the EASY Product Center, you begin a long partnership with us. EASY isn't going anywhere. We're here to stay. We want to help you now because we want to be there when you expand your business so that you will always be ready for new growth and larger profits.

Now that I've covered some of the superficial questions, I'd like to bite into the meat of the presentation. I will briefly identify and comment on six of the main concerns that you people have told me are problems in your offices.

First, eliminating overtime in your office: How would you like to be able to do paperwork five times faster? Mass mailings can be completed in a fraction of the time. Second, the problem of the secretary having to retype proposals: Would it benefit you if your secretary never had to retype your proposals? Word processors allow you to make changes to, revise, edit, and delete documents in just seconds. Third, accounts receivable is out of control: Would it save you any time or money if you could cross-reference your receivables on a day-to-day basis? No more bulky ledger, stacks of invoices, or out-of-balance figures. Fourth, restoring old-fashioned quality: Would you be pleased to have up-to-the-minute status on your business finances? How would you like reports that are printed flawlessly in manuscript form? No problem! Fifth, twice a month or more, the budget sheet must be updated, requiring up to 75 entries: If you had a way to automatically update

---

Margin notes:

The speaker points out the benefits that will come from acquiring the product.

The speaker makes use of audience analysis to get some information about the listeners in order to apply the information in the presentation.

The speaker emphasizes additional benefits of purchasing the product.

The speaker answers audience objections and stresses the company's service as well as its product.

The speaker outlines the specific objections and counters each with an argument emphasizing how the product can overcome it.

The speaker concentrates on specific problems customers are likely to have experienced and points out how the product will solve specific problems.

The speaker presents some final evidence to convince the prospects of the product's value and use to them.

The speaker answers some final objections.

The speaker offers an incentive to buy now.

The speaker closes with a remark intended to seal the new partnership between seller and buyer.

your budget sheet on a daily basis, would that benefit you? Maybe it would eliminate an accountant or free up a secretary. Finally, an efficient way to keep information on clients: Wouldn't you like to know which customers are 90 days past due? While you're at it, print an "overdue invoice" and envelope for each one of these customers. All this takes only a few minutes.

Now I realize that some of you have more questions. Most of you are sitting there trying to weigh the advantages and disadvantages of acquiring this new technology. Just remember that if an EASY Personal Computer can streamline just one aspect of your company, it will probably save you money, manpower, and precious working time.

My marketing staff will be available in just a few minutes to answer your more specific questions. Also, be aware that you are welcome to come to the EASY Product Center at any time, for any reason.

There is one more incentive for you. From now until the end of the month, we will honor a 20 percent discount on any computer equipment purchased by those of you who attended this seminar today.

I'd like to ask you now to move to the various computer stations around the room where you can direct any further questions to the marketing representatives. They will also be filling your orders and arranging for delivery and set-up. Orders placed today will be filled on a first come, first serve basis because of the high demand.

Thank you all for being here this afternoon. I've certainly enjoyed my visit and I look forward to seeing all of you at the EASY Product Center.

SUMMARY

Persuasion through motivation deals with emotional appeal, an appeal to the listeners' needs, wants, desires, and values. The goal of persuasion through motivation is to get the listeners to do something, that is, to motivate them to change behavior. Various theories have attempted to explain motivation, which is defined as the moving force behind a person's behavior. The theories most applicable in explaining persuasion through motivation are those of rewarded behavior, hierarchy of needs, group identification, and self-image. The speaker who understands and applies the theories of motivation is well equipped to motivate listeners. The persuasive speaker must decide which motivational approach or approaches will work best with a particular audience.

Appeals to security, knowledge, power, prestige, accomplishment, aesthetics, and love are motives a speaker can tie to the listeners' needs, wants, desires, and values. The formula for organizing a motivational speech includes six steps: getting attention, stating the point, pointing out the benefits, giving examples, restating the point, and answering questions and objections.

One example of persuasion through motivation is the sales presentation. No matter what the specific objective of the presentation, the general goal is to motivate the listeners to do something—to buy a product, to subscribe to a service, etc. The personal qualities most expected in a salesperson are honesty, knowledge of the product, belief in the product, friendliness, enthusiasm, a sense of humor, emotional stability, and an acceptable appearance. Developing these qualities will enhance the prospective salesperson's chances for success.

Certain established sales procedures have proven to be effective. Six time-tested steps include: beginning with the listener's interests, pointing out the benefits, presenting the evidence, demonstrating the product, answering objections, and closing the sale. Notice how many of these are similar to the six-step formula for organizing a speech of motivation.

ASSIGNMENTS

1. Listen to a speech of motivation. Determine how the speaker tried to motivate you. Examples of motivational speeches might be a church sermon, a commercial on radio or TV, and a candidate for political office encouraging you to vote for him or her. Give an oral report of your findings in class.

2. Make a speech in class in which you motivate your listeners to do something: see a movie, read a book, take a course, buy a product, contribute money to a charitable organization, or vote for a candidate. What benefits can you illustrate?

3. Give a sales talk in which you attempt to sell a product you have used: a purse, wallet, watch, tool, gadget, razor, camera, cordless phone, or anything else of a concrete, practical nature. What benefits can you illustrate?

4. The role-playing exercises suggest situations in which you use a motivational appeal to persuade someone to do (or not to do) something.

   a. You have one minute to persuade someone not to jump from the twelfth floor of a building. What persuasive arguments will you use? Before attempting this exercise, you may want to talk to someone in your local police department who has had experience with this problem.

   b. In five sentences persuade an armed burglar not to shoot you. What persuasive arguments can you use?

NOTES

1. W. Phillips Davison, "On the Effects of Communication," *Public Opinion Quarterly* 23 (1959): 359.

2. George C. Homans, *Social Behavior: Its Elementary Forms* (New York: Harcourt Brace and World, 1961), p. 18.

3. Abraham H. Maslow, *Motivation and Personality* 2nd ed. (New York: Harper and Row, 1970), pp. 35–72.

General Types of Evocative Speaking	Speeches of Inspiration	Be Sensitive to Others
		Get Stirred Up
		Find Some Heart-to-Heart Way of Helping
	Speeches of Entertainment	The Factors of Interest
		Building a Background of Humor
		Understanding the Types of Humor
		Do's and Don'ts in Using Humor
Specific Types of Evocative Speaking: Speeches for Special Occasion	Frequently Delivered Special Occasion Speeches	Announcing a Coming Event
		Introducing a Speaker
		Nominating a Candidate
		Extending a Welcome and Making a Response
		Making a Presentation and Accepting It
	Less Frequently Made Special Occasion Speeches	Commemorative Speeches
		Formal Occasions

13 Evocative Speaking

OBJECTIVES

When you have finished this chapter, you should be able to:

1. define an inspirational speech;
2. make a short inspirational speech that arouses noble human emotion;
3. explain what an entertaining speech is and describe nine ways to generate interest in a speech of entertainment;
4. make a short entertaining speech in which you use one or more of the factors of interest to get and keep the audience's attention;
5. describe the characteristics of each of the specific types of evocative speeches, the speeches for special occasions; and
6. make a special occasion speech—an announcement, introduction, nomination, welcome, response, presentation, acceptance, tribute or eulogy, dedication, anniversary speech, invocation, benediction, inaugural address, or farewell speech.

13 Evocative Speaking

Edwin Kendziorski, teacher of carpentry at the Kilbourn Junior Trade School, went to his friend who teaches speech and said, "I've got to make a presentation at the Trade School Teacher's Association banquet. Could you write a speech for me?" The speech teacher asked a half dozen questions to get the facts. The next day he presented a one-page manuscript to Ed, who looked at it and said, "How can you put something like this together?" "The same way you make originally designed cabinets," was the reply.

Ed took the manuscript gratefully, thinking to himself that he could teach his friend how to build cabinets much more easily than his friend could teach him how to construct this kind of speech.

Why did Ed feel this way? Why did he have such doubts about his ability to write and deliver an evocative speech? In this chapter we will attempt to answer that question by examining the nature of evocation, the kinds of evocative speeches, and the way to build them.

What is evocative speaking? Evocative speaking calls forth an emotional response from within the listener. In this chapter we will discuss the general types of evocative speaking—inspiration and entertainment. We will also look at several examples of specific types of evocative speeches, which are often called speeches for special occasions.

GENERAL TYPES OF EVOCATIVE SPEAKING

The general types of evocative speeches are speeches of inspiration and speeches of entertainment. The knowledge and use of these general types will serve as a background and enrichment of the specific types of speeches for special occasions, which we will discuss later in the chapter.

Speeches of Inspiration

Lew Sarett, a well-known professor of speech at Northwestern University, concluded a letter to a former student with these words:

Again, thank you so much for writing to me. You fired up my spirit a lot. Every man's energies drag now and then. Mine too. A letter like yours does one enormous good. Thank you.

Faithfully,

Lew Sarett[1]

The man who received this letter was amazed to learn that his note to his former teacher had "fired up the spirit" of a famous person who had taught for over thirty years, had written extensively on personal adjustment, and had created some of the nation's warmest poetry.

The bellows of inspiration need to be directed to the waning inner fires of every individual from time to time. The football coach stimulates the losing squad at halftime. The sales manager paints promising pictures for the sales staff. Clergy encourage their congregations to see more vividly and believe more deeply. Wherever human beings are found, inspiration is often the answer to flagging energy.

Knute Rockne, football coach at the University of Notre Dame for many years, understood this human need for inspiration. One afternoon, after his players had played a ragged first half and were resting in the locker room expecting to receive a severe tongue lashing, Rockne said nothing. He just paced back and forth, his jaw set, his eyes narrow slits. As the seconds ticked by, the silent tension increased. The players occasionally lifted their eyes from a futile inspection of the concrete floor, exchanged brief glances, and wondered. Finally, as the signal to begin the second half sounded, Rockne turned to the players and barked, "All right, little boys, let's go!!!" Stung and inspired at the same time, the Notre Dame team came from behind to win the game.

Speeches of inspiration are usually given on a theme that the listeners already understand and believe in. The football team wants to win. The sales staff believes in the product and wants to sell. The members of the congregation have faith and want to lead better lives. They do not have to be informed or convinced. It is true that the inspiring speaker can help the listeners understand even more clearly by offering better explanation and help them believe even more intensely by presenting stronger evidence. However, the main function of inspirational speaking is to re-awaken what is sleeping, to fire up what is dying, to rekindle what may be nearly gone.

Three steps to becoming an effective inspirational speaker include: be sensitive to the problems of others, get stirred up over them, and find some heart-to-heart way of helping others.

Be Sensitive to Others.   "I know how you feel." You as a speaker can say these words honestly because you do know how other people feel. You know because you have had the same kinds of feelings. You have faced the same kinds of problems. When you let this knowledge rise to the surface of your consciousness, you are developing a sensitivity toward others and a philosophy of life.

The search for a philosophy of life has occupied human thinking for many thousands of years. People have asked deep, searching questions and, from the answers, have evolved sets of values. Values are individual matters, but the problems that give rise to them are universal.

In order for inspiration to be effective, it must reach deep into a person's basic philosophy. It must concern a consideration of such universal questions as:

- Is there a God?
- What is patriotism?
- Where do I belong?
- What does home mean to me?
- What is love?
- Who is my true friend?
- Where is security to be found?
- What is my special and satisfying place in the world?

Our attempts to find answers to such questions result in our formulating the values that give meaning to life. Speeches of inspiration can reinforce these values.

A belief in God can be fortified through the sacred writings of various religions. The Psalms of David, Jesus' Sermon on the Mount, the revelations to Muhammad recorded in the Koran, and the *Analects* of Confucius have often been sources of inspiration because they show an understanding of and a compassion for humanity.

Belief in a common humanity evokes inspiration. Imagine how you would feel if, as a new immigrant to the United States, you stood below the Statue of. Liberty and read the words of Emma Lazarus inscribed there:

> *Give me your tired, your poor,*
> *Your huddled masses yearning to be free,*
> *The wretched refuse of your teeming shore,*
> *Send these, the homeless, tempest-tost to me:*
> *I lift my Lamp beside the golden door.*

If daily living seems a burden sometimes, inspiration can ease the load. When President John F. Kennedy gave his inaugural address, he was sensitive to the inspirational moment at hand.

> . . . the same revolutionary beliefs for which our forebears fought are still at issue around the globe—the belief that the rights of man come not from the generosity of the State but from the hands of God . . .
>
> We dare not forget today that we are the heirs of that first revolution. Let the word go forth from this time and place, to friend and foe alike, that the torch has been passed to a new generation of American-born in this century, tempered by war, disciplined by a hard and bitter peace, proud of our ancient

> heritage—and unwilling to witness or permit the slow undoing of those human rights to which this nation has always been committed and to which we are committed today. . . .
>
> And so, my fellow Americans: Ask not what your country can do for you. Ask what you can do for your country.[2]

Get Stirred Up.   Sometimes people who want to appear sophisticated get the idea that a sophisticated person never shows emotions. Such people believe that showing enthusiasm, for example, is naive and somehow childish. They believe that they should wear a deadpan expression and act rather bored.

Nothing could be further from the truth. Any person, sophisticated or otherwise, can be enthusiastic. Enthusiasm is not fanaticism. It is a zest for living.

When you are aware of someone else's problems and get stirred up over them, it shows that you care enough to want to do something to help. Because you care, you focus your energies toward working things out, not as a duty but as an exciting and joyous experience of life. This is enthusiasm. It can be interpreted as an attraction for something good, noble, or of great value—something that brings out the best in us. When this best is brought out, then we can, in turn, impart it to others as we give inspiration. Enthusiasm begets enthusiasm.

Find Some Heart-to-Heart Way of Helping.   Often the best way to help people is not to solve their problems for them but to inspire them so that they can solve the problems on their own. One way to accomplish this is to tell them where you stand. Speaking out of your own experience and beliefs, you can be sincere. You can speak of your feelings, and your listeners can be inspired by knowing that you care enough to share with them some deep and meaningful part of your life.

The speaker in the following example inspired his listeners to believe more fully that every person must have an island—a place of escape from everyday stress.

> My wife and I some years ago inherited from my uncle an island two miles off the coast of Maine. Outside of bottled gas for cooking and refrigeration, it is primitive. We draw water from the well, chop wood for the fireplace, and live in splendid isolation during the summer months. We do have a telephone, but it is useful only for outgoing calls! Here we can escape from the pressures of modern living, from the automobile, the telephone, the television, the importuning of faculty and students. Here we can refresh our souls, reassess our values, and commune with the sea, the air, the pines, and the stars.

> If this is an escape, I make no apology for everyone must, I believe, have
> an escape. Each person must have an island. We all need that release from
> the too-pressing tensions that surround us. From where will this judgment
> of comparative values come, this sense of direction that will supply our
> hypothetical pilot of the supersonic bomber with a compass and a celestial
> chart? It can come, I believe, only from the search for God, from the search
> for beauty as well as truth, from the search for the meaning and purpose of
> life. It can come only from a faith in the sanctity of the human spirit, from
> a belief in our importance in the grand design.

The speaker did not attempt to help his listeners by telling them exactly
what to do. Instead, he expressed his own beliefs and the solution he had
found. Perhaps some of his listeners were helped by his experience and
perhaps others were not. In either case, they were free to choose a course
of action. This is the essence of inspiring others to help themselves.

Frequently listeners need a lift. In your inspirational speech you can
supply this lift by being sensitive to their emotional needs, getting stirred
up yourself, and finding something in your life that can set off a spark in
the lives of your listeners.

Speeches of Entertainment

While we may find many things entertaining, most of us think little of
our own ability to entertain others. We need not sing, dance, or be a
professional comedian in order to hold the attention of an audience. Our
own interests, when told in a thoughtful, orderly, and enthusiastic manner, can be interesting and entertaining to others.

In this section we will examine not how you can become a paid professional entertainer, but rather how you can make your speeches now in
the classroom and later in your professional career more interesting and
entertaining.

The Factors of Interest.   We can discuss at least nine methods you
can use to develop an entertaining speech. These nine methods, which
we refer to as the factors of interest, are the vital, the unusual, the uncertain, the similar, the conflicting, the animated, the concrete, the beautiful, and the humorous. We will examine each of these factors in more
detail.

1. The *vital*. When someone hands you a photograph of a group of
people and you're among the group, for whom do you look first? You
probably look for yourself. When you pass a mirror, can you avoid the
temptation to look at your reflection? When a speaker refers to you by
name, can you resist paying attention? People may feign embarrassment,
but secretly most of them love being in the spotlight. If you as a speaker

want to make something vital to your listeners, talk about something that is vital to their interests. Talk about tuition increases and watch your class members sit up and pay attention.

2. The *unusual*. In the early days of television, all programs were done "live." Nowadays, most programs are taped or "taped in front of a studio audience." Today when a program is done live (for example, "Saturday Night Live"), a sign or announcement indicates that the show is being performed live. The advantage of the live performance is that anything can happen. The audience stays alert, waiting for the unexpected or the unusual to occur. If a student speaker brings a monkey to class for use as a visual aid, everyone in the class is fascinated.

3. The *uncertain*. When the football score is 33–0 and there are two minutes left in the game, you don't see many fans left in the stadium, but when the basketball underdog is leading the number one team by one point with only twenty-two seconds left to play, no one moves. When the speaker is about to describe what happened when the raft was running out of control down the rapids, even the bell sounding the end of the class can't influence the audience to leave.

4. The *similar*. Thorton Wilder's play *Our Town*, considered by some to be America's finest play, is about the everyday activities in a small town— growing up, gossiping, churchgoing, romance, marriage, birth, and death. An actor who played the part of the stage manager in the play has reported that the comment most frequently heard after performances was "the play reminded me so much of my hometown (or my neighborhood)." As a public speaker, you can use the similar as a factor of interest anytime in your speech, but using it in the introduction is especially helpful to establish common ground with the audience.

5. The *conflicting*. Life is a drama, and the essence of a dramatic plot is conflict. Wherever we look we can find conflict. Young children fight over a toy. Teenagers vie for popularity. Adults compete for promotions or for jobs. The public speaker draws interest by speaking for or against a person, principle, cause, or institution. The person against society, the forces of nature against the individual, and a terrorist society against the rest of the world are some examples of situations that engender interest through conflict.

6. The *animated*. Watch several television commercials and analyze their visual elements. Notice how effectively the automobile salesperson moves in and out and around the various models of cars. Turn to the Saturday morning cartoons and see how large a part movement plays in their presentations. Transfer that principle to public speaking. The speaker who just stands there is boring, but the speaker who moves with a purpose, gesticulates descriptively, and uses showmanship and dramatization can have the audience listening attentively.

7. The *concrete*. To be effective, your speech should be as concrete as the subject allows. You can talk about nutrition, but it is much more effective to describe the benefits of a fresh fruit salad made with sliced bananas, juicy pears, crisp apples, succulent oranges, and tart grapefruit.

8. The *beautiful*. A grandfather wrote a birthday poem for his two-year-old granddaughter and recited it for family and friends. The group listened intently as he spoke:

> *Little Becky on a star,*
> *How I love you from afar.*
> *Underneath the moonlit blue*
> *Let me find a cloud for you*
> *Where we can play some hide and seek,*
> *And when I find you, kiss your cheek.*
> *Then for your birthday find a nail*
> *So we can pin a comet tail*
> *Against the deep blue midnight sky*
> *For flying saucers passing by.*
> *Little Becky on a star*
> *Congratulations from afar.*
> *Happy Birthday way up there*
> *For all your angel friends to share.*[3]

Beauty is not communicated only through poetry. We can appreciate the visual beauty of odd cloud formations alchemized by the setting sun or the ghostly mist rising over a lake at dawn. Sometimes we can communicate beauty through a single word, "The fisherman had a faraway *lake* in his eye."

9. The *humorous*. When asked by a jazz neophyte what jazz is, Louis Armstrong is alleged to have replied, "If you don't know what it is when you hear it, how can I tell you what it is when you don't?" Many comedians have experienced the same difficulty in trying to define humor. It's hard to pinpoint just what tickles the funnybone.

One academic definition of humor describes it as "the incongruous, coming as a surprise." That definition may cover many cases of humor, but isn't an automobile accident incongruous and don't many auto accidents come as a surprise? Certainly we wouldn't describe an automobile accident as humorous. The dictionary defines humor as "the quality that makes something seem funny, amusing, or ludicrous." But what is that "quality"?

No matter what the definition of humor, humorous passages in a speech must be carefully prepared. They should be written out, not to be read or memorized, but to be thought about thoroughly. The tag line, the line that triggers the laugh, should be memorized or at least known so well that the briefest glance at your notes will be sufficient to spark your memory so that you can deliver the line naturally and directly to your audience.

You may wonder if all this work is really necessary just to get a few laughs. Once you've experienced the thrill of having your listeners laugh along with you, you'll appreciate that the time spent preparing is well worth the effort. Humor breaks tension and helps the speaker make friends with the listeners. Listeners like speakers who make them laugh. Because using humor to generate interest is such a difficult skill to master, in the next section we'll discuss some ways to make the task easier.

Building a Background of Humor. The first step in developing a humorous approach is building a background of humor. You are surrounded daily by humorous incidents. It isn't always easy to see the humor when you are under stress, but you can try. Don't let yourself be upset by trifles. Try to find the humor in life.

There are a number of practical ways to build up a humor file. Recall as many jokes and humorous stories, quotations, anecdotes, and analogies as you can. Write out each one on an index card and devise a classification system for the cards. Every time you read a pertinent item in a newspaper or magazine or hear an item on the radio or television, write it down. Some items may fit under several classifications. If so, make a cross-reference for the item.

Understanding the Types of Humor. Before you can learn to become humorous, you should understand the different types of humor. We can identify nine common types of humor: the pun, the overstatement, the understatement, satire, sarcasm, wit, mimicry, burlesque, and irony.

1. The *pun* is often called the lowest form of humor because it is a play not on an idea but on a word or a sound. For example, a supermarket customer asked the butcher to cut a skinned rabbit in half, and the butcher replied, "Sorry, we don't split hares here." Now you can see why the pun is called the lowest form of humor. One person's pun may be another's punishment.

2. *Overstatement* is exaggeration. It's comedian Bob Hope's trademark: "I wouldn't say it was cold coming up to Alaska, but . . ." You can fill in your own exaggeration.

3. *Understatement* gets the laugh through downplay or restraint. For example, a great thunderstorm poured buckets of rain, forcing postponement of a scheduled outdoor concert. The public address announcer opened the concert by saying, "I welcome you to tonight's concert postponed because of last night's 'moisture.'"

4. *Satire* pokes good-natured fun at something. For example, "human beings are described as rational animals, but in reality they are animals, slightly tinged with rationality."

5. *Sarcasm* is biting humor. For example, "That's a lovely dress, dear. Too bad they didn't have your size."

6. *Wit* is a clever remark expressed in a sharp but amusing way. For example, the professor remarked to his class, "The capacity of the human mind to resist the introduction of needed information is infinite."

7. *Mimicry* is the imitation of another person's idiosyncracies in a light-hearted manner. Comedian Rich Little is well known for his many impersonations. A familiar one is Little's mimicry of President Reagan, which begins with a smile, a shake of the head, and the vocalized "Well, . . ."

8. *Burlesque* is extreme exaggeration for comic effect. Perhaps the most obvious example is the circus clown enjoyed by children and those who have not forgotten childhood's joys.

9. *Irony* is saying one thing but meaning another—usually the exact opposite of what is said. For example, a student who doesn't like a particular teacher may ask (with a vocal inflection), "Is he a *teacher?*"

Do's and Don'ts in Using Humor.   When you attempt to use humor in your speeches of entertainment, keep in mind these do's and don'ts.

Do's
1. If you can, use the joke, story, or anecdote to illustrate a point. Then even if there is no laughter, you still have the illustration.
2. Try to be original and creative. If you can't come up with a new joke or story, tell an old story in a new way.
3. Make sure the joke or story you plan to use has not been used by another recent speaker or that your humorous remarks are not so timeworn that everyone in the audience is sure to have heard them a number of times.
4. Direct your humor to your specific audience.

Don'ts
1. Don't force humor or try too hard to get a laugh. The listeners may not always respond with vocal laughter. Sometimes you can see them smiling with their eyes.
2. Avoid attempts at humor that are offensive or off-color. Be aware of the sensitivities of your listeners, and let your remarks be in good taste.
3. If in doubt about a joke, don't tell it. Losing the respect of your listeners is not worth a momentary bit of laughter.

As we mentioned at the beginning of this chapter, speeches of inspiration and speeches of entertainment are general types of evocative speaking. Some very good examples of speeches that use inspiration and entertainment are the ones we will study in the second part of this chapter, the specific types of evocative speeches called speeches for special occasions.

SPECIFIC TYPES OF EVOCATIVE SPEAKING: SPEECHES FOR SPECIAL OCCASIONS

Speeches for special occasions are characterized by these general considerations:

1. They are the outgrowth of a specific occasion, such as a banquet honoring someone for achievement.
2. They are usually brief, one to two minutes, because they are in the context of a longer program.
3. They are nonargumentative and promote goodwill.
4. Their primary purposes are to inform, to inspire, and to entertain.

There are many types of speeches for special occasions. Some types, of course, are more frequently made than others. In the next section we will examine the more frequently delivered special occasion speeches.

Frequently Delivered Special Occasion Speeches

The more frequently made speeches for special occasions are the announcement, the introduction, the nomination, the welcome and response, and the presentation and acceptance. In the following sections we will examine the characteristics of these special occasion speeches and look at some examples of each type.

Announcing a Coming Event. Rare indeed is the speech of announcement in which the vital information given is fully and correctly remembered by the audience. All too often the speech of announcement is not well made. Frequently, after the speaker finishes, the listeners inquire of one another, "What time did he say?" or "How much does a ticket cost?" or "Where is it going to be held?" Remember the tools of reporting: who, what, where, when, why, and how. Use them to give complete information in your announcements.

There are many ways to make a speech of announcement. One method that fits many situations consists of five steps:

1. Give the time, place, date, and price if applicable.
2. Tell what will take place.

3. Point out what benefits the listeners will receive by attending.

4. Repeat the time, place, date, and price.

5. Repeat once again the time, place, date, and price.

A speech of announcement might resemble the following example.

> Friday night, December 18, at 8 P.M., in the gym, for only two dollars, you are invited to attend the annual student-faculty fund-raising basketball game. You'll see some of your friends and classmates pitted against the fearsome faculty in a game of skill and intelligence.
>
> In addition to having a good time, you'll be helping the American Field Service raise money for some worthy student to enjoy a one-year scholarship on foreign soil.
>
> That's next Friday night, December 18, 8 P.M., in the gym, for only two dollars.

If the time, place, date, and price seem repetitive, they are! And they have to be, if you want your listeners to remember.

Introducing a Speaker.   The speech of introduction has two major purposes: to build up the confidence of the person who is being introduced and to let the audience know that the person is worth listening to. Understanding the purpose of the speech will help you remember the following do's and don'ts in speeches of introduction.

Do's
1. Be brief, no longer than one minute.

2. Be happy to make the introduction, although you need not say so in words.

3. Present your best informal self. There is no need to sound like you're making a speech.

Don'ts
1. Don't try to be funny.

2. Don't try to be more important than the speaker.

3. Don't drag in favorite ideas of your own that are unrelated to the occasion.

4. Don't trespass on the speaker's content.

5. Don't use worn-out introductory phrases such as, "It gives me great pleasure," "a speaker who needs no introduction," or "without further ado."

6. Don't use adjectives for special pleading such as "our able, talented, capable speaker."

Use the following four-step guide to prepare your speeches of introduction.

1. Give a brief history of the speaker's accomplishments, but only those that relate to this speech, this audience, and this occasion. Avoid long recitations of accomplishments that, no matter how impressive, have little or no bearing on the present situation. Don't underplay or exaggerate; give the facts. To get the facts, you may have to interview the speaker before the program begins.
2. Show how the listeners will benefit by listening to the speaker.
3. Announce the title of the talk.
4. Enunciate the speaker's name clearly to the audience. Then turn to the speaker, smile, and nod. Do not announce the speaker's name to him or her. The speaker already has that information.

The following example shows how the four steps are used in the speech of introduction.

> Members of the Student Senate, I'm honored to introduce a graduate of our university, someone who majored in speech and debated for four years on our varsity debate team. She is now a communication consultant for several industries in the city. Sometimes we think of debaters as arguers, persons who want to win an argument by hook or by crook. I think you'll be surprised at the subject our speaker has chosen. It is one that all of us can benefit from. Her title is "How to Win the Argument Without Losing the Friend." Members of the Senate [speaking to the audience first and then nodding to the speaker], Ms. Janet Mallory.

Nominating a Candidate.   Members of organizations are frequently nominated for office by a simple statement, "I nominate Elena Ramirez for vice-president." In more formal nominating situations, however, the need arises to present the nominee's qualifications. The big weaknesses frequently found in speeches of nomination are too many generalities without sufficient facts, and too many superlatives that indicate more enthusiasm than evidence. To counteract these weaknesses, follow this method:

1. Present the candidate's qualifications by indicating what was accomplished. Brief examples are effective.
2. Refrain from overstating your case by referring to the nominee as the best, the most qualified, the greatest candidate of all. If you omit elaborate superlatives, you will stand a better chance of having your listeners believe you.
3. Withhold the nominee's name until the end.

Notice how, in the following example, the speaker presents evidence to support a nomination.

> Fellow students, I wish to nominate someone for chairperson of the homecoming committee for two reasons—her record of service and the enthusiasm she has to get things done. Her record of service you remember well. She served as secretary last year, coordinated our alumni party at the Union, and served as hostess to greet incoming students this fall. You know she has the drive to get things done. Much of the success of the outdoor campus party resulted from her efforts. For her service and enthusiasm, I nominate Sarah Shapiro.

Extending a Welcome and Making a Response.   The speech of welcome is similar to the speech of introduction. The difference between the two, however, is that the speech of welcome assumes that the guest of honor "needs no introduction." Instead, the emphasis is on receiving the person gladly. This key concept of gladness provides the tip-off as to how the speech of welcome should be made. The salutatory address given at commencement exercises is one example of a speech of welcome.

These suggestions will help you make a good speech of welcome:

1. Remember that the person being welcomed, not the welcomer, is the important one.
2. Be warm and friendly in your greeting.
3. To make the guest feel welcomed, give reasons and examples. Here is an opportunity for inspiration and humor, even slight teasing.
4. Some token of welcome may be presented. It may be an engraved admission pass, the familiar key to the city, or any gift that signifies the message, "We're glad you're here, and we welcome you with all our hospitality."

The following is an example of a speech of welcome.

> To complete our halftime festivities this afternoon, we welcome back one of our stars of seven years ago, someone who brought us honor during his years at Ohio State, and who continues to make us proud in every game he plays with the Cleveland Browns. John Stockhausen, you're as welcome here today on this field as the spirit of fine fellowship and good sportsmanship that you exemplified as a student and that you have continued to demonstrate in professional football. John, many hopeful young men on our squad look at your retired uniform in the trophy cabinet and are inspired by what they read beneath it, "John Stockhausen, gentleman, athlete, and friend."

> We reserved a special seat for you today, on the old bench where you seldom sat. As you can see, it still needs a good paint job, but we're proud to say that your presence will make it shine anew.
>
> Welcome back, John Stockhausen.

The person being welcomed makes a speech of response, taking the cue of response from the speech of welcome itself. In order to prepare in advance, the speaker responding to the welcome should try to anticipate what the welcomer might say and prepare a broad, general response on this basis.

Speakers must listen carefully to the actual speech of welcome so that they can see how well the prepared response fits. As speakers get up to talk, they can make whatever changes are necessary, and they can include some specific references to the welcomer's remarks.

The responding speaker should speak humbly, show happiness, and express sincere appreciation by complimenting those present. In the following example, notice how well the speech of response relates to the speech of welcome.

> Thank you very much, all of you. There are many memorable days in the life of a player. This is one that your warm welcome will help me remember always.
>
> I'm deeply grateful to my coaches at Ohio State, to the homecoming committee who extended this invitation, and to all of you here today who came out to cheer our team to victory. Thank you for the special seat on the bench. I couldn't think of a better seat anywhere. Thank you.

Making a Presentation and Accepting It.

The thoughts and feelings behind the speeches of presentation and acceptance are very similar to those accompanying speeches of welcome and response. However, the presentation of a gift is made with the thought that it will be lasting and of some value.

When presenting a gift, which may be in the form of an award, a citation, or a material offering, you should examine the recipient's background to discover reasons for the presentation. In your speech, stress those reasons but don't overplay them in exaggerated language. Try also to find some enjoyable association between the recipient and the gift.

In the following example, a graduating senior, representing his class, presents the graduates'.gift to the college at the graduation ceremony.

> President Gagliano and members of the faculty, we, the graduating class of 1987, wish to present at this time our graduation gift to the college. We know that a gift from the seniors is something traditional. That is not why

we are making this presentation. Our reasons are based on our appreciation for what you have done for us.

We appreciate, first of all, the fact that you have dedicated your lives to education. We know it isn't always easy to meet a group of unbridled, inexperienced, untamed freshmen and to try in four short years to make them worthy graduates. Yet, year after year, you accept this same challenge and meet it. Second, we appreciate the extra time that you gave us over and above the call of duty. Often after you did your work once, we asked you to do it again in the form of extra and special help.

To show our appreciation, we would like to present to you and the college our class gift, this painting entitled *Autumn in the Country*. We thought that, perhaps, next fall when the day is pleasant and the students are a bit noisy and wearing on your nerves, you might like to look at it and wish you were— "in the country."

Just as the speech of response takes its cue from the speech of welcome, so does the speech of acceptance take its cue from the speech of presentation. The speaker accepting the presentation should try to have some idea in advance of what the presenter will say, at least generally, and

A speech of acceptance takes its cue from the speech of presentation. If possible, the accepting speaker should know in advance what the presenter will say. If advance information is not available, the accepting speaker should pay close attention to the presentation so that the response can be as specific as possible.

then listen carefully to the actual presentation so that the reply can be somewhat specific.

A few additional rules to follow in the speech of acceptance include:

1. Express gratitude. Don't forget to say "thank you."
2. Comment on the significance of the act of giving.
3. Accept the gift as a representative of all who share in its reception.
4. Look at the giver and not at the gift while listening to the speech of presentation.
5. If the gift is fairly small, accept it in the left hand so that you can shake the right hand of the presenter.

In the following sample speech of response, the president of the college in our example accepts the graduates' gift to the college and makes a speech of acceptance.

> Thomas O'Toole and members of the graduating class, in the name of the College of Speech, its students, faculty, and administrative staff, I accept your gracious and thoughtful gift. *Autumn in the Country*—that's a good idea, a very good idea. In fact, the idea is so provocative that I'm almost tempted to say, "In memory of this class, we hereby declare a special day each fall to be devoted to the outdoors for art work, nature study, science, and rural sociology." We might even invite the mathematics department to help us determine the shortest route to wherever we choose to go. There is one hitch in this kind of proclamation, however. Next year's graduating class might present us with *Winter in the Country*, and if I understand the imagination of students, we might even be accepting *Springtime at Muskego Beach*.
>
> We are grateful for your gift. We shall hang it in a prominent place in our hallway where all who pass by can enjoy its beauty and be reminded of your thoughtful generosity. Thank you.

Speeches of announcement, introduction, nomination, welcome-response, and presentation-acceptance are the kinds of special occasion speeches you will probably be called on to deliver most frequently. There are other kinds of occasional speeches, less frequently made, and some-day you may need to know how to make these kinds of speeches.

Less Frequently Made Special Occasion Speeches

Special occasion speeches less frequently made by the average speaker are conveniently grouped under the categories of commemorative speeches and speeches on formal occasions. These speeches are no less important than the types already discussed, but the opportunities for giving them do not occur very often. They are, however, important in commemorative and formal situations.

Commemorative Speeches. Commemorative speeches honor the memory of a person, place, or thing. A tribute or eulogy, a dedication, and a speech celebrating an anniversary are examples of commemorative speeches.

When we wish to praise someone living or dead and to draw inspiration from that person's life, we make a speech of tribute or deliver a eulogy. A tribute is given for the living, a eulogy for the deceased. A poor eulogy or tribute covers too much ground, narrates merely a series of facts, attempts to deify the person, or is sentimental. A good eulogy or tribute develops a theme around one or more related ideas, using inspiring illustrations from the person's life to support the ideas within the theme.

The following excerpt is from a eulogy delivered on behalf of Mr. Kerrigan, a neighbor of the speaker.

> The person we miss most in our neighborhood is our former neighbor, Mr. Kerrigan. Hardly a week goes by without one of the children or teenagers bringing up his name. The apple tree in his backyard still reminds us of his generosity and patience toward the children who loved to climb its branches. He enjoyed having children in his yard, and it seemed evident enough that the children, sitting on various levels of the branches, were more important to him than the apples themselves.

The following tribute was spoken on behalf of Dr. William M. Lamers, an assistant superintendent of the Milwaukee Public Schools, at a testimonial dinner.

> Ladies and gentlemen of the Milwaukee School Association, tonight at this testimonial dinner for Dr. Lamers, we would like to present this scroll to him. It reads:
>
> This testimonial has been presented to Dr. William M. Lamers in recognition of his outstanding leadership in the profession of education, his many contributions to the advancement of learning, his long and distinguished service as Assistant Supervisor of Schools for Milwaukee, and his wholehearted support of the precepts to which this organization subscribes. May this scroll serve as a permanent expression of our warm regard and high esteem for an associate who is a true friend, complete gentleman, superior administrator, and ideal educator.

Many things are officially dedicated to the public in our society. At the national, state, and local levels are monuments, bridges, dams, and cornerstones of all sorts of buildings—churches, schools, libraries, courthouses, and hospitals. You may have witnessed dedications at your college for an athletic field, a cornerstone for a new building, a theater, a science laboratory, a recreation hall, or a trophy room.

You may never be called on to make a speech of dedication for a million-dollar building. However, as an officer of an organization or as a chosen representative of a group, you may be asked to dedicate something important to your particular circumstances.

Regardless of the amount of importance attached to the occasion, the structure of the dedication speech is usually the same. The effective speech of dedication answers three questions:

- What is the meaning of this event?
- Who is responsible?
- What will it mean to those who follow?

The following example is a speech commemorating the dedication of the United States flag in a school library.

> Mr. Bouvier and fellow students, this is our flag. It stands here as a vivid symbol of our country, as an expression of your generosity, and as a patriotic inspiration to those who will study in this library now and in the future. You will see many flags in the future, but this one you will always remember because it was purchased out of your generous contributions. Today, as we dedicate this flag of our country to this library, we do so knowing that it will be ours to enjoy while we are here and theirs who follow us after we are gone. This is our flag. I dedicate it to this, the Brooks Memorial Library.

A third type of commemorative speech is the speech celebrating an anniversary. Anniversaries make vivid some past event. Our memories grow dim, and the significance of great days of the past fades away. To revivify the past, therefore, we celebrate anniversaries. Birthdays, patriotic holidays, wedding anniversaries, years on the job—all are possible subjects for anniversary speeches.

The anniversary speaker usually reflects on the past event that is being commemorated, analyzes its meaning, and projects its significance into the future. In the following example, notice how the speaker mentions several highlights of the past and ties them to the future.

> Today, Professor Alfred J. Sokolnicki, we celebrate your fortieth anniversary at Marquette University. Our researchers found that you entered the university in 1945 to take the position of Director of Speech Therapy and continued in that position for over twenty years. At that time you were elevated to the position of Dean of the College of Speech, a post you held for twelve years, during which time the student enrollment climbed to an all-time high. After resigning from the deanship, you became director of the

teaching assistants of the basic public speaking course, a position you still hold today. Congratulations for making your vast experience available to these teaching assistants who will remember you as well as thousands of others who enjoyed your memorable friendship and guidance.

In addition to the commemorative speeches of tribute or eulogy, dedication, and anniversary, evocative speeches may also be delivered on formal occasions.

Formal Occasions.   A formal occasion is a situation in which fixed customs or ceremonies are followed. Many of the speeches for special occasions could be discussed in this category, but the kinds of speeches that are usually given on formal occasions are the invocation and benediction, the inaugural address, and the farewell speech. The invocation and benediction are religious presentations. The invocation, given at the beginning of a program, asks for divine assistance in the program's success. The benediction, or prayer of thanks, is also a request for divine help as the occasion ends. The speaker, often a member of the clergy, gets ideas from the occasion itself. Both the invocation and the benediction may be original prayers enriched by the speaker's religious heritage. The following is an example of an invocation.

> Eternal God, we ask your help on this graduation day. Bless the graduates who have labored long in academic halls and classrooms; bless the many parents, relatives, and friends who have borne the responsibility of support; and bless the administration and faculty who have imparted the wisdom of the ages. Let this day be special in its celebration because of your vigilant help, Almighty Father. From you we have our strength; from you we receive fresh water in the desert and bread with the setting sun. For all these signs of your unending love, we praise you and thank you.

The following benediction was given by the Reverend Floyd A. Lotito, O.F.M., of the St. Boniface Franciscan Community at the 1984 Democratic National Convention in San Francisco. We quote the opening and the closing of the benediction.

> Sisters and Brothers, peace be with you! Your work here for this day is done. You have earned the right to rest and recreation. May memories of our City of St. Francis remain with you and the lessons that you have been learning here.
> St. Francis had a vision of a world at peace and in love, where we were all sisters and brothers—one family of humankind. Here the United Nations was founded. Here the nations voted to outlaw war as an acceptable way to settle their differences. . . .

Lotito concludes his benediction with these words:

> Dear God, trusting in your mercy and love, we cry "No more war! No more weapons of war!" Let us cherish your people as our nation's greatest asset.
>
> Give us your guidance that we may serve your people well, especially the poor, the outcast, the unwanted, that there may be justice for everyone without exception, and on earth peace, goodwill to all. Amen.[4]

After an election it is customary to hold a ceremony for the inauguration of the new officers. The newly elected president is usually the officer called on to make the inaugural address. In making an inaugural address, the president should:

1. Express gratitude for the trust expressed by the organization but refrain from saying, "I want to thank those who voted for me."
2. Avoid reference to campaign controversies to avoid polarization within the group. If possible, compliment the opponents for a fair and hard-fought campaign.
3. Concentrate on common beliefs and review the purposes of the organization.
4. Look to the future with optimism by promising to do the job well with the help of all.

The following is an example of an inaugural speech that might be given on a typical college campus.

> Thank you, Mr. Chairman, and thank you fellow members. I am very grateful and honored for the trust you have placed in me. By your vote of confidence you have given me an opportunity to re-examine with you the purpose of the Student Senate, which, according to our constitution is "to encourage students of Mayflower College to take an active interest in curricular, cocurricular, and social affairs through their duly elected representatives" who are found here in this group today. It should be our pledge, therefore, to represent the student body. We are their servants, and to this end we should devote our best energies. I promise you my best efforts and look forward to working with all of you.

Of all the speeches for special occasions, perhaps the most delicate is the speech of farewell. Out of sadness, the speaker must extract the elements of joy. This challenge requires a careful, balanced selection of material. The speaker must try to avoid slipping into the extremes of aloofness on the one hand and into sentimentality on the other.

One typical speech of farewell is that given at a commencement exercise by the valedictorian, the student who ranks highest in scholarship. In the speech of farewell, the speaker should show appreciation, express regret at leaving, and promise to remember. The speaker should recall pleasurable past associations but also look happily ahead. Whatever the circumstances, the speaker can meet the challenge by taking time to think, anticipate, and maybe even meditate. If the meeting of minds is important in communication, perhaps the meeting of hearts is even more so in the speech of farewell. In the following example, a graduating senior says farewell to the members of a drama group.

> Fellow Players, it is hardly necessary for me to tell you in so many words that I leave the Players with regret or that I shall miss you. No one could be active in an organization for three years without leaving part of oneself behind. But if I leave part of myself behind, I shall take equal parts of this organization with me. The memories of six plays—trying out, rehearsing, building sets, making costumes, experimenting with makeup—all these can never be forgotten, of course. But these are only things.
>
> My warmest memories are of you, my friends and colleagues. How can I ever forget your cooperation in *Our Town* and *Oklahoma* and the help you gave me in memorizing lines. These are the experiences I treasure most and shall remember longest.
>
> I'm looking forward to trying my luck in New York. Whatever success I may have there, if any, I shall always remember that the seeds were planted here, and that they grew in the fertile soil of my association with you. If ever you are looking for someone to buy a ticket so that you can complete your selling assignment, be sure to call me. I'll be back to see you perform, and in the meantime, I promise to remember all of you.

SUMMARY

Included in the category of evocative speaking are the general types of evocative speeches—the speech to inspire and the speech to entertain—and the specific types, the speeches for special occasions. In speeches of inspiration, the speaker reaches into his or her heart and into the hearts of others to find material to inspire audiences to live more fully. To reach these goals, the speaker must be sensitive to others' emotional needs, get stirred up over them, and find some heart-to-heart way of helping others.

There are nine methods that can be used to develop a speech of entertainment. These nine methods—referred to as the factors of interest—are the vital, the unusual, the uncertain, the similar, the conflicting, the animated, the concrete, the beautiful, and the humorous. Use of the humorous is a difficult skill to master: the speaker must develop the proper attitude to be able to see the humor in life. The speaker should also prepare for the use of humor by building a humor file of jokes and amusing stories, anecdotes, and analogies. Understanding the types of humor is another step in learning how to use it. Nine common types of humor are the pun, the overstatement, the understatement, satire, sarcasm, wit, mimicry, burlesque, and irony. Following the guidelines of do's and don'ts in using humor is a third step in developing a humorous approach.

Specific types of evocative speeches are often called speeches for special occasions. These speeches reach down into the wellsprings of inspiration and entertainment for mood and flavor. Special occasion speeches include announcements, introductions, nominations, welcomes and responses, and presentations and acceptances. Speeches for special occasions may also be delivered in commemorative or formal situations. Some types of commemorative speeches are the eulogy, the tribute, the dedication, and the anniversary speech. Speeches delivered on formal occasions include the invocation, the benediction, the inaugural address, and the farewell speech.

ASSIGNMENTS

1. Choose one of the following topic suggestions and give a two-minute inspirational speech.
   a. Look into your life for some noble, emotional moment. By telling the class what happened, inspire them to feel as you felt.
   b. Prepare a talk that could be called "This I Believe." Begin with a concept such as democracy, education, happiness, worship, courtesy, or brotherhood/sisterhood. Work out a specific purpose to clarify the foundation of your belief. Use an example or two.
   c. Share with your audience your admiration for a person who faces obstacles with courage or who has overcome handicaps. An account from a newspaper or magazine is acceptable, but personal experience is better.
   d. Choose one of the holidays and, by using a vivid example or two, inspire the class to appreciate the significance of the day more than they do at present.
   e. Stimulate in your listeners an interest in and appreciation for a little-known person whose life has in some way affected yours.
   f. Recall a poem, story, motion picture, or television drama that affected you deeply. Extract the important message and then apply it to daily living with a fresh example.

2. Choose one of the following suggestions and give a two-minute entertaining speech.
   a. Recall an incident from one of your travels in a speech that appeals to the beautiful.
   b. Give a talk emphasizing human interest. Relate a great thrill, an embarrassing moment, or an interesting anecdote from your own life.
   c. Tell about a humorous incident from your own life.
   d. If you think you can do a successful job, try telling a joke. Use the joke as an illustration of a point you wish to make.
   e. Rewrite an old joke to fit a situation with which your listeners can identify.

3. Give a one- to two-minute speech for a special occasion. Your instructor may assign one of the types of individual speeches to each class member or you may be asked to choose the one you feel you can handle best.

4. For an integrated educational experience, plan a banquet. Select one member of the class to be the emcee. Let each of the other class members make one of the speeches for special occasions.

NOTES

1. Lew Sarett, letter to the author, January 23, 1949.

2. *Public Papers of the Presidents of the United States: John F. Kennedy.* Washington, DC: Government Printing Office, 1961.

3. Joseph M. Staudacher.

4. Rev. Floyd A. Lotito, O.F.M., 1984 Democratic National Convention, San Francisco, CA.

Some Introductory Considerations	Definition of Impromptu Speaking
	Negative Aspects
	Positive Values
	Advice for Impromptu Speaking

Confidence in Impromptu Speaking	How Impromptu Is Impromptu?
	What Is Preparation?
	Can You Avoid Panic?

Basic Principles in Impromptu Speaking	Speaker Credibility
	Audience Analysis
	Purpose
	Research
	Organization
	Development
	Style
	Visual and Vocal Technique
	Adjustment to Feedback and Questions

Preparation Techniques for Impromptu Speaking	Background Considerations
	Introductory Comments
	Audience Analysis
	The Point
	Structure
	Examples
	Conclusion
	Brevity

Specific Patterns of Organization in Impromptu Speaking	Alan H. Monroe
	Richard C. Borden
	Dale Carnegie
	Lynn Surles

14 Impromptu Speaking

OBJECTIVES

When you finish this chapter, you should be able to:

1. define impromptu speaking;
2. list the negative aspects of impromptu speaking;
3. describe the positive values of impromptu speaking;
4. explain how you can build confidence in impromptu speaking;
5. list and explain the basic principles that underlie effective impromptu speaking;
6. list and explain the preparation techniques for impromptu speaking;
7. describe the patterns of organization proposed by Alan H. Monroe, Richard C. Borden, Dale Carnegie, and Lynn Surles; and
8. demonstrate your ability in impromptu speaking by making an impromptu speech on any subject you are assigned.

14 Impromptu Speaking

A young sociology instructor about to teach her first college-level course was nervous. It wasn't her opening lecture that bothered her. She had prepared well through long years of study and several recent hours of specific preparation for her first class. What bothered her was the uncertainty of what would follow the lecture itself, the time for questions. Some of the questions would be directly related to the lecture and would pose no problem, but this young sociology instructor knew from her own student days that some of the questions would "come out of left field."

Would she be able to make a good impression on her class? Would she be able to exhibit poise, analyze the question, separate its parts, reach into her background for information, particularly examples, and give an answer satisfying to students with the spirit of inquiry?

Someday soon in a public speaking situation you will be asked to say a few words without much chance to prepare. Will you be able to meet the challenge to your satisfaction? In this chapter we will discuss some methods and techniques that can help you meet and master that challenge.

SOME INTRODUCTORY CONSIDERATIONS

Impromptu speaking is the most frequent kind of communication used in social and business conversation. The impromptu challenge in public speaking is constant. You make a date, apply for a job, answer in class, answer questions after a speech, and make a point at a meeting. All of these situations are impromptu.

In the first part of this chapter we will define impromptu speaking and consider both the negative aspects and the positive values of the impromptu experience.

Definition of Impromptu Speaking

Impromptu speaking is not written out word for word and read aloud from a sheet of paper, nor is it memorized and then recited. It is not researched and extemporized from a carefully prepared outline. Impromptu speaking is spontaneous and unrehearsed, given on the spur of the moment. In essence it is thinking on your feet with almost no formal preparation.

Do not be misled by the dictionary definition of impromptu. The dictionary uses extemporaneous as a synonym for impromptu. While it is true that extemporaneous speakers choose many words, phrases, and even sentences on the spot, extemporaneous speakers are prepared and organized in advance, an advantage denied the impromptu speaker.

Someone once said there are two kinds of speeches: those made when you have something to say and those made when you have to say something. When you speak impromptu, you have to say something, and your prayer is that you also have something to say.

One kind of impromptu speaking is a creative game played in the classroom. Your instructor gives you a situation and you do the best you can. In the other kind of impromptu speaking, you are called on at a meeting and expected to stand up and make your contribution before a large audience. The chances are very good that if you handle those classroom practice situations well, you will meet the challenge outside the classroom too.

In whatever situation you find yourself, it is helpful to determine your purpose: to report, explain, convince, motivate, inspire, entertain, or solve a problem. Each purpose requires a different means of developing your point, although the one general life preserver in most impromptu speaking is to reach into your own experience for an example.

Negative Aspects

At the present moment, you may find that impromptu speaking is a problem. To solve any problem, we look to the facts, both bad and good, to work out a solution. Impromptu speaking is not without its negative aspects. Perhaps by discovering what these disadvantages are you can learn how to overcome the problems associated with impromptu speaking.

Former British Prime Minister Benjamin Disraeli once observed, "Impromptu talks on the spur of the moment are difficult since the moment often arises without the spur." While you may be expected to say something, you may not be inspired to say anything. Another disadvantage is making a mistake or a tactless remark. Leaders of political parties often try to stop their candidates from making impromptu comments. It is so easy to say something regrettable. For example, President Gerald Ford, in debating presidential challenger Jimmy Carter, suggested that freedom was not a problem in Eastern Europe. The remark drew much unfavorable response.

The impromptu speaking situation can create anxiety and defensiveness. The impromptu situation may reveal weaknesses in the speaker's informational storehouse. As a result, speakers shy away from these defeating experiences. The most obvious disadvantages of impromptu speaking is in the lack of opportunity to practice the speech in advance. Your mental computer must do triple time.

Positive Values

Despite all its negative aspects, you can meet the challenge of impromptu speaking just as thousands of others have, and like these others, you'll be glad you did. Twenty-five years ago a young man in a basic public speaking course was subjected by his instructor to numerous impromptu speaking situations. Many years later, this man, an officer in the U.S. Navy, wrote to the president of the university he attended:

> I don't know whether my old speech instructor is still teaching, but I want you to know that he got us upon our feet frequently with little preparation. While I didn't enjoy it too much at the time, I can tell you now how valuable I found the training.
>
> One evening at a military banquet our featured speaker took ill and a substitute had to be found. The commanding officer asked me if I could fill in with a five-minute speech. I must confess I didn't enjoy the meal too much, but I did scribble a few words on the tablecloth. I'm happy to report that the speech went over quite well, and I must say I couldn't have done the job without the training I had received in my speech course. To top things off, I was invited to be the featured speaker the following year.
>
> This fall I am sending my son to my alma mater, and if my old speech prof is still there, I want my son to be in his class.[1]

The experience of this Navy officer could be yours someday. To be as successful as he was, you might consider the old slogan: the more you practice, the better you get.

Versatile Steve Allen, an actor, writer, comedian, singer, composer, and producer, kept a pack of cards on many different subjects on the front seat of his car. As he drove along, he would pick a card at random and make a speech on the subject. This procedure helped him develop fluency in impromptu speaking.

As we have seen, there are both negative and positive aspects of impromptu speaking. While there are inherent difficulties with the process of impromptu speaking, these problems are not insurmountable. In fact, many people have met the challenge.

Advice for Impromptu Speaking

Knowing both the negative aspects and the positive values of impromptu speaking may help you overcome some of your misgivings about your ability to deliver an impromptu speech. Some specific advice, however, may be even more helpful to you. Just as in other types of speaking, there are rules to follow in impromptu speaking.

The most important thing to avoid is speaking when you have nothing to say. You may not have to speak every time you are asked. A simple, "I don't know," or "I have no comment," may suffice. This kind of response may not go over too well in the classroom, but it could prove effective in the real world.

Imperfections in impromptu speaking can be multiplied many times. Almost any mistake that can be made in speaking will be made more frequently in impromptu situations. Mark Twain once joked, "It usually takes more than three weeks to prepare a good impromptu speech."

When you are asked to make an impromptu speech, remember not to venture into high-risk areas. Stay within the confines of your own experience. Talk about something you've earned the right to talk about. Don't start with an apology. Take a positive attitude even though you may feel that you have little to offer. Be proud of your contribution, no matter how small it may seem. Probably the most important way to become proficient in impromptu speaking is to develop confidence in your ability to speak impromptu. We explore this important topic in the next section.

CONFIDENCE IN IMPROMPTU SPEAKING

You can begin to develop self-confidence by remembering that most of the speaking you do is impromptu. For example, the day may begin with your roommate saying, "This room is a mess. Do you think we could arrange it more efficiently?" "Well," you reply, taking a few seconds to collect your thoughts, "yes, I think we could. We could do at least three things. We could . . . ." You develop your "three things" approach with reasons, examples, demonstrations, and a very brief conclusion. You have just made an impromptu speech.

The same procedure takes place in ordinary conversation, interviews, small groups, panels, and large meetings. Some of the best communication occurs when individuals are moved to respond naturally and without realizing that they are making a speech.

The important thing for you to do is to see impromptu speaking in its essence, its simplicity, its easy application. You may not believe it now, but after some exciting experiences, you may begin to enjoy the impromptu challenge because of its unpredictable creativity.

The answers to three questions may help you learn how to develop self-confidence in impromptu speaking: How impromptu is impromptu? What is preparation? Can you avoid panic?

How Impromptu Is Impromptu?

Sometimes we hear a speaker perform very well in a seemingly impromptu manner. The question is, how impromptu was the speech?

In 1830 Senator Robert Hayne of South Carolina, speaking in the Senate chamber, advanced the doctrine of state supremacy, declaring that states had the right to nullify federal laws and even the right to secede from the Union. Senator Daniel Webster of Massachusetts, replying to Hayne, defended the sovereignty of the Constitution and the Union. In his closing paragraphs Webster stated:

> When my eyes shall be turned to behold for the last time the sun in heaven, may I not see him shining on the broken and dishonored fragments of a once glorious Union; on states dissevered, discordant, belligerent; on a land rent with civil feuds, or drenched, it may be, in fraternal blood! Let their last feeble and lingering glance rather behold the gorgeous ensign of the republic, now known and honored throughout the earth, still full high advanced, its arms and trophies streaming in their original luster, not a stripe erased or polluted, nor a single star obscured, . . . [2]

When Webster was asked how he had been able to deliver such a magnificent oration, he answered, "I've been preparing that speech all my life."

We can draw an analogy between playing jazz solos and speaking impromptu. The jazz soloist improvises around the melody, supposedly never doing that solo in exactly the same way. To a neophyte jazz disc jockey, Duke Ellington once stated, "There's not as much improvization as you think." Bill Ehlert, a jazz cornet player, when complimented on his improvisational creativity said, "I've been working on that passage for five years."

The same holds true for impromptu speaking. Do not be misled by someone who makes an excellent, seemingly off-the-cuff speech. The speaker may have made those remarks many times before in all kinds of situations. Do not let this display of excellence create within you a feeling of inadequacy. What seems so impromptu is not as impromptu as you may think. An impromptu speech is *not* always unprepared.

What Is Preparation?

Impromptu preparation seems to be a contradiction in terms because we define an impromptu speech as one given spontaneously and without rehearsal. And yet there is preparation in the impromptu situation, the preparation of our own experiences.

Dale Carnegie tells the story of a man in his adult speaking class who met the impromptu challenge on the subject of "What, if anything, is wrong with religion?"[3] The man proceeded to tell how devastated he was at the death of his mother. Even when the sun was shining, the day seemed dreary. One day he passed a church and entered. He sat down in the back and said nothing. After sitting there for awhile, he felt a strong urge to say, "Thy will be done," and a deep peace came over him. As a concluding statement he said to his classmates, "Ladies and gentlemen, there is nothing wrong with religion. There is nothing wrong with God's love."

Dale Carnegie congratulated the man for making that speech, and the speaker replied, "Thank you, and I did it without any preparation." Preparation?" said Carnegie. "What is preparation? You were preparing to make that talk when you looked down into your mother's casket. You were preparing that talk when you felt devastated on a bright day. Preparation is thinking, feeling, breathing and suffering the slings and arrows of outrageous fortune."

One of the strongest sources for impromptu speeches is personal experience or reporting the experiences of others. Earning the right to talk about something is the first step in impromptu preparation.

Can You Avoid Panic?

Reaching for a personal experience may be difficult if you are panic-stricken. If you find your emotions in a whirl, try to relax. Remember, however, that relaxation is not "doing nothing"; it is doing something positive. Think. Take control. Relax your muscles.

A magnificent story of emotional control is told of Harry Houdini, the magician and escape artist. Houdini was put in a straight jacket and lowered into a hole cut in the ice in the Detroit River. The escape from the straight jacket would be easy, and Houdini would climb up through the hole in the ice. But he failed to take one circumstance into account —the flow of the river. When he escaped from the straight jacket, he had moved downstream under the ice. Houdini did not panic. He thought. He remained calm and remembered there is an air space between the ice and the water. Taking a deep breath he began swimming upstream until he saw a shaft of light in the water from the open hole. He swam to the hole and escaped from what seemed certain death because he did not panic.

Think about Houdini's experience. What would you have done in those circumstances? Can you extract a principle of learning from this experience? Can you keep your cool, relax, think, let your mind rule over your emotion? If you can, even to some degree, you are over the psychological hump, ready to grow and develop more self-confidence.

Remember that what you can do once, you can do twice, and what you can do twice, you can develop into a habit. Self-confidence is built through a series of successful experiences.

BASIC PRINCIPLES IN IMPROMPTU SPEAKING

Practice in impromptu speaking can produce better results faster with the application of basic principles. Something, of course, can be learned from a random, hit-or-miss approach, but the application of basic principles will be more productive in the long run.

The best training for impromptu speaking is much practice in extemporaneous speaking. It can work the other way around too; practice in impromptu speaking can enhance your ability to speak well extemporaneously. Developing skill in impromptu speaking, however, stems largely from developing skill in extemporaneous speaking.

Earlier in this text we examined the basic principles used in extemporaneous speaking. In this section we will review those principles and see how they apply to impromptu speaking. The principles we will consider are speaker credibility, audience analysis, purpose, research, organization, development, style, visual and vocal technique, and adjustment to feedback.

Speaker Credibility

Be a person of sound moral principle, one who is upright, honest, and sincere. Do not fabricate or misrepresent. Be truthful and emotionally secure and stay within the confines of your competence.

Audience Analysis

Analyze the audience and the occasion. Ask yourself what kind of response you want from your listeners. Is it understanding, belief, action, enjoyment, or a solution to a problem? Ask yourself what kind of approach you can use to gain the response you seek. Are there any circumstances you should take into account, such as the purpose of the meeting, the mood of the listeners, or the formal or informal nature of the situation?

Purpose

Determine your general and specific purpose and try to state the specific purpose in a single, concise sentence. You may not be able to do this immediately, but after a few introductory comments, you should be able to determine and state your specific purpose.

Research

You'll have no time in the impromptu situation to run to the library or conduct interviews. You'll have to cull through your own background and experience for your material. Try to recall what you can from your reading and from talking to others.

Organization

Many general patterns of organization are possible: chronological, spatial, topical, pro and con, logical, psychological, and problem-solution. These patterns are described in detail in Chapter 3 (pp. 44–45). Later in this chapter we will discuss some specific patterns of organization in impromptu speaking.

Development

The easiest way to develop a point is to use an example from your personal experience. As we discussed in Chapter 10 in the section on "Illustrating" (pp. 182–84), a number of techniques can be used in developing or explaining a point. You might use an analogy, correlation, anecdote, or story. You might choose to cite statistics or quote an expert on your subject. If you use statistics or quotations, however, make sure that they are accurate.

Style

Keep your approach simple and try to speak in an oral, conversational style, rather than a written, formal style. Do not try to be cute or appear oversophisticated. Avoid long and involved sentences. By keeping your presentation simple, you will be able to keep it clear.

Visual and Vocal Technique

When you are delivering your material, think of what you are saying, but try to be alive and enthusiastic. Make sure that you are loud enough to be heard easily. Be conversational, but enunciate clearly so that all can understand you. Use gestures and facial expression to reinforce your points.

Adjustment to Feedback and Questions

Pay close attention to your listeners. Watch their nonverbal cues and listen to their questions. Keep a positive attitude. Most of the time listeners are not hostile, but if someone should be hostile, try to be objective, friendly, and fair. Avoid emotionalism.

A knowledge of these basic principles of speaking can promote a good start in impromptu speaking just as they helped you get started in extemporaneous speaking. In addition to these basic principles there are a number of specific preparation techniques that can be useful in impromptu speaking. We'll discuss these preparation techniques in the next section.

PREPARATION TECHNIQUES FOR IMPROMPTU SPEAKING

Mastery of some specific preparation techniques can help you become an effective impromptu speaker. By applying these techniques you can learn how to present a unified, coherent, and proportionally developed impromptu speech. You might wonder how the professionals meet the challenge of impromptu speaking. One writer interviewed fifteen speech professors and asked them what they thought a speaker should do in an impromptu situation. Their comments covered eight categories: background considerations, introductory comments, audience analysis, the point, structure, examples, the conclusion, and overall brevity.

In this section we will examine each of these categories. We will consider how speakers should approach each category and what questions they should ask themselves when called on to speak in an impromptu situation.

Background Considerations

In any impromptu situation, you need to listen carefully to what is being said. In anticipation of being called on or volunteering, you should think positively and trust yourself. In an impromptu situation you are not expected to give an excellent talk, only a good one. You can't solve the whole problem in a minute or two but you can make a contribution.

Introductory Comments

One way to begin is to start with an amusing remark or story. You may get yourself off the hook by saying, "In my opinion . . ." Respond to the context of the situation by asking yourself how much has already been said and then determining what your contribution will be. Do you want to add, subtract, or evaluate what has been said? Is this a classroom exercise or a real-life situation?

Audience Analysis

Look over the audience and consider the nature of the occasion. What are the listeners like? How do they relate to you? Are they open to leadership or do they want you to say what they want to hear?

The Point

State your point simply and clearly. It's good to give a definition or make a distinction, but don't get complicated. Arrive quickly at your main point.

Structure

Use organization to help you remember. Jot down a few notes if you have time. Print them in large, well-spaced letters so you will be able to read them easily.

Examples

Probably the most effective technique in impromptu speaking is a vivid example. If you can't give an example, try to find an analogy of a similar situation.

Conclusion

Be specific. Don't start the speech over. Summarize key points. End on a solid final note.

Brevity

Try to limit your speech to one or two minutes. If you go on longer, others eager to talk may become restless and you may begin to wander. Consider these instructive points:

1. Think positively.
2. Determine what you want to do.
3. Analyze your audience.
4. Make a simple point.
5. Organize your material in some way.
6. Use an example from your personal experience.
7. Summarize your key points.
8. Do not speak longer than one to two minutes.

SPECIFIC PATTERNS OF ORGANIZATION IN IMPROMPTU SPEAKING

Probably the biggest problem in impromptu speaking is the organization of material. The speaker has ideas but frequently doesn't have a clear notion of how to put that material in a coherent sequence. As you will recall, we discussed general patterns of organization in Chapter 3 on speech preparation. You will find that those general patterns apply to impromptu speeches as well as to extemporaneous, manuscript, or memorized speeches.

In this section we will consider some specific patterns of organization that you may find particularly helpful in organizing your impromptu speech. These patterns are those developed by Alan H. Monroe, Richard C. Borden, Dale Carnegie, and Lynn Surles. The value of these patterns of organization lies in their simplicity and easy application and use. They have been used for many years with student success and instructor approval.

Alan H. Monroe

In 1935, Alan H. Monroe wrote *Principles and Types of Speech*, in which he outlined his motivated sequence approach, a sequence of steps that follows the normal processes of human thinking and motivates an audience to respond to the speaker's purpose.[4] Monroe explained that a speech has five steps:

1. Attention: get the listeners' attention.
2. Need: establish a need for a change.
3. Satisfaction: present a plan, a solution.
4. Visualization:
   a. Help the listeners visualize what will happen if the proposal *is* accepted.
   b. Show what will happen if the proposal *is not* accepted.
5. Action: ask for brief change or something the listener can do.

Suppose you were given the subject of *grades* for an impromptu exercise. Using Monroe's formula, you might use an organizational plan such as this one.

1. *Attention*
   How many of you would like to get an A in this course?
2. *Need*
   All of us could increase our grade point average. I know I'd like to have a B average, and an A in this course would help.
3. *Satisfaction*
   I have a plan that will help you do better in your tests and speeches. The plan is group study. You get together with two or three of your friends and study the textbook together and listen to each other's speeches before delivering them in class.
4. *Visualization*
   If you try to do this work all by yourself, you may succumb to laziness and take a nap or watch TV. With a group of friends around, you may find study more stimulating and profitable.
5. *Action*
   Could I get two or three of you to join me in a group to try this idea? How many would like to join me?

Richard C. Borden

In 1935, the same year that Monroe published his motivated sequence, Richard C. Borden wrote *Public Speaking As Listeners Like It*.[5] In it Borden presented his four steps for effective speaking:

1. Ho-hum: break down listeners' yawns.
2. Why bring that up? establish a need.
3. "Fer" instance: give an example.
4. So what? tell your listeners what you want them to believe or do.

Suppose you were given the subject of *jobs* for an impromptu exercise. Using Borden's formula, you might use this organizational plan:

1. *Ho-hum*
   There's an old saying, getting a job is only half the battle. It's keeping the job that really counts.
2. *Why bring it up?*
   I've noticed a number of times that my friends have been fired from jobs that took a long time to get. It even happened to me last year.
3. *"Fer" instance*
   Last year I got a cleaning job in one of the downtown offices. And just to get that menial opportunity, I had to go through two interviews. I suppose my attitude wasn't right. I came late several times and even tried to get away with mediocre work. You guessed it. I was fired. But that experience taught me a lesson. I am now working as a waitress at the Campus Lunch Counter. My attitude is altogether changed. I get there ten minutes early, smile, do little extra things I don't have to do, and the results have been rewarding. I'm happier, my tips are very good, and my boss asked me if I'd like to work full time in the summer.
4. *So what?*
   You could learn from my experience. If you want to keep your job, put a little more into it than you have to. You may be asked to stay on the way I was.

Dale Carnegie

A few years after Borden published his book, Dale Carnegie sought Borden's services for the Dale Carnegie Course. Together Carnegie and Borden then modified Borden's formula to include five steps:

1. Ho-hum: get attention.
2. Point: declare proposal.
3. Reason: need.
4. Example: "fer" instance.
5. So what? ask for action.

Several years later the formula was simplified to a three-step approach:[6]

1. Example
2. Point
3. Reason

Here is an example of how this three-step approach might be used. The speaker is urging students to drive more carefully.

1. *Example.*

There were seven children in our family. Margie was the youngest. At the age of twenty-three she decided to pursue her career as a beautician in California. Her first step was to move in with her aunt in Carmel, California.

Carmel was an artists' colony at the time, and there were no lights at night. As Margie proceeded down the road for her walk before bedtime, she walked on the left side of the road facing the oncoming traffic. Driving in the opposite direction, at a high rate of speed, was an eighteen-year-old soldier from nearby Fort Orr who had been stopped by a police officer the night before but was let go because he was in uniform. The officer told him, however, "You're going to kill someone driving that way."

The following night that same officer was pursuing that same young man as he hit Margie from behind. The officer called for an ambulance. Margie still had a pulse but was dead on arrival at the hospital.

The following day my aunt called me rather than my mother. I got the family together and we went to see my mother. She was writing a letter to Margie.

When my mother was told the news, she began to cry. It was the strangest cry I had ever heard. It sounded like hysterical laughter, and we were all deeply moved.

2. *Point*

When you get behind the wheel of your car, please remember the awful responsibility you have.

3. *Reason*

You could prevent someone's crying from sounding like hysterical laughter.

An example from the speaker's experience

Lynn Surles

In 1954, after several years of college teaching, Lynn Surles began teaching communications courses to business and industry. In these courses he experimented with various patterns of organization for impromptu speaking. In 1960, in *The Art of Persuasive Talking* Surles reported the formula for impromptu speaking that his students had found most useful:[7]

1. Point
2. Example
3. Action

Let's examine how that pattern works in the following case. In this situation homeowners in a cooperative housing development are meeting to adopt rules and regulations to safeguard their properties. One of the proposals up for discussion would require periodic inspection of all homes in the development to eliminate fire and accident hazards. Several homeowners oppose the proposal as an invasion of their privacy. But Bob Upjohn favors it. He makes the following impromptu remarks:

1. *Point*

I feel I must speak up on this issue. Here's my point: There's too much at stake—the lives of our children, our investment in our homes, and our own safety—for us to turn down this opportunity for making this a model neighborhood. To some extent, each of us holds the safety and well-being of his neighbors in the palm of his hand.

2. *Example*

My experience is very much to the point here. Three weeks ago I inspected my own house and garage. I found a lot of booby traps that might have injured my own children—or yours if they had been playing at my house. Some of the hazards might have kept me from going to work someday.

First I went to the garage. I found a wooden box full of paint cans—some of them open—in a spot where the sun could focus. Some brushes were soaking in turpentine. I also found a rickety stepladder that my wife sometimes uses.

Then I went to the basement. I found my incinerator and piping only a foot from a wooden partition. There was a clothesline close by.

In my attic I found an electrical outlet that looked like an octopus. That's where my six-year-old boy plays on rainy days. In a second-floor bedroom I found a broken window-screen latch. That's the room where my two-year-old sleeps and plays. The medicine cabinet in the bathroom contained a large bottle of aspirin and a bottle of Lysol—all within reach of my four-year-old "Tarzan." And,under the kitchen sink I found a bottle of ammonia—a grand prize for any kid.

3. *Action*

My little inspection trip made me aware of booby traps right in my own house. And I'm not sure my unpracticed eye caught all of them. I wouldn't say I'd been careless—just indifferent, maybe. But I would say I could be ignorant of many hazards because I'm just not a professional hazard hunter. I've got things pretty well cleaned up now at my home. But I'd like to have a professional troubleshooter come around once in a while and inspect my home. And I believe most of you here would like to do the same thing, and I'm going to vote for the proposal. I hope you will, too.

As we have seen, there are many different kinds of patterns. Is there any one pattern that fits all kinds of situations? If by that you mean all kinds of speech situations, the answer is a flat no. There are too many different kinds of situations in speechmaking to justify one particular formula. By experimenting with the various patterns of organization discussed in this chapter, you may find the particular pattern or variation that works best for you.

The following pattern has proven helpful in both speaking and teaching. Try it. You can also experiment with other combinations to find a pattern that works for you.

1. Get attention with an interesting opening.
2. State your point clearly in a few words.
3. Give an explanation or reason if it will support your point.
4. Give an example or analogy.
5. Ask for some kind of response: a deeper understanding, further study, a change of attitude, a modification of belief, or some kind of action.

These specific patterns of organization work. Practice using them. At first you may feel uncomfortable just as you felt the first time you tried to ride a bicycle or drive a car. But look at you now!

SUMMARY

All of us are heirs to the challenge of impromptu speaking: that is, speaking in public with little immediate preparation. By examining the nature of impromptu speaking, both its negative and positive aspects, we can learn to meet this challenge. Specific guides on what to do and what to avoid in impromptu speaking can also be helpful.

We can develop self-confidence in impromptu speaking by realizing that we deliver many impromptu speeches throughout each day. Our challenge is to deliver effective impromptu speeches in the public speaking situation. We can meet the challenge by avoiding panic and recognizing that impromptu does not mean "unprepared."

The basic principles of extemporaneous speaking apply as well to impromptu speaking. These principles include speaker credibility, audience analysis, specific purpose, research, organization, development, style, visual and vocal technique, and adjustment to feedback. Knowledge and application of these principles can lead to success in impromptu speaking.

Preparation techniques for impromptu speaking include the need to listen carefully to what is being said before beginning to speak. The effective impromptu speaker determines the point to be made, analyzes the audience, makes a simple and clear point, uses an easy-to-follow organizational pattern, uses examples, and summarizes key points in the conclusion. Above all, the successful impromptu speaker learns to keep his or her talk brief.

The specific patterns of organization proposed by Alan H. Monroe, Richard C. Borden, Dale Carnegie, and Lynn Surles may prove especially helpful in organizing the impromptu speech. As a speaker, you should practice and experiment with various patterns of organization to find the pattern that works best for you.

ASSIGNMENTS

1. Your first assignment is to take advantage of impromptu speaking opportunities that present themselves in real life situations: in informal conversation or at meetings.

2. Your second assignment is to take advantage of impromptu opportunities presented by your instructor in the classroom.

3. Your third assignment is to practice speaking impromptu by yourself or with others. Try using one of the organizational patterns presented in the chapter or create your own. With practice you'll soon discover how much fluency you can generate.

NOTES

1. Personal communication.

2. *The Writings and Speeches of Daniel Webster*, Boston, 1903, Vol. 6, pp. 3–75, as quoted in *The Annals of America*, Vol. 5, 1821–1832. *Steps Toward Equalitarianism* (Chicago: Encyclopaedia Britannica, 1968), pp. 354–55.

3. Dale Carnegie, *A Quick and Easy Way to Effective Speaking* (New York: Association Press, 1962).

4. Alan H. Monroe, *Principles and Types of Speech* (Glenview, IL: Scott, Foresman, 1935).

5. Richard C. Borden, *Public Speaking As Listeners Like It* (New York: Harper & Row, 1935).

6. Dale Carnegie, *A Quick and Easy Way to Effective Speaking.*

7. Lynn Surles and W. G. Stanbury, *The Art of Persuasive Talking* (New York: McGraw-Hill, 1960).

Definition of Discussion

Types of Discussion

Round Table

Panel Discussion

Symposium

Types of Discussion Questions and Methods of Analysis

Questions of Policy

Steps of Reflective Thinking

The Problem-Solving Approach

Questions of Fact

Questions of Speculation

Questions of Degree

Questions of Value

Preparation Steps for Discussion

Criteria for Selecting Subjects

Stimulating Subjects

Worthwhile Subjects

Interesting Subjects

Controversial Subjects

Multisided Subjects

Suitable Subjects

Statement of the Question

Duties of the Chairperson

Study the Question

Prepare an Outline

Be a Leader

Duties of the Discussants

Be Well Prepared

Be Emotionally Adjusted

Be Socially Minded

Show Discussion Etiquette

The Deliberative Public Speaker

15

Deliberative Speaking

OBJECTIVES

When you finish reading this chapter, you should be able to:

1. define discussion;
2. explain the types of discussion formats: round table, panel, and symposium;
3. list the steps of reflective thinking used to analyze questions of policy;
4. describe the steps used to analyze questions of speculation, degree, and value;
5. explain the criteria for selecting subjects;
6. participate in a discussion either as a leader or a discussant; and
7. give a public speech based on one of the discussion patterns of analysis

15 Deliberative Speaking

Five students sat in the student union, wondering how they could improve their grades in conversational Spanish. No one received higher than a C for a mid-semester grade, and there were two D's and one F.

They started to talk about their problem of low grades, wondering what they could do about it. They began to think about reasons for the problem and even some excuses that they soon disregarded. They deliberated about possible ways to improve the situation. After much discussion and several possible solutions, they settled on one. They decided to meet for one hour after the evening meal each day to converse but only in Spanish.

It wasn't easy. At first the conversations were halting and not very fluent, but as time went on, they began to improve. At the end of the semester, no one of the five got lower than a C for a final grade.

What is the point of this example? What does the example have to do with public speaking? The five students described in the example formed a discussion group to analyze their problem and to find a solution. This type of discussion, in which the participants talk about a question and decide on an answer, is a deliberative process. Such deliberative speaking often takes place in a group context. In this chapter we will explore the nature of group discussion and the ways in which you might make an individual public speech using the deliberative process. We will begin our explanation of group discussion by defining discussion and explaining its types. We shall explore the types of discussion questions and the methods of analysis. Finally, we will consider the preparation needed for discussion.

DEFINITION OF DISCUSSION

Discussion requires an open-minded attitude toward an open-ended question. A typical discussion question might be, "How can we improve our study habits?" Specifically, discussion is a cooperative effort by the members of a face-to-face group, usually under the leadership of a chairperson, to share information or to analyze questions by using the steps of reflective thinking or some other pattern of thinking more easily adapted to the question.

Let us examine each of the phrases in this definition:

1. *A cooperative effort.* The members try to be open-minded in the discussion, even though they may be inclined toward some preconceived ideas. The members try to be fair and listen to all sides with a view toward

sharing information or finding answers that are in the best interests of the group as a whole.

2. *Of a face-to-face group.* The members react better and communicate more fully when they can see each other's faces. They catch the nonverbal cues.

3. *Usually under the leadership of one person.* Anyone in the group is free to exert leadership at times but that quality is usually vested in one person to give disciplined flow to the procedure.

4. *To share information or answer questions.* In sharing information, a study group may use the discussion process to hear various sources of information and varying viewpoints. In the discussion process, many viewpoints can be shared.

When discussion addresses a question, there is more than the sharing of information. The discussion is geared to a plan of action. Suppose the question is "What can be done about the excess number of nuclear weapons?" The President of the United States, the Secretary of Defense, and the Joint Chiefs of Staff can discuss this question and determine a national policy. A group of college students can discuss the same question and determine that they will write to their national representatives in Washington.

5. *By using the steps of reflective thinking or some other pattern of thinking more easily adapted to the question.* In general the steps of reflective thinking are defining the problem, determining its causes, identifying possible solutions, evaluating the solutions, and creating a plan of action. The other patterns relate to questions of fact and value. We will discuss all these types of questions and methods of analysis later in this chapter.

TYPES OF DISCUSSION

A discussion can take place in any one of several different formats. The formats most commonly used are the round table, the panel discussion, and the symposium. In this section we will describe the characteristics and give some examples of each of these formats.

Round Table

The round table is the most fundamental type of discussion. Usually consisting of five to six members, the group is small enough to enable the members to engage in face-to-face conversation as they sit around a table or in an informal circle or arc. A five- to six-member group encourages enough viewpoints and also gives each member a chance to participate frequently. Each member is expected to prepare for the discussion. The leader or moderator of the group can be appointed or chosen by the members.

Round-table discussion is widely used in our society. Because it is essentially informal and conversational, it is not conducted before large audiences except on radio or television. Through these media, however, the round table has become a widely used and popular format for discussion. You have probably seen many televised round-table group discussions of important questions.

Panel Discussion

In a panel discussion, a group of speakers discusses a topic in the presence of an audience. Panel discussions are essentially informal, like round-table discussions, and are conducted before listeners who constitute the forum.

In ancient Rome, the forum was a public square serving as the center of the community's judicial and business affairs and as an assembly place. Today a forum has come to mean an assembly for the discussion of questions of public interest. A panel discussion becomes a panel-forum when the audience participates. The typical panel-forum consists of two parts. The first is a discussion among the panel members themselves. The second part opens the discussion to all those present, panel and audience alike. In this second part of the discussion the audience members are permitted to comment, criticize, and ask questions of the panel members.

Symposium

A symposium is a meeting in which several persons express their opinions on a given topic. Unlike the informal conversation among the participants in a panel discussion, the members of a symposium present a series of prepared speeches. Frequently, there is a further distinction that more accurately describes the nature of a symposium: each member of the panel represents or supports a particular aspect or position with respect to the topic. For example, suppose there is a symposium on "How can X University better involve itself in the problems of the community?" The members of the symposium might be the university's academic vice-president, a faculty social scientist, the director of continuing education, a representative from the community—perhaps the mayor, and a student, each speaking from a particular viewpoint. The unique value of a symposium is that it formally recognizes different positions and viewpoints.

Like the panel discussion, the symposium has two parts: the formal presentation of the symposium speakers who make individual, prepared speeches and the open forum in which the listeners participate through comments and questions.

TYPES OF DISCUSSION QUESTIONS AND METHODS OF ANALYSIS

Discussion, as we have seen, is largely concerned with questions and analysis of the questions in order to find answers. Three kinds of questions have been traditionally recognized among authorities: questions of policy, questions of fact, and questions of value. In a real-life situation, these three kinds of questions sometimes run into one another. For example, to determine a policy, facts must be assembled, and values must be considered. To illustrate, consider the question of smoking and the policy of what should be done about it. Consider the fact that smoking causes cancer. Consider the conflicting values of enjoyment and the risk taken. Policy, fact, and value, therefore, can become intertwined. We separate these three types of questions for purposes of clarity and study.

Questions of Policy

A question of policy is concerned with what should be done in a given situation. The following are some typical questions of policy:

1. Who should be considered as a presidential candidate?
2. Where should the line be drawn between the protection of children and censorship?
3. When can moral law take precedence over civil law?
4. Why should liberal minority viewpoints be aired at a conservative majority meeting?
5. How should discipline be administered in kindergarten?

These are questions of policy. You can usually spot a question of policy when you see the words "should," "could," or "can" in the question.

To understand how to analyze a question of policy, we need to examine the steps of reflective thinking and demonstrate the problem-solving approach with an example.

Steps of Reflective Thinking. Reflective thinking is a strategy for problem solving originally developed by American philosopher and educator John Dewey.[1] Dewey identified five steps in the process. These steps are procedures by which we can analyze a problem and reach a solution. The five steps involve asking the questions:

1. What is the problem?
2. What are the causes of the problem?
3. What are some possible solutions?
4. What is the best solution(s)?
5. What is the plan of action and implementation of the best solution(s)?

The Problem-Solving Approach.   To analyze the question of policy, take the five steps of reflective thinking through the problem-solving approach. Suppose your question concerns how to lessen the number of traffic deaths on the nation's highways. The five-step problem-solving approach might analyze and attempt to answer the question in the following way:

1. *What is the problem?* Over 52,000 persons are killed annually on our highways. Are these persons primarily drivers? Passengers? Pedestrians? Is this primarily city traffic? Freeway driving? Country driving? Daytime driving? Night driving? Are the vehicles that are involved primarily passenger cars? Trucks? Motorcycles? Buses?

2. *What are the causes of the problem?* What are the causes to which traffic deaths might be attributed? Reckless driving? Inattentive driving? Excessive speed? Highway conditions? Weather conditions? Teenage drivers? Drinking? Mechanical failure? Unsafe automobiles? Drugs? Which causes—causes for which remedies may be prescribed—are responsible for most traffic deaths? The evidence found may be conflicting and not quite conclusive, but let us say we find alcohol to be a major cause of traffic deaths, excessive speed second, and inattentive driving third.

3. *What are some possible solutions?* With alcohol, excessive speed, and inattentive driving as key causes, what are some possible remedies? Are more severe penalties needed for the drunken driver, speeders, and inattentive drivers? Do we need more traffic officers patrolling streets and highways?

Is there anything we can do to deal with the other causes of traffic deaths? Do we need a national seat belt law? Can we make a major breakthrough in eliminating poor highway conditions? Winding roads? Two-way traffic on lanes that are too narrow? Do we need more traffic signs? Signs that are easier to understand? Should we have wider median strips? Better illumination for badly lighted areas? Better engineered freeways and tollways?

4. *What is the best solution(s)?* What are the best ways to reduce drunken driving? Excessive speed? Inattention?

5. *What is the plan of action and implementation of the best solution(s)?* What specific steps should be taken? What is our timetable? Where do we place the responsibility for carrying out this program?

The steps of reflective thinking and the problem-solving approach apply to the analysis and solution of questions of policy. There are other kinds of questions, such as questions of fact and questions of value, which do not follow the steps of reflective thinking in their solution. In the next sections we will consider questions of fact and questions of value and the methods used in the analysis and solution of these types of questions.

Questions of Fact

A question of fact is concerned with whether something exists or to what extent it exists. Whether something exists is called a question of speculation. To what extent something exists is called a question of degree. For example, a question of speculation might be, "Is there life on other planets?" A question of degree might be, "Is our athletic program meeting the needs of our students?"

Questions of Speculation.   To speculate is to consider matters that call for much conjectural thinking and some theorizing. We are faced with questions of speculation when we seek to draw conclusions from incomplete evidence. The answers, at best, are likely to be theories. Groups sometimes take up questions of speculation because they find them intriguing and stimulating. Sometimes they discuss them out of necessity. They have to make a practical judgment in spite of incomplete information. In such cases, a theory—defined as a set of assumptions that can explain data and predict behavior—is frequently helpful and certainly better than nothing.

Questions of speculation do not lend themselves to the same analysis as questions of policy do, the steps of reflective thinking. In analysis of questions of speculation, the following steps may prove useful:

1. Clarify the terminology.
2. Hear the available information and evidence.
3. Weigh the significance of the evidence.
4. Select the most reasonable conclusion.

Applying these steps to a discussion of the question, "Is there life on other planets?" we can arrive at the following outline:

1. *Clarify the terminology.* What is meant by "life"? Do we mean plant life? Animal life? Human life? Can we conceive of life entirely outside these categories? What is meant by "other" planets? Are we speaking only of those within our solar system?

2. *Hear the available information and evidence.* As far as astronomers can determine, the universe is made up of tremendously large star systems called galaxies. Our own galaxy, the Milky Way, which is shaped like a gigantic pinwheel, has a diameter of roughly 100,000 light years and a "thickness" of roughly 20,000 light years. This means that someone traveling at the speed of light (186,000 miles a second) would require 100,000 years to cross our galaxy from rim to rim and 20,000 years to go through it from "top" to "bottom."

There are billions of galaxies like the Milky Way. Each has billions of suns like our own sun, called stars. Although these galaxies seem to be in clusters, they are thousands of light years apart from each other, and some of them are as far as 25 billion light years away from our own galaxy.

The question is "What evidence do we have that there is anything like a habitable planet outside our solar system?" There are many nonluminous masses that have been detected revolving about stars outside our solar system and within our galaxy. Astronomers are not sure what these masses are. Could they be habitable planets? One of these masses was detected in 1963, circling Barnard's star. It is a nonluminous mass, more than 400 times the weight of the earth, traveling in orbit around the star (its own sun) once in each 24 earth years.

3. *Weigh the significance of the evidence.* With all these billions of suns in billions of galaxies, is it possible that somewhere there is at least one planet circling one of these suns that has life on it?

4. *Select the most reasonable conclusion.* Speculation will not lend itself to a succinct and orderly summary and will call for some skill on the part of the chairperson. At best the leader may be able to provide only a listing of the major theoretical and speculative statements that have been agreed on and hopefully some general conclusions.

Questions of Degree.   The second kind of question of fact is a question of degree, which we defined as the extent of something's existence. Let's clarify our definition with an example.

When John's mother says, "Johnny can read," we understand "read" to mean to a greater or lesser extent. We would normally not interpret his mother's statement to mean that Johnny can read everything. We assume that Johnny can read "to a degree," and we make a similar assumption in all questions of degree.

Analysis of questions of degree calls for a somewhat different approach than that used with questions of speculation. One useful approach covers these five steps:

1. Define the terms.
2. Point out what is adequate or satisfactory.
3. Point out what is inadequate or unsatisfactory.
4. Derive a balance sheet.
5. Propose specifics.

Applying these five steps to the question "To what extent is our athletic program meeting the needs of our students?" might result in the following outline:

1. *Define the terms.* What is our athletic program? What varsity teams

do we have? What is the number of students who participate in them? What percentage of students is involved? What physical educational courses do we have? What intramural activities? Do all students need physical recreation? What facilities are available for play and games? To what extent are they used?

2. *Point out what is satisfactory and adequate.* Our varsity program encourages large ticket sales, builds school spirit, furnishes good examples of athletic ability, and by good example encourages others to participate in sports. Our intramural program includes teams organized by classes, teams organized by fraternities and clubs, and independently organized teams. Many courses are offered in physical education. There are supervised classes in aerobics several times a week. Facilities include tennis, handball, racquetball and basketball courts, Ping-Pong tables, and an indoor track.

3. *Point out what is unsatisfactory and inadequate.* More than two thirds of the athletic budget and three fourths of the time of the physical education staff are devoted to the varsity teams. Less than 5 percent of the student body participates in varsity competition. The playing field, gymnasium, track, and tennis and basketball courts are largely monopolized by the varsity teams. Less than half the student body participates in the intramural program; little is done to encourage participation. The so-called available facilities are not easily accessible or convenient to most students.

4. *Derive a balance sheet.* Is our overall athletic program serving the needs of the mass of students? A majority do not participate in physical recreation. Specific inadequacies and shortcomings call for drastic measures.

5. *Propose specifics.* Should the basic goal be more active participation by all students? Should efforts be made to achieve broader participation in the intramural program—more teams, more leagues, more games? Should the physical education facilities be made more accessible and readily available? Is more efficient scheduling of varsity team practice indicated? Should additional personnel be hired to increase the availability of the facilities, particularly on weekends, evenings, and during short vacations? Should facilities be more widely advertised? Should an educational program concerning fitness for all be initiated?

Questions of Value

Questions of value emerge when individuals and groups are confronted with conflicting standards (criteria, principles) based on varying needs, wants, desires, and benefits. The following four steps are suited to analysis of questions of value:

1. Define and clarify the terms.
2. Determine values, criteria, standards, and principles.
3. Propose the choices.
4. Make the best choice.

Suppose the question of value is, "What is the best buy among low-priced cars?" Using the four steps, you might analyze the question in the following way:

1. *Define and clarify the terms.* What do we mean by "best buy"? Initial cost? Upkeep? What are the "low-priced" cars? How much? Are we considering new cars only or used cars as well?

2. *Determine the values, criteria, standards, and principles.* What criteria of value are involved? High mileage? Maintenance guarantee? Good styling? Trade-in value? Relatively infrequent need for repairs? Safety?

3. *Propose the choices.* Which cars suit the criteria? Small foreign cars? American compacts? American standard models? Do some used cars suit the criteria?

4. *Make the best choice.* Which car most nearly meets all criteria? Does one car stand out? Are several about equal? Because a choice must be made, on what basis will it be made?

In the foregoing section, we have examined the types of discussion questions—questions of policy, of fact (speculation and degree), and of value—and their various methods of analysis. No matter what the type of question, however, each discussion demands preparation. In the next section, we will look at some of the tasks involved in preparing for discussion.

PREPARATION STEPS FOR DISCUSSION

In preparing for discussion, we need to consider the criteria for selecting subjects, statement of the question, the duties of the chairperson, and the duties of the participants.

Criteria for Selecting Subjects

Six criteria frequently are correlated with interesting discussion and profitable learning experiences. These same criteria also have value in determining questions that can profitably be discussed outside the classroom.

Stimulating Subjects.   A stimulating subject arouses interest and challenges exploration. Good subjects stimulate reflective as opposed to directive thinking. They produce deliberative rather than argumentative

speaking. Stimulating subjects raise issues about which we are genuinely puzzled—issues for which a quick and easy answer is not possible. A stimulating subject for a discussion with people of various ages might be, "What is good music?"

Worthwhile Subjects.   Subjects for discussion should be worthwhile, that is, worth the time and effort of both discussants and listeners. Timeliness gives importance to subjects. What is in the headlines, on the editorial pages, and widely talked about is at least of current interest and probably important.

   Some subjects are more aptly called timeless. They seem always to be with us. Among these are crime and punishment, taxes, and the generation gap, to mention a few. Timeless questions might be, "What is appropriate punishment for convicted murderers?" "What should the new tax plan include?" "Should all popular music be played on the air?"

Interesting Subjects.   If the subject is both stimulating and worthwhile, it will probably be interesting, too. However, some subjects are stimulating to some people but not to others. Some subjects that you agree are worthwhile and important may not interest you. For example, some people are Civil War enthusiasts and some are not. University students have their special interests, and subjects for classroom discussions should be selected with these interests in mind. The special interests of each discussant should also be considered. In many ways, the makeup of the group determines the desirability of the subject.

Controversial Subjects.   The most suitable subjects for good discussion should be controversial, but not overly so. Controversy need not be avoided, but subjects that cannot be considered calmly and objectively will generate more heat than light. This is particularly true if controversy has divided people into two groups, pro and con. Such groups are ready for a confrontation of the issues in a formal debate. Their minds are made up from the beginning. Discussion will not work for them.

Multisided Subjects.   Discussion subjects should be multisided. A question such as "Should dormitory closing hours at this university be extended to 3 A.M.?" is not an ideal discussion question because it admits only two answers, yes or no. As such, it tempts the discussants to take sides. This situation encourages directive thinking and discourages reflective thinking and deliberation. The question might be reworded: "At what time should dormitory visiting end?" This question is open-ended with multisided possibilities.

Suitable Subjects.   Subjects for discussion should be suited to the time, place, circumstances, and people involved. Since class discussions rarely extend beyond thirty or forty minutes, a discussion of the question "How can we improve our American educational system?" is hardly suitable for so short a time period. A speech class of students recruited from many areas of a university is hardly the appropriate place for a technical discussion of psychology or a problem in theology; perhaps only a few members of the group would consider such topics interesting, worthwhile, and suitably controversial. Suitable subjects for discussion must meet the needs of the group members. Only those groups can say what those subjects are.

Statement of the Question

When a group has selected a question for discussion that satisfies as nearly as possible the criteria we have just discussed, the next step is to determine the best way to state the question. A properly phrased question is clear, unbiased, and focuses on the problem, not the answer. It should be stated as a complete interrogative sentence. There is nothing thought-provoking, for example, about topics expressed as "interracial problems," "teenage drivers," or "conserving our natural resources." When these topics are expressed in the form of suitable questions, however, it is a different matter. For example, "How can this university assist in easing interracial tensions?" is a suitable question for discussion.

Nor should the discussion question be prejudiced, loaded, or biased. "How can we eliminate senseless examinations?" or "How can we improve our outmoded educational system?" are questions involving partiality and bias. They take for granted a part of what they should attempt to answer.

Finally, as we have already noted, the phrasing of a discussion question should focus on the issue, not the answer. "Should we increase the income tax?" is obviously a question for formal debate. "Should we raise taxes to help balance the state budget?" is more nearly a discussion question, although it focuses on an answer. "How can we increase our state revenues?" is the best of the three questions because it focuses precisely on the issue: how to replenish the state treasury. These criteria for stating the question can streamline discussion. A well-phrased question is like the right ticket to a desired destination. It gets the group off to a good start.

Duties of the Chairperson

Probably the key to this chapter on deliberative speaking and discussion is the word "chairperson." In a typical discussion group, the chairperson starts the discussion and serves as its rudder, directing the process toward a pointed and courteous conclusion. Good chairpersons alone, however, do not make good discussions; the participants, too, must cooperate.

We can list three duties of the chairperson, although we must recognize that the participants share responsibility for beginning well and keeping the discussion flowing in a unified, coherent, and mannerly fashion.

Study the Question. It is not necessary for the chairperson to be the best-informed individual in the group, since there may be others who know more about certain aspects of the question. Nevertheless, the chairperson, like all the discussion participants, should make a reasonable effort to become better informed. In this way, the chairperson and the discussants will find it easier to ask pertinent questions, evaluate contributions, engage in further questioning, and summarize what has been said.

Prepare an Outline. To prepare a good outline, the chairperson should determine what kind of question (policy, speculation, degree, or value) the group will be discussing and what method of analysis will be used to study it. From this base the chairperson can fill in other questions that arise from further thinking, reading, and talking to others, especially to the discussion participants themselves.

In preparing the outline, the chairperson should leave large blank spaces after each major step (causes, main causes, possible solutions, for example) so that summaries can be written down during the discussion. Wide margins are also helpful so that adaptations to meet unforeseen situations can be noted. An experienced chairperson knows that a planned outline is necessary but that frequently the group will get off the prepared route and make a few detours. The following sample outline might be used by the chairperson of a discussion.

A Sample Outline for a Discussion Leader

The question: How can beginning public speaking students acquire self-confidence?

I. What is the problem?
   A. Do people lack self-confidence?
      1. Are there any specific cases?
      2. Does anyone have any statistics?
   B. How big a part does anxiety play?
      1. Any cases?
      2. What are the specific signs, hints, or clues of anxiety?
II. What are the causes behind this anxiety?
   A. Does heredity play a part?
      1. Any examples?
      2. Any statistics?
      3. Any authoritative statements?
   B. Does environment enter the picture?

       1. Did the anxious person have any negative experiences?

       2. Is the anxious person devoid of any experience at all?

    C. Are there any other causes or reasons for this anxiety?

III. What are some possible solutions to conquering anxiety?

    A. Is there a distinction between a feeling of inferiority and an inferiority complex?

       1. Could this distinction lead to different kinds of therapies?

       2. What might these therapies include?

    B. Do most people feel inferior in some way?

       1. Is the "you're not alone" theory helpful?

       2. Has it been helpful to any in this group?

    C. Is seeing a therapist helpful?

       1. A psychologist for counseling?

       2. A psychiatrist for medication?

    D. Would taking other performance courses be helpful?

       1. Acting?

       2. Dancing?

    E. Would thorough preparation for each speech be helpful?

    F. How important is frequent performance in developing self-confidence?

IV. Of all the possible solutions, which one is best? Or are there several?

    A. _____

    B. _____

    C. _____

V. What plan of action can be taken to implement the best solution(s)?

    A. _____

    B. _____

    C. _____

Be a Leader.   After the chairperson has studied the question and prepared an outline, he or she is ready to lead the discussion. The leader should not try to take over the discussion, but when the need to lead arises, the chairperson should have the courage to step in.

The key words here are "to lead." By delicately blending rightful authority with considerate, tactful direction, a leader can bring out in others a desire to contribute their best.

Both the discussion leader and the discussion participants should guard against becoming dictatorial or bossy, injecting personal views, or telling other people how or what to think. If a person becomes dictatorial, the timid may withdraw, the mature become embarrassed, and the emotionally unstable grow belligerent. On the other hand, the chairperson who lacks the courage to exercise rightful authority when necessary runs the risk of losing the position of leadership, thus inviting confusion or even mutiny.

To know when to exercise authority and when to exercise restraint depends, in part, on the kinds of personalities within the group. Therefore, any information that the chairperson possesses about the backgrounds of individual members and the factors that influence their thinking will help in better understanding their contributions. The more mature the members are, the more they can untangle the conflict themselves; the less competent they are, the more the leader must step in and take hold.

At times, any member of a group may be in a position to take over as chairperson and lead the discussion for a short time. The official chairperson should welcome such ability and interest and be happy if several members react in this manner. When discussion is going well, the leader should let it continue, stepping in only if needed. Nothing chills the warmth of good discussion more than the drafty interruption of an openmouthed chairperson preoccupied with an enlarged ego.

The group, not the chairperson, should solve the problem. Wise leaders ask questions. Instead of evaluating answers that are given, they ask others for their opinions of the contributions. In this way, a crisscross of group dynamics develops. Members know what other members are thinking, and ideas get out into the open. It's true that conflict may develop, but without some conflict, the discussion may stagnate.

Sometimes, when discussion is moving well, the chairperson may notice that only two or three members are doing most of the talking. When this happens, the leader should tactfully bypass the overtalkative and draw out the silent members with well-directed questions. The fact that someone is not talking is no indication that he or she isn't thinking. More often than not, the silent member may have an excellent contribution to make. All participants in a discussion should encourage all members of the group to talk.

Sometimes members are silent because they represent a minority viewpoint. Discussion is democratic, however, and the fair chairperson will encourage the expression of minority views. The chairperson will realize that the whole truth is not necessarily found in a majority vote and that, conversely, at least part of the truth is sometimes found in a minority appraisal.

Finally, the chairperson should try to have a good time and get the members of the group to have a good time. A sense of humor, an occasional anecdote, the light touch—all can help ease group tensions. In fact, all group members should attempt to relieve any tensions that develop.

In addition to the responsibilities that group members share with the chairperson or discussion leader, all discussion participants have further responsibilities for contributing to a good discussion and lively exchange of ideas. In the following section, we will describe some of these duties and responsibilities. Of course, the chairperson, as a member of the group, also shares these responsibilities.

Duties of the Discussants

The main duty of the participants is to answer the question in the best interests of all concerned. Some persons who agree to participate in discussion really have little reason for being there. These are the people who don't believe that discussion is an efficient method of getting things done.

There are others who could participate if they understood what discussion is. They don't know the rules of the game. Still others come ill-prepared, with little to contribute except personal opinion. Although it is conceded that everyone has a right to voice an opinion, it is likewise fair to ask, "What is the opinion worth?" Experience demonstrates that effective discussants are those who are well prepared, emotionally adjusted, socially minded, and show proper discussion etiquette.

Be Well Prepared.   Speakers assigned to a debate spend hours reading and preparing their case. Those same speakers assigned to a discussion often feel their participation is adequate if they talk "off the top of their heads," offering personal opinion supported by limited experience. Since the ingredients of good discussion are facts and expert opinion, it becomes the first duty of the discussant to reinforce his or her limited experience with outside reading and study.

In other forms of speaking, the speaker prepares an outline and puts information on note cards when necessary. Discussion participants should do the same. The outline will be similar to the one the leader uses, although it need not be so detailed. An orderly arrangement of the note cards containing important factual information or quotations from authorities supplements the outline.

Be Emotionally Adjusted.   Very few persons in this world are perfectly adjusted emotionally. Almost everyone has some feelings of inferiority, inadequacy, or mistrust. A person acts on these feelings most commonly either by becoming overly quiet and withdrawn or by fighting the situation and becoming overly talkative and domineering.

The first principle of emotional adjustment is Socrates' wise counsel, "know yourself." If someone is more competent or informed than you are, admit it. If you are more qualified than someone else, be gracious.

The following suggestions are helpful in achieving emotional balance in discussion:

1. Don't be aloof. Cooperate with the chairperson and your colleagues. A little effort on your part will bring you a rewarding interest.

2. Don't try too hard. Don't identify yourself too much with the problem. In discussion, group interests take precedence over personal interest.

3. Don't feel that people are against you. An antagonist probably is not attacking you personally. He or she may have a feeling of inferiority, become defensive, and lash out first.

4. Be a good competitor. Like a duck in a surging rapids, enjoy the challenge of competition but let the waters of conflict run off you.

5. Watch your language. Beware of emotionally loaded words that distort the truth and antagonize others. Look at facts as they are. Then use words that express those facts.

6. Listen to the sound of your voice. If the volume, pitch, quality, and rate suggest too much personal involvement, remember that a displeasing voice can turn sound ideas into sour notes.

7. Watch the faces of others. Frequently, they reflect your own.

Be Socially Minded. As the discussion group works to answer a question in the best interests of the group itself or others, the members should avoid two extremes—an overly cautious fear of offending others and an overly aggressive desire to get things done.

All discussants should recognize that they have a right to talk but that they must grant the same right to others. All should assume that they have something worthwhile to contribute, but they must also listen to the contributions of others. "Listen not to contradict but to weigh and consider" is thoughtful advice.

All should assume that they have a right to disagree, but they must not forget to respect the opinions of others. Someone else's answer to the question might turn out to be the right one.

In disagreeing with someone, it is wise to disagree with the contention but never with the person. If John is an emotionally adjusted individual, he can accept the statement, "John, I disagree with your conclusion." But he may bristle if someone says, "You're wrong, John."

Discussion participants should welcome conflict that arises but remember to keep it within the confines of good judgment, diplomacy, and tact. When disagreeing with others, pinpoint a specific area to challenge. If someone is guilty of broad and sweeping conclusions, ask for a specific, typical example. If a person is overly agreeable, ask how he or she could reconcile opposing viewpoints. If someone is extremely negative, ask what solution that person can offer.

It's often easy to spot different personal characteristics but difficult to know how to deal with the people who have them. Sometimes, as in the cases of the sarcastic, the opinionated, the mistrustful, and the surly, the only practical method is to listen as they talk and let it go at that. Any attempt to change their views often makes the situation worse than it was before. Tolerance, tact, and good example often offer the best chance for success.

In presenting views, the discussants should remember that most people want to do what is best. Most people will usually be receptive to ideas that are presented with evidence and without prejudice. So long as sound principles are in the foreground, so long as good values lead the way, so long as facts and acceptable expert opinion support a viewpoint, so long as the welfare of the group is considered first, the proposal stands a good chance of being accepted.

Show Discussion Etiquette. The following practical suggestions are considered good etiquette in discussion:

- Don't interrupt. If necessary, raise your hand if you want to talk.
- Don't talk too long or too frequently.
- Acknowledge that anyone who hasn't as yet spoken has a prior right to talk.
- Avoid introducing ideas, even though good, that are irrelevant.
- When speaking, make eye contact with many, not just one or two.
- Treat all members alike. Don't play up to those in power or look down on others.
- Listen.
- When the group wants to move on, don't lag behind regrinding hamburger or sawing sawdust.
- Be conversational in tone and manner.

THE DELIBERATIVE PUBLIC SPEAKER

The question raised at the beginning of this chapter concerned the relevance of the deliberative process to public speaking. We can use an example to illustrate the usefulness of an understanding of the deliberative process for the public speaker.

A speech instructor received a phone call from a successful real estate sales manager very much involved in community affairs. He found himself speaking at many meetings, club luncheons, and even some local banquets. While land development and the sale of commercial buildings were his major interests, he enjoyed his involvement in civic affairs. He frequently spoke before what he called "very influential people."

"My problem is to find an effective way to present my material," he told the speech instructor. "I want you to start from the beginning and tell me everything you know about different ways of organizing material."

The instructor spent half a dozen hours at various intervals explaining the different purposes and types of speaking. A few weeks after the sessions were completed, the instructor asked the community-minded public speaker what ideas he had found helpful.

"I liked them all," he said, "but the last part on deliberative speaking I liked best. I think I'll get the most use out of that pattern."

"Why?" the instructor inquired.

"Because this kind of speaking can help me use a problem-solution approach. The kinds of people I talk to will listen to that kind of approach," replied the sales manager.

In this chapter we described three types of discussion questions and the various methods of analysis used to answer the questions. You, as a deliberative public speaker, could use any one of these methods, depending on the particular question you wish to address. For example, let's suppose that your topic is "How can we decrease alcoholism among teenagers?" Applying the steps of reflective thinking and the problem-solving approach related to a question of policy, you might construct the following outline:

I. What is the problem?
   A. Begin with an illustration, a case study.
   B. Let this illustration lead into the problem.
   C. State the problem: A fourth of the population, ages twelve to twenty, suffers from alcohol abuse.
II. What are the causes of the problem?
   A. Family history
      1. Heredity versus environment
      2. Mental health
      3. Abuse
      4. Incest
      5. Neglect
      6. Divorce
   B. Failure
      1. In school
      2. On the job
   C. Breaking up with a loved one
   D. Escape from reality
III. What are the possible solutions?
   A. Join Alcoholics Anonymous
   B. Enter an adolescent treatment center in a hospital
   C. Attend educational programs on alcoholism
      1. Damage to liver, heart, and brain
      2. Difficulty with employers
      3. Romantic loss
      4. Family conflict
   D. Find a friend
   E. Become other-people-oriented

At this point, the speaker could summarize the possible solutions and let the listeners choose the method of rehabilitation, or the speaker could go on through step 4 to find the best possible solution and step 5 to determine a plan of action and implementation. Much depends on the nature of the question, the listeners' needs, and the circumstances of the occasion. The point is simply this: the public speaker can use the deliberative pattern in speechmaking. Some day you may be asked to help answer questions that deal with discord between religious outlooks, capital and labor, capitalism and communism, wealth and poverty, people's inhumanity to people, or a thousand and one other issues. In your creative enthusiasm for the betterment of the world, you can use your knowledge of and skill in public speaking to attempt to answer these questions.

SUMMARY

Discussion requires an open-minded attitude toward an open-ended question. Discussion occurs when several persons exchange views and information to solve a problem or to reach a common understanding. The three most common types of discussion formats are the round table, the panel (or panel-forum), and the symposium (or symposium-forum).

Four main types of discussion questions are those of policy, speculation, degree, and value. Each type of question is also associated with a particular pattern of analysis. Policy questions use the five steps of reflective thinking: what is the problem, what are the causes of the problem, what are some possible solutions, what is the best solution(s), and what plan of action can be used? These steps of reflective thinking are the most commonly used in discussion aimed at getting something done. Other methods of analysis are used for questions of speculation, degree, and value.

In preparing for discussion, select subjects that are stimulating, worthwhile, interesting, controversial, multisided, and suitable. Phrasing of the discussion questions should be clear, precise, and unbiased. The question should be focused on the issue, not the answer.

Good chairpersons and good discussants together make good meetings. The responsibilities of the chairperson, shared with the participants, are to study the problem, prepare an outline, and try to exert leadership by bringing out the best in others.

Good discussion participants do their homework by studying the question and its related issues, by being emotionally adjusted to developing conflicts, by being socially minded in their relations with others, and by showing discussion etiquette.

ASSIGNMENTS

1. For this exercise the class is divided into groups of five or six and chairpersons and recorders are appointed for each group. All groups discuss simultaneously for a given period of time (to be determined by the instructor). Each recorder then gives a one- to two-minute report on the question under discussion, the analysis of the question, the answers proposed and determined, and the reasons for the group's answer. Some possible topics for discussion are:
   a. What courses should be required for a liberal arts and sciences college?
   b. What will the United States be like in 100 years?
   c. How should first-degree murderers be dealt with?
   d. How can parents combat the effects of TV violence on their children?
   e. What is the greatest value that guides your life?
   f. If you won the lottery, how would you use the money?
   g. How many children make the ideal family?
   h. How best can the world be improved?
   j. Who should be our next president?

2. A panel of five or six is seated in the front of the room and discusses a question (to be assigned by the instructor) for a given period of time. After the discussion, the forum (audience) comments and asks questions of the panelists.

3. A symposium of five or six persons is appointed. Each member delivers a short, prepared presentation on a separate aspect of the question to be discussed. After all the presentations, the forum (audience) asks questions and makes comments.

4. For this public speaking exercise, make a five-minute deliberative speech in which you use one of the methods of analysis for discussion questions. Use any one of these patterns or formats:
   a. For a question of policy: problem, causes, possible solutions, best solution, plan of action.
   b. For a question of speculation: clarification of terminology, available evidence, evaluation of evidence, selection of most reasonable conclusion.
   c. For a question of degree: definition of terms, satisfactory aspects, unsatisfactory aspects, determination of balance sheet, specific answers.
   d. For a question of value: definition and clarification of terms, criteria for decision, possible choices, best choice.

NOTES

1. John Dewey, *How We Think* (Boston: D. C. Heath, 1910).

Appendix **A**

Evaluation Forms and Critique Sheets

LISTENER'S EVALUATION FORM

SPEECH CRITIQUE SHEET

SPEAKER'S CREDIBILITY CRITIQUE SHEET

You can use the following forms to evaluate speakers, speeches, and yourself as a listener. The third form is a critique sheet you can use to evaluate a speaker's credibility (see Chapter 6).

LISTENER'S EVALUATION FORM

Name of Speaker _____

Speech Title _____

Rate the speaker by using the following scale:

5	4	3	2	1	0
excellent	good	average	fair	poor	uncertain

Introduction

Gained interest of audience   _____

Stated purpose clearly   _____

Started to build credibility   _____

Used transition to connect introduction and body   _____

Body

Identified major points   _____

Identified supporting points   _____

Used sound evidence   _____

Supported ideas   _____

Used appropriate language   _____

Related message to audience   _____

Summarized key points   _____

Organized points in the body   _____

Conclusion

Used transition to connect body and conclusion   _____

Summarized key points   _____

Restated major points   _____

Provided a strong concluding statement   _____

Delivery

Established sufficient eye contact   _____

Spoke confidently   _____

Appeared interested   _____

Used appropriate vocal qualities   _____

Adapted to feedback   _____

General Evaluation

Used visual aids effectively   _____

Adapted message to specific audience   _____

Accomplished purpose   _____

Developed ideas adequately within time limit   _____

Established interest in the message   _____

General Comments

_____

_____

_____

_____

Rate yourself as listener. Use the same scale.

5	4	3	2	1	0
excellent	good	average	fair	poor	uncertain

Listening Habits

Displayed good listening habits   _____

Minimized bad listening habits   _____

Benefits of Listening

Gained new information   ———

Helped to stimulate better speaking   ———

Improved note taking   ———

Enjoyed listening   ———

General Comments

————————————————————————————

————————————————————————————

————————————————————————————

————————————————————————————

————————————————————————————

SPEECH CRITIQUE SHEET

Name of Speaker _____

Title of Speech _____

Rate the speaker using the following scale:

excellent	good	average	fair	poor
5	4	3	2	1

Research

The speaker's own experience   _____

The experience of others   _____

Additional comments _____

_____

_____

Organization

Specific purpose   _____

Outline   _____

Introduction   _____

Conclusion   _____

Additional comments _____

_____

_____

Development

Clear explanation   _____

Evidence   _____

Reasoning   _____

Motivation   _____

Additional comments _____

_____

_____

Adaptation to Audience

Interests   _____

Needs   _____

Additional comments _____

_____

_____

Style of Speaking

Conversational   _____

Extemporaneous   _____

Fluent   _____

Creative   _____

Additional comments _____

_____

_____

Visual

Appearance   _____

Movement   _____

Gesture   _____

Facial expression   _____

Eye contact   _____

Additional comments _____

_____

_____

Vocal

Volume   _____

Conversational   _____

Melody pattern   _____

Variety in tone color   ————

Pace   ————

Pronunciation   ————

Enunciation   ————

Additional comments ————————————————

SPEAKER'S CREDIBILITY CRITIQUE SHEET

Name of Speaker _____

Title of Speech _____

Place a check mark in the appropriate space.

1. If provided, did the introduction of the speaker increase your perception of the speaker's initial credibility?

Great increase	Moderate increase	Uncertain	Minor increase	No increase
_____	_____	_____	_____	_____

2. At what level did the speaker display competence on the subject?

High level	Moderately high level	Uncertain	Moderately low level	Low level
____	_____	_____	_____	____

3. At what level do you trust the speaker?

High level	Moderately high level	Uncertain	Moderately low level	Low level
____	_____	_____	_____	____

4. At what level did the speaker display goodwill toward the audience?

High level	Moderately high level	Uncertain	Moderately low level	Low level
____	_____	_____	_____	____

5. At what level did the speaker display dynamism?

High level	Moderately high level	Uncertain	Moderately low level	Low level
____	_____	_____	_____	____

6. At what level do you identify with the speaker?

High level	Moderately high level	Uncertain	Moderately low level	Low level
____	_____	_____	_____	____

7. At what level do you identify with the speaker's message?

High level	Moderately high level	Uncertain	Moderately low level	Low level
————	————	————	————	————

8. Additional comments concerning the speaker's credibility:

————————————————————————————

————————————————————————————

————————————————————————————

————————————————————————————

Appendix **B**

Suggested Speech Topics

Often the biggest problem facing beginning public speaking students is finding a topic for a speech. "What should I talk about?" they ask. "I can't think of any suitable topic." The suggestions provided here are meant to be a starting point for possible speech topics.[1] There is, of course, no completely exhaustive list of topics for each type of speech. The following list may stimulate you to explore a specific topic or a related topic of interest. Don't hesitate to add your own topics to the list for possible future use.

The suggestions are divided into the types of speeches discussed in the text. There are topics for demonstration speeches, informative speeches, persuasive speeches, evocative speeches, speeches delivered impromptu, and group discussions. Some topics may be listed under more than one category. Often a single topic can be developed in a number of different ways, depending on the type of speech to be given. When you select a speech topic, be sure that you can develop your ideas and convey your meaning within the time allowed. Often this will mean narrowing a broad, general topic to a single, significant aspect of the topic. For example, suppose you choose the general topic of the sport of tennis. There are any number of aspects of tennis you can talk about. You can discuss the history of tennis, the rules of tennis, singles versus doubles tennis, tennis strategies, proper form in tennis, various tennis strokes, a particular tennis player, your experience in playing tennis, the duties of various tennis officials, famous tennis competitions, types of tennis court surfaces, tennis equipment, and so on. Just as in this example and with most of the suggestions in the following list, you can develop a topic in a wide variety of ways.

TOPICS FOR DEMONSTRATION SPEECHES

Forecasting the weather

Types and use of sporting equipment

Photography

Collections (coins, stamps, etc.)

Playing musical instruments

Firefighter and police equipment

How to play games (chess, backgammon, etc.)

Assembling terrariums

Making animals from balloons

Applying makeup

Card tricks

Handcrafts (knitting, macramé, découpage, crocheting, etc.)

Cooking

Art (sketching, collage, etc.)

How to read the stock market page

Taking your own blood pressure

Scuba diving

Giving first aid to a choking victim (Heimlich maneuver)

Making a lamp out of a bottle

Surfing

Practicing to be a drum major

How to perform magic tricks

Finger painting

How to set a table

Hitting a baseball

Anatomy of the eyes

The art of theatrical or other makeup

Trends in women's (or men's) fashions

Freeway (or other transportation) networks

Optical illusions

How to read blueprints

Urban planning

How a communications satellite works

Polishing a car

Flower arranging

Modeling in clay

Good form in bowling, tennis, swimming, fencing, or golf

Handling a firearm

How to use home electrical tools

Color mixtures and combinations

The speech and hearing mechanisms

Human communication models

How to do a given dance step

On being attacked by bees

Movie stunts

Modeling clothes

Dribbling and shooting in basketball

Body-building exercises

Different ways of walking

Cheerleaders' routines

Orchestra conducting

Measuring the size of this room

Shadowboxing

Military marching

Archery

Automobile racing

Bingo

Bridge

Canoeing

Cycling

Football

Gymnastics

Field hockey

Ice hockey

Horse racing

Ice skating

Polo

Pool

Rowing

Skiing

Sky diving

Volleyball

Weight lifting

Yachting

Making flowers

Making puppets

Mechanical drawing

Surveying

Morse code

CPR

Operating a switchboard, computer terminal, typewriter, or photocopier

How to outline

Uses of a pocket calculator

Use of visual aids

Fingerprinting

Changing a flat tire

Watercolor painting

Sculpture

Square dancing

Making ice cream sundaes

Making tossed salad

Barbecuing

Signals of officials in football, basketball, baseball, soccer, hockey

Yoga

Videotape recording

Audiotape recording

Stage movement

How to make bread

How to make wine

Japanese paper art

Polish paper cutouts

Ukranian Easter egg decorating

Croatian embroidery

Italian pastamaking

Eating with chopsticks

TOPICS FOR INFORMATIVE SPEECHES

College Life and Activities

Life in a college fraternity or sorority

Running for a campus office

Values of military training

An extracurricular activity

Tests: bane of college life

The veteran goes to college

What teaching assistants do

Editing a college newspaper

Working in the bookstore

Selecting a vacation job

Acting in a school play

How to get good grades

How to relax on weekends

Living in a college dorm

Values of college debating

Getting off probation

Public Issues

Universal military training

Causes of juvenile delinquency

The welfare state: good or evil?

Conserving our natural resources

Industry's role in our economy
Readjusting our tax structure
Government management of news
Race relations
Narcotics control
Capital punishment
Marriage and divorce
Veterans' legislation
Medicare

Professions and Jobs

Accounting
Music
Medicine
Acting
Law
Architecture
Insurance
Real estate
Journalism
Mechanical engineering
Commercial art
Professional tennis
Gas station operation
Landscape architecture
Camp counseling
Television announcing
Banking
Librarianship
Fashion designing
Movie production
Dietetics
Auto mechanics
Dental technology
Teaching

PEOPLE

Lawyers

Louis Brandeis
Rufus Choate
Clarence Darrow
Thomas Erskine
Abraham Lincoln
Lord Mansfield
Thurgood Marshall
Daniel Webster

Novelists

Louisa May Alcott
James Baldwin
Saul Bellow
Colette
Charles Dickens
Feodor Dostoevski
William Faulkner
Alex Haley
Ernest Hemingway
Sir Walter Scott
Aleksandr I. Solzhenitsyn
Leo Tolstoy
Mark Twain
Kurt Vonnegut, Jr.
Robert Penn Warren
Edith Wharton

Poets and Playwrights

Maxwell Anderson
Gwendolyn Brooks

Emily Dickinson
Robert Frost
Lillian Hellman
Langston Hughes
Amy Lowell
Arthur Miller
Ogden Nash
Eugene O'Neill
Edwin Arlington Robinson
Carl Sandburg
William Shakespeare
George Bernard Shaw
Gertrude Stein
Tennessee Williams

Preachers, Spiritual Leaders

Thomas á Becket
Buddha
John Calvin
Confucius
Mary Baker Eddy
Billy Graham
Anne Hutchinson
Jesus
Martin Luther
Martin Luther King, Jr.
Mohammed
Moses
Norman Vincent Peale
Savonarola
John Wesley
The pope

Scientists, Inventors

Marie and Pierre Curie
Thomas A. Edison

Albert Einstein
Enrico Fermi
Sir Alexander Fleming
Robert Fulton
Charles Goodyear
Samuel F. B. Morse
Isaac Newton
Louis Pasteur
Jonas E. Salk
Gottfried Wilhelm von Leibnitz

Speakers

Susan B. Anthony
William Jennings Bryan
Edmund Burke
Stokely Carmichael
Shirley Chisholm
Sir Winston Churchill
Henry Clay
Benjamin Disraeli
Frederick Douglass
Charles James Fox
J. William Fulbright
William E. Gladstone
Patrick Henry
Barbara Jordan
John F. Kennedy
Abraham Lincoln
David Lloyd George
Golda Meir
Eleanor Roosevelt
Franklin D. Roosevelt
Theodore Roosevelt
Margaret Chase Smith
Woodrow Wilson
The president

NATIONAL AND INTERNATIONAL POLICY

Health

New vaccines
Pediatrics
Geriatrics

Population Control

Diets
Contraception
Abortion

Trade Policy

Wheat
Arms
Automobiles

Education

Progressive versus traditional
IQ and testing
Busing

Agriculture

Farm subsidies
Futures
Inflation control

Housing

Low-cost
Mobile homes
Condominiums

Ecology

Recycling
Water pollution
Pesticides

Transportation

Train
Airplane
Automobile

Technology and Modernization

Retooling of industry
Refuse as energy
The modern city

Exotic Places

Easter Island
Katmandu
Olduvai Gorge
Mount Kilimanjaro
Inca ruins
Mount Everest
The Nile
Kyoto
New Zealand
Transylvania

Economics

Inflation, recession, depression
Cost of energy
Psychology of the stock market
The gold standard
Unemployment

Public work
Guaranteed national income
World monetary system
Free trade

Myth Versus Fact

Witchcraft in Salem
Visitors from outer space
The Loch Ness monster
The history of Dracula
Ghosts in England
Davy Crockett
Indian wars and battles
Voodooism
Houdini
The discovery of America

Notorious Criminals

Adolf Hitler
Adolf Eichmann
John Wilkes Booth
Lee Harvey Oswald
Charles Manson
John Dillinger
Bonnie and Clyde
Jack the Ripper
Al Capone
Nero

Futurism

Cloning
Space travel

Radiational mutations
Artificial organs
Futuristic art
Lasers
A.D. 2500
Atomic energy
Underwater habitation
Earthquakes and holocausts

Sports

The spawning of professional teams
The nationalization of the Olympics
College recruitment
Famous moments in sports
Famous coaches and players
The history of sailing
Sports scandals
Broken bones and artificial turf
Women versus men, boys versus girls
The abolition of violent sports
The dangers of skydiving

Morality and Ethics

Censorship and the law
Moral versus national interests in the making of foreign policy
Prostitution
The future of organized religion
Zen Buddhism
Karma
Euthanasia
Capital punishment
White-collar crime
Vivisection

Military History

Gettysburg

Battle of the Bulge

D-Day, the sixth of June, 1944

The bombing of Hiroshima

Stalingrad

Pearl Harbor

Iwo Jima

The Alamo

The Six-Day War

The Boston Massacre

ADDITIONAL TOPICS FOR INFORMATIVE SPEECHES

A discovery or invention (DDD, transistorized ignition, lasers)

Molecular biology

Analyzing the outcome of an election

How to hedge against inflation

Safeguards for color TV

Detergents (fertilizers, pesticides) that recycle

Rackets and pools

The U.S. investment in Panama (El Salvador, Israel, etc.)

Safety engineering the automotive industry

When disaster strikes

Diversification in stock buying

Catastrophe insurance

New methods of weather forecasting

New ideas on prison reform

Courtesy on the freeway

Winning an argument without too much arguing

Legalized gambling

How benzedrine (or some other drug) acts

How a satellite is launched (or operates)

Building the Alaska pipeline

The hunger crisis

Causes of inflation (unemployment, recession, etc.)

Some aspect of modern art (music, poetry)

How something works (electronic brain, offset printing, transistors, radar, photoelectric cell, investigation of credit, insurance applications, etc.)

The chemical revolution on the farm

New trends in (church, hospital, home, office building) architecture

Danger of high-altitude explosions

Peacetime uses of the atom

New discoveries about diet

Fighting forest fires

Proper gear for mountain climbing

Increasing traffic on the lakes

Keeping up with new books

Financing state government (sales tax, income tax, state lotteries)

What the Egyptians (Russians, Chinese, Israelis) want

Malpractice insurance

Fraudulent advertising

New nations of Africa (or one of the new nations)

DNA: What we have learned about heredity

Why traffic fatalities are increasing (decreasing)

Poverty, slums

Rights of smokers (nonsmokers)

Crime and criminals

Terrorism

Option trading: Chicago Board of Exchange (and others)

Solar energy

The gold (silver) coin boom

Citizen-band radios

Opinion polls

Trends in fashion (art, literature, music, etc.)

Guidelines for better grades

Recruitment on campus

Computer-assisted career exploration

National (world) population trends

Birth control

Pragmatism

How bigotry is born

Preschool education

Social class and educational achievement

Sensitivity training (Esalen)

Charisma of great leaders

Federal and state support to local schools

Developments in hydraulic (energy-absorbing) automobile bumpers

Recycling petrodollars

Islam (Judaism, Buddhism, Christianity, etc.)

An endangered species

The national debt

The declining dollar

Improvements in camera design

The Concorde (B-1 bomber or other advanced aircraft)

Alaska's future (or future of any state)

New ski gear (new methods of instruction)

The danger of meltdown in nuclear plants

Why the MBA degree is popular

The computer-game industry

Secrets of the fast-food business

The rise of casinos

The back to the land (back to the inner-city) movement

Volcanic eruptions (or other natural disasters)

Amending the Constitution

The importance of Ghana in African politics

The greatest blunder of the Civil War (World War I, Korean War, etc.)

How to succeed in business

Aviation safety

Standards of judging textbooks

Refugees

Improving the postal service

Boating

Drugs

Stereotyping (races, personalities, religions, social institutions)

The Delphi method of forecasting the future

Dieting

Intercultural communication

Bunko artists (confidence men, investment funds, sales, pyramid schemes)

Safety engineering (automotive, color TV, home appliances, toys)

Single-parent families

Television commercials

Privileged information given to reporters

Moratorium on space exploration

Universal fingerprinting

Voiceprints in legal evidence

The intoxicated driver

What is agribusiness?

Food irradiation

Etiquette

Rappelling

Aerobic conditioning

First aid

Obesity

What coins are made of

My visit to

Communicating with dress

The penalty for drug possession

Underground homes

College alcoholics

Salt in your diet

Automobile accidents

Chiropractors

The basics of interviewing

Anorexia nervosa

The autistic child

Eye surgery

The Irish universities

UFOs

Exam anxiety

The dormitory system

Door-to-door sales

Personality tests

Soft drinks

What is *habeas corpus*?

Who are the Libertarians?

Substance abuse centers

Natural childbirth

Grounds for divorce

The minimum wage

The social security system

What is a pacifist?

Pewter

Salt water aquariums

Comparing popcorn poppers

Winterizing your car

Unique wood products

Clearcutting in forestry

Ski boots

What is an engineer?

Sleep and the college student

Handling handguns

The concert business

Adventures of a bartender

My pet

Generic labeling

What is construction management?

Writing your résumé

How computer science makes your job easier

What is active listening?

Food preservatives

What is a finance major?

Motorcycle safety

Radiation and plutonium

Evolution and the Bible

What is political philosophy?

More about Iran

Solar energy for your home

Police codes

Cricket

Simple automobile repairs

Hair styling made easy

TOPICS FOR PERSUASIVE SPEECHES

Parole should be abolished.

Standardized tests should (should not) be used as a main criterion for college admission.

Campus security personnel should be allowed to carry weapons.

Trade unions should (should not) be abolished.

Youth gangs who harass defenseless citizens should be jailed.

Public speaking courses should be required of all university or college students.

Defense spending should (should not) be increased.

Women should (should not) be admitted to the Roman Catholic priesthood.

The Roman Catholic clergy should (should not) be allowed to marry.

All high school students should (should not) be required to study foreign languages.

Parents of students in private schools should (should not) be permitted to deduct tuition and living costs from their taxable income.

College athletics should (should not) be abolished.

U.S. athletes training for the Olympics should be federally subsidized.

The United States should (should not) withdraw from the United Nations.

Retirement should (should not) be mandatory.

There should (should not) be a set age for retirement.

The United States should (should not) limit its foreign aid to third-world countries.

There should (should not) be a national health insurance program.

Our welfare system is driving all of us to the poorhouse.

Smoking (drinking) is harmful to health.

Commercials advocating alcoholic beverages should (should not) be abolished.

Sex education classes in high school should (should not) be abolished.

Plans to build the "star wars" defense system should (should not) be abolished.

Offshore oil drilling should (should not) be allowed.

The major baseball leagues should (should not) ban use of the designated hitter.

Nuclear power plants should (should not) be built until a method can be found to dispose of atomic waste.

Marxist governments in the Americas should (should not) be opposed by every available means, including military.

"Oddball" religious sects should (should not) be banned in the United States.

Castration should (should not) be the punishment for convicted rapists.

Competency tests should (should not) be required for college graduation.

Poverty should (should not) be abolished at home before giving foreign aid abroad.

The United States should (should not) adopt a constitutional amendment making deficit financing illegal.

High school dropouts should be drafted into the armed forces.

Social fraternities and sororities should be banned.

Most college students drink too much.

Gambling should be legalized in our state.

Marijuana should be legalized.

Men are (are not) unduly discriminated against in divorce proceedings.

Future manned exploration of space is (is not) worth the expenditure.

Graduating seniors should be excused from final examinations.

The university should establish a cooperative (bookstore, grocery, etc.)

Vote in the next election.

Teachers, police, fire fighters should (should not) be permitted to strike.

Military recruiting should (should not) be permitted on campus.

Required college subjects should (should not) be abolished.

The presidency of the United States should be restricted to one six-year term.

All millionaires should be required to pay income taxes.

Big government is bad.

A politician's private life should remain private.

Professors should exempt "A" students from taking final examinations.

The presidency is too big a job for one person.

Capital punishment should (should not) be abolished.

Cheating on an examination should be punished by expulsion from the college.

Alcohol should be prohibited (permitted) on college campuses.

The U.S. postal service needs competition.

Buy (don't buy) a particular product.

Don't drink and drive.

Fad diets are dangerous.

Compulsory education should be abolished.

Rent control should be curtailed (instituted).

People are lazy.

Religion is important in life.

Junk food should be removed from all school (public) buildings.

Grades are necessary to motivate students.

Wearing a seat belt can reduce injury.

Every student should volunteer time to a hospital (nursing home, etc.).

Older citizens should be treated equally.

Everyone should give to charity.

Retirement should (should not) be mandatory.

Teenagers should not be allowed to marry.

Pollution controls are too rigid.

Campus food services should be improved.

Support the college theater (athletics, music, fine arts) program.

Personal firearms should be permitted (prohibited).

This country should establish comprehensive medical insurance for all citizens.

Universal free legal service should be instituted by our government.

Court decisions are "handcuffing" the police.

Oil (other) prices should be decontrolled.

Cigarettes (liquor) should be taxed more heavily.

All freeways should be converted to toll roads.

Congress should enact legislation setting the nationwide legal drinking age at twenty-one.

The Olympic games should be cancelled permanently.

Our economy can (cannot) support full employment.

Students should (should not) be allowed to evaluate professors.

Prisons should be for punishment, not for rehabilitation.

U.S. immigration quotas should be reduced.

We must have wiretapping.

Everyone should be fingerprinted at birth.

Judges should be elected, not politically appointed.

Additional Topics for Persuasive Speeches

Should news be entertaining?
Gay liberation
The megavitamin myth
Training for parents
Child abuse
Equal rights for women
Political apathy
Selecting wines
Youth gangs
Affirmative action
Ghetto housing
Buying used cars
Cured meats and cancer
The truth about pesticides
Improve nutrition
Do we need trade unions?
Sex bias on the job
Selling automobiles
Against the minimum wage
TV and public needs
Tipping in restaurants
Intelligence tests
Religious instruction in public schools
Science versus religion
Organized labor
Credit cards
Billboards on highways
Water resources
Study habits
Mental health as a community problem
Killing harp seals
Strengthening our national defense
Marijuana is dangerous

Advantages of ROTC
Why you shouldn't vote
Celibacy
Against football
Hiring the handicapped
Buying real estate
Inexpensive travel
The facts about hunting
Watch less TV
Cohabitation
X rays are dangerous
Legalize gambling
Cocaine
Misbehavior at games
Be assertive
Volunteer your time
Generic drugs
Against jogging
Vegetarianism
The grading system
Animal protection
Automation
"Know yourself"
Equal opportunity
Overeating
Fallacies in reasoning
The greatest baseball (football, tennis, etc.) player of all time
A third political party
Poetry reading
Peaceful coexistence
Studying a foreign language
Wasting time
The jury system
A liberal arts education

TOPICS FOR EVOCATIVE SPEECHES

Survival on the freeway

How to drive in Rome (Paris, London, New York, Los Angeles, etc.)

The hand is quicker than the IQ

Prospecting for a spouse

Lost on a used-car lot

A new code for pedestrians

How to fail in business

Shortcuts to success in society

I was an investigator for the FBI

How I got into the computer business

A strange experience at boot camp

A female reporter in the locker room

How not to make Phi Beta Kappa

How not to win a man's (or woman's) attention

Learning to sell the hard way

Working in a factory

My German (Vietnamese, Cambodian, etc.) spouse in the United States

The championship finals

Advantages of being a minister's son (or daughter)

Passing final examinations

Losing my passport

Experience in selling Bibles

Five sisters are too many

A trip to Disneyland

I am not superstitious, but _____

The fable of the wise fox

Prisoner of war for a day

Why I collect autographs

The incident that sent me back to school

How to stop drinking (smoking, overeating, etc.)

Computerized dating bureaus

New rules for rushing

If I were president (or the boss)

Some of the splendors of love

My tastes, alas, are expensive

How to cash a check in a strange place

Kid brothers (sisters) should be leashed

Noise pollution in dorms

Twelve countries in twelve days

My grandparents

My trip to _____

Twenty-four hours left to live

My special sister (brother)

Trouble at my junior prom

The funniest movie I've seen

Belief in rainbows

What a bad day is like

My trip across the United States on a limited budget

My first blind date

The politician I most respect

The death of my favorite pet

He (she) was handicapped but not crippled

On first learning to drive a car

The joys and pains of learning a new sport

The tragedy of car accidents

Humorous fishing trip experience

My first real "culture shock"

Getting a speeding ticket

Fun at a surprise birthday party

The actor (actress) I most admire

How alcoholism affected my family

Giving a eulogy for a close friend

Hardships that my family overcame

Excitement of auto racing

Thrill of flying for the first time

The beauty of a train ride through scenic parts of the United States

Acceptance speech on receiving an important honor

The beauty of birth

The first time my parents left me alone

Experiencing sexism

Honoring war veterans

My first drinking experience

Lasting influence on me by a teacher

Not having enough money on an important date

My first time attending a symphony

TOPICS FOR SPEECHES DELIVERED IMPROMPTU

Communications

Should TV programming be supervised more closely? If so, how?

Should political parties be charged broadcasting fees during an election year?

Should we abandon "summit meetings" as an instrument of international communication?

Should the news be managed by our government in time of crisis?

Are traditional American values endangered by television and the movies?

Do contemporary visual arts "communicate"?

Should the federal government become an active competitor in the field of commercial broadcasting?

Do electronic media personnel bias the news?

Economics

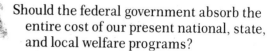

Should the federal government absorb the entire cost of our present national, state, and local welfare programs?

How shall we combat inflation?

How can we ensure full employment?

Are fair trade laws really fair?

Should the federal government be empowered to control prices and wages?

Should the stock market be further regulated?

What, if anything, should be done about conglomerate industries?

Do consumers need additional protection?

"Pay-to-pollute" laws: necessary or expedient?

Has truth-in-lending legislation accomplished its intended goals?

How can the United States ensure a favorable balance of trade?

What changes, if any, should our government make in its foreign aid programs?

What should be U.S. economic policy toward oil-producing countries?

What changes should be made in social security laws?

Do Medicare and Medicaid offer sufficient protection for all citizens?

What should be done about financial extravagance in the Pentagon?

Should professional athletics fall under antitrust legislation?

What can be done to control organized crime in the United States?

Have wiretapping laws created an infringement of privacy for U.S. citizens?

Should loyalty oaths be abolished?

Should the federal government further regulate the drug industry?

Should there be a stricter code of ethics for Supreme Court justices?

Education

Have sex education programs met their intended goals?

Should all college undergraduates be required to register for a common basic program of studies?

Academic freedom: necessity or luxury?

Should textbooks used in public education be "asexual"?

What can be done to reduce student stress in higher education?

What role(s) should students play in educational decision making?

Have intercollegiate athletics outlived their usefulness?

Is a liberal education worth pursuing? If so, is it available in American colleges and universities?

Do universities meet the needs of contemporary society?

Should team teaching be universally adopted (revised, abolished)?

What should be done about the grading system in American education?

Does the study of sensitivity training deserve academic support?

Borrowing to pay for a college education: indenture or privilege?

I chose a major in _____ because . . .

My obligation as a student

My responsibility to the school community

Student responsibilities in the dormitory

The university's responsibility to the student

The university's responsibility to the community

The real value of education

What faculty can expect from students

What students can expect from faculty

Student evaluations of faculty

Ethical conduct among students

Religion as a base for ethical conduct

Punctuality

The ideal part-time job for a college student

An ideal work-study-recreation schedule

Recommended leisure time activity

An alternative to drinking

Advice to my professors

Joining campus organizations

Academic cheating

Interest in campus politics

Asking for a date on the phone

Computers in my life at college

Judicial, Legal

What action(s) should be taken to improve the quality of present law enforcement?

Should the investigative powers of Congress be curtailed?

Should euthanasia be legalized?

Should traffic in certain types of drugs be legalized?

Should legal statutes relative to criminal insanity be revised?

Is firearm legislation adequate? If not, what changes are necessary?

Should marriage and/or divorce laws be changed? If so, how?

What tangible legal steps should be taken to minimize violence in this country?

Must our liberties be curtailed in order to maintain the safety and security of a majority of our citizens?

Labor

Should public employees be allowed to unionize and strike?

Have labor unions outlived their usefulness?

Shall we adopt a federal "right-to-work" law?

Military

The lottery: better or worse than the draft?

Should ROTC be abolished, modified, or retained on college campuses?

Shall NATO be continued? If so, how?

Are current U.S. military training programs outdated?

Does the military have excessive power in the United States? If so, how can it be curtailed?

Should homosexuals be allowed in the armed forces?

Has the volunteer army met its expectations?

Political

Does the political system of checks and balances really work?

What disarmament programs, if any, should the United States pursue?

Should there be a federal energy program?

How can we avoid further Vietnams?

What policies should the U.S. pursue in regard to the Communist countries of Eastern Europe?

What policy should the U.S. adopt toward the nonaligned nations of Asia and Africa?

What policy should the U.S. pursue in regard to China—Communist China and Taiwan?

Should there be a limit on expenditures for presidential campaigns?

What policies should the United States pursue in regard to the Soviet Union?

Is the United Nations worth saving?

Pollution control devices for automobiles: a necessity?

Should the United States intervene in conflicts that occur between Communist bloc nations? If so, how?

What should be the U.S. policy regarding the Arab-Israeli conflict?

Should presidential candidates be nominated by another system, such as through direct primaries?

How can U.S. governmental policies relative to native Americans be improved?

Should the Environmental Protection Agency be granted greater freedom and powers?

Religious

Do churches, as religious institutions, practice what they preach?

Should the clergy be protected by law in their right to refuse to divulge information?

Should prayer be permitted in public schools?

Should churches continue to be exempt from taxation? Why?

Should religious institutions, or their leaders, ever support the concept or activities of war?

Should clergy be allowed a role in politics?

What effect would female priesthood have on Roman Catholicism?

Rural

What farm policies should be altered or adopted by the federal government?

Are our conservation laws adequate?

Should there be greater controls placed on the activities of the Nuclear Energy Commission?

What should be the governmental policy toward protection of wildlife?

Scientific

Do agricultural chemicals represent a threat to national health?

Is "mind control" the next frontier of science?

Should the scientist be considered "amoral" or "extrajudicial"?

Should we lend merit to the study of behavior modification?

Is science dehumanizing humanity?

Under what conditions, if any, should animals be used in experimentation?

Does further support need to be given to the development of "test tube babies"?

Should medical doctors be required to face peer evaluation of their practice?

Genetic engineering: an end for the unfortunately deformed or a tool for a "master race"?

What should be done about the high cost of hospitalization?

Should the medical profession be held legally accountable for its medical practices?

What is the future of mass transit?

Organic gardening: safety or silliness?

Should treatment of the mentally ill be revised? If so, how?

Can we lend merit to the study of witchcraft?

What's next for commercial aviation?

Are our airways safe for travel?

Urban

What, if anything, should we do about urban renewal?

Planned cities: hope or fantasy?

What, if anything, should be done about civil disobedience in our cities?

Day care centers: freedom for parents or forced socialization for children?

How can cities better obtain needed financial support?

Do zoning ordinances accomplish their objectives?

What should be the role of the county in relation to the city?

TOPICS FOR GROUP DISCUSSION

Does the United States need to import oil?

Is the United States facing a drought?

Should pornography be prohibited?

Do X rays of the head or neck cause cancer of the thyroid gland?

Is a person's social standing directly related to his or her wealth?

Should we spend less money on weapons?

Should employees determine their own work schedules?

Should women retain their own names when they marry?

Should saccharin (aspartame, cyclamates) be banned?

Does regular exercise lengthen your life?

Should the federal government regulate the use of energy?

Should everyone have the right to get married?

Does unemployment fall disproportionately on the young?

Are abortion laws too liberal (too strict)?

Should right-to-work laws be repealed?

Should a limit be placed on jury awards in malpractice suits?

Should we increase our supply of conventional weapons?

Should we give more attention to consumer education?

Should we reduce the consumption of sugar?

Should medical students be required to study nutrition?

Should casinos be allowed (banned) in this state?

Should Puerto Rico be given statehood?

Should welfare benefits be decreased?

Should the consumer pay for industrial pollution?

Should student health services dispense birth control pills?

Should state educational institutions be governed by trustees, regents, or curators?

Should suburbs be integrated?

Should pleasure-boat drivers be licensed?

Should you join the Rod and Gun Club (Toastmaster's Club, Le Cercle Français, etc.)?

Will communism expand in Latin America (or Africa)?

Should all instructors be required to take a course in speech communication?

Should less emphasis be placed on final examinations?

Should the wage scale for student employees be increased?

Should students be more widely represented on college committees?

Should regulations against wiretapping be further modified?

What should be governmental policy about informing the public on matters of national security?

Should access to higher education be available to all?

Should the rating system (industrial, military) be modified?

Should we change the state divorce laws?

Should industry hire the handicapped?

Should punitive antipollution legislation be enacted?

Should we boycott the products of countries that fail to join in fishing and whaling conservation practices?

Does Congress have the right to investigate individuals?

Should high schools prepare their graduates for college entrance examinations?

Is the criticism of modern art justified?

Should capital punishment be mandatory for hijackers and other terrorists?

Are term papers an effective way of learning?

Should divorces be made easier to acquire?

Should the history of minority groups be taught?

Is due process too slow?

Should students be bused to achieve school integration?

Should every American be guaranteed a minimum wage?

Should we recognize the government of . . . ?

Should federal aid scholarships be based entirely on need?

Should more strict gun control legislation be enacted?

Should this state adopt (increase, repeal) the sales tax?

Should early marriages be encouraged?

Should teachers have scheduled salary increases plus merit increases?

How can juvenile delinquency be lessened?

Should parents be allowed income tax deductions for college expenses?

Should we raise standards of admission to this institution?

Should science education be improved?

Are the humanities sufficiently emphasized?

Should the sales tax be extended to include services?

Should students buy insurance while they are in college?

Should we amend the state liquor laws?

Should the college course be shortened to three or three and a half years?

NOTES

1. We would like to thank Professor Alfred Sokolnicki of Marquette University and Dr. Doug Losee of Humboldt State University for their help in compiling these lists of suggested speech topics.

Index

dry-run, 96
focus group, 95
questionnaire, 96–97
Methods of reporting, 177–80
description, 179
narration, 178–79
simple explanation, 179–80
Mimicry, 258
Monroe's Motivational Sequence, 285
Monroe, Alan H., 285–86
Monthly Catalog of United States Government, 76
Motivation, 230–46
Movement, 114–20
Myths about listening, 25–27
hearing is listening, 26
higher intelligence, 25
listening means agreement, 26–27
natural ability, 26
passive process, 27
speaker and message, 26

N

Narratives. *See* stories
New York Times Index, 75–76
Newspapers, as sources, 75–76
Newsweek, 71
Noise, 8–9
defined, 8
environmental, 9
physiological, 8

psychological, 8
semantic, 8
Notetaking, 31–32

O

Ogden, Charles, 159
Oral style, 188–90
avoid excess, 190
avoid redundancy, 189
be accurate, 189
be specific, 189
bridge gaps, 190
keep it simple, 189
personalized style, 188
Outlining, 45–49, 185–88
Overgeneralization fallacy, 218

P

Pacing, 144–45
Patterns of organization, 44–45, 184–85
chronological, 44
logical, 45
pro and con, 45
problem-solving, 45
psychological, 45
spatial, 44
topical, 44–45
Pausing, 145
Pearson, Judy Cornelia, 164

Pei, Mario, 161
Personality, 134–35
Persuasion, 198–247
argumentation, 199, 210–17
credibility, 102–11, 199, 230
defined, 199
develop speech of conviction, 219–21
organizing motivation speech, 239
motivation, 230–46
sales techniques, 242–44
salesperson's qualities, 241–42
sample speech of conviction, 221–24
sample sales talk, 244–46
Pitch, 139
Poe, Edgar Allan, 149
Pons, Lily, 55
Practice, 54, 279
Preparation steps for discussion, 302–10
duties of chairperson, 304–8
duties of discussants, 308–10
interesting subjects, 303
multisided subjects, 303
selecting topic, 302
statement of question, 304
stimulating subjects, 302
suitable subjects, 303–4
worthwhile subjects, 303
Presentation. *See* delivery
Problem-solving approach, 298
Pronunciation, 142–44